A PICTORIAL HISTORY OF THE UNIVERSITY OF IOWA

A Pictorial History of the
UNIVERSITY OF IOWA

By John C. Gerber

With Carolyn B. Brown, James Kaufmann,
and James B. Lindberg, Jr.

University of Iowa Press ⑂ Iowa City

University of Iowa Press, Iowa City 52242

Copyright © 1988 by the University of Iowa

Printed in the United States of America

First edition, 1988

Book and jacket design by Richard Hendel

Typesetting by G & S Typesetters, Austin, Texas

Printing and binding by BookCrafters, Chelsea, Michigan

Library of Congress Cataloging-in-Publication Data

Gerber, John C.

A pictorial history of the University of Iowa / John C. Gerber;
with Carolyn B. Brown, James Kaufmann, and James B. Lindberg, Jr.—

1st ed.

p.   cm.

Includes index.

ISBN 0-87745-189-3

1. University of Iowa—History.   2. University of Iowa—
Description—Views.   I. Title.

LD2568.G47   1988

378.777'655—dc19   87-30769

CIP

Contents

Publication of this book was made possible by a generous grant from the University of Iowa Foundation

Preface

The intent of this volume is to recapture selected moments in the life of the University of Iowa since its beginning in 1847. It contains over 320 photographs, each with its own caption. Each of the six sections concentrates on one or more presidencies, and within them the 70 self-contained vignettes, or subsections, provide background for the photographs. What finally emerges is a mosaic that not only exhibits the growth of the University but also suggests the courage and resourcefulness of those who have been associated with it. Iowans have a right to be proud of their university. (A note to old-timers: To avoid confusion, we refer to the University throughout the book as the University of Iowa or simply Iowa and not, even in the earlier pages, as the State University of Iowa or SUI.)

Laurence Lafore of the Department of History was originally commissioned to create this work but died before he had finished more than a general introduction. His sound judgment and good humor have been a continuing inspiration.

Our debts are many. Particularly we are obligated to Earl M. Rogers, the University archivist, who attended our editorial meetings and helped check the manuscript; to Irving B. Weber, the popular Johnson County historian, who read the manuscript for omissions as well as commissions; and to such members of the faculty and staff as Dr. William B. Bean, Samuel L. Becker, Willard Boyd, Charles W. Davidson, Ruth B. Dawson, Samuel M. Fahr, Ray L. Heffner, Margery E. Hoppin, Richard Jordison, Margaret N. Keyes, Carl H. Klaus, Lloyd A. Know-ler, Cleo Martin, Baldwin Maxwell, Mary Jane McLaughlin, Dee W. Norton, Mary F. Parden, Stow Persons, Larry Rettig, Evelyn D. Robison, Frank Seiberling, James A. Van Allen, David H. Vernon, and Darrell D. Wyrick, all of whom supplied pertinent information and some of whom read and corrected portions of the manuscript. Others, such as Barbara Kent Buckley, John M. Harrison, and Margaret Zimansky, donated books and documents that proved invaluable.

President James O. Freedman commissioned the book; later, Interim President and Vice-President for Academic Affairs Richard D. Remington and Associate Dean of Faculties Fredrick Woodard supported our research. The University library staff members were unceasingly helpful. In addition to Earl M. Rogers, we are especially grateful to Dale M. Bentz, the University Librarian who, before he retired, helped us to get the book started, Robert A. McCown, head of Special Collections, Margaret E. Richardson, stacks librarian, Frank Allen in government documents, and Vevalee Voots, secretary in Special Collections.

Picture credits appear at the end of the volume. Information in the captions and vignettes comes primarily from the resources of the University of Iowa libraries and, to a lesser extent, from the holdings of the State Historical Society of Iowa. Major unpublished sources included doctoral dissertations, presidential addresses, minutes of faculty meetings, transcripts of interviews, and correspondence and directives by administrative officers. Published sources included University catalogs, directories, course schedules, departmental and college announcements and newsletters, business records, regents' reports, student newspapers (the *Vidette-Reporter*, the *S.U.I. Quill*, and the *Daily Iowan*, for example), news journals and bulletins (including the *FYI*, the *Spectator*, and the *University of Iowa News Bulletin*), the *Iowa Alumnus*, the *Iowa Alumni Review*, the *Hawkeye* yearbooks, and student humor magazines such as *Frivol*. Other helpful journals were the *Annals of Iowa*, the *Iowan*, the *Iowa Historical Record*, the *Iowa Journalist*, the *Iowa Journal of History and Politics* (after 1948 the *Iowa Journal of History*), and the *Palimpsest*. The files of the *Des Moines Register* and the *Iowa City Press-Citizen* were essential for pinning down many names and dates.

An indispensable tool for research was Earl M. Rogers's carefully indexed *Bibliography of the History of the University of Iowa, 1857–1978* (with a supplement that extends the latter date to 1986). There is no general history of the University, either scholarly or popular, but in a section of his bibliography Rogers lists the more comprehensive accounts that do exist. Especially useful were the writings of Clarence Ray Aurner, Thomas Hart Benton, Jr., Vernon Carstensen, Ryland V. Crary, Frederick G. Davies, Ruth A. Gallaher, William J. Haddock, Marie Haefner, William C. Lang, Bruce E. Mahan, Leonard F. Parker, Larry Perl, Josiah L. Pickard, and Harrison John Thornton.

John C. Gerber
Carolyn B. Brown
James Kaufmann
James B. Lindberg, Jr.

ONE

Johnson County High School, 1847–1859

The Mechanics' Academy, first home of the University of Iowa, as sketched by George H. Yewell in 1854.

The University came close to dying in its infancy. With little money, an inexperienced board of trustees, a part-time president, one rented building, and almost no students from outside Johnson County, the small school in the brand new town of Iowa City was a university in name only. Beginning in 1855, it lasted for three years and then, except for the teacher-training classes, closed down for the next two. Given the advent of the Civil War, it is a wonder that it reopened at all.

Iowa City

The territory of Iowa came into being in 1838 when by an act of Congress it was detached from Wisconsin Territory. At the first meeting of the Legislative Assembly of Iowa Territory, Governor Robert Lucas proposed that Burlington be made its temporary capital and Mount Pleasant, three years later, its permanent capital. Members of the assembly agreed with him on Burlington, but some thirty of them offered their hometowns as substitutes for Mount Pleasant. After long and tiresome wrangling, a brilliant idea caught hold: have a group of three commissioners select a site for a permanent capital in Johnson County. Named for the Indian fighter and vice-president of the United States Richard Mentor Johnson, Johnson County was proposed because it was centrally located in what was then defined as Iowa Territory. So it was that Chauncey Swan, John Ronalds, and Robert Ralston—since immortalized in the names of a downtown plaza, a street, and a creek—were elected commissioners. On May 4, 1839, they selected a location on an elevation just east of the Iowa River and roughly two miles north of Napoleon, the county seat.

About where the Old Capitol now stands, they erected a sign saying "Seat of Government, CITY OF IOWA, May 4th, 1839." Thus did the eventual home of the University get its name.

Later that summer the surveyors gave the city its basic shape. They divided it into blocks 320 feet square with lots 80 by 150 feet. The streets were all 80 feet wide except Iowa Avenue, which was 120 feet, and Washington, Jefferson, Capitol, Clinton, and Madison, which were 100 feet. Alleys were 20 feet. The surveyors reserved a four-block square for the capitol building and its grounds, and one block each for Governor's Square, the Park, the College Green, and the North, Center, and South markets. Four half-blocks were reserved for three churches and a school. The first auction of lots occurred on the third Monday in August, 1839, a jolly occasion, with the crowd repairing to Lean Back Hall to fortify themselves between sales. The first lot, near where Old Brick now stands, was sold to L. D. Phillips for $330. Later, Matthew Teneyck built the first house, a two-story cabin of hewed logs on the southwest corner of Dubuque Street and Iowa Avenue. By January 1, 1840, about twenty families had settled within the limits of the town, and Jesse Berry had opened a school on College Street. Henry A. Usher was the first blacksmith, Hutchinson and Williams the first carpenters, Dr. Henry Murray the first physician, and Andrew J. Gregg the first horse thief. With federal authorization, Samuel H. McCrory, the postmaster, changed the name of the post office from Napoleon to Iowa City.

By 1855, when the University first opened its doors to students, the population of Iowa City was roughly four thousand, mostly people from states to the east and south, with a liberal sprinkling of Bohemians, Germans, Irish, and Welsh. With its seventy business establish-

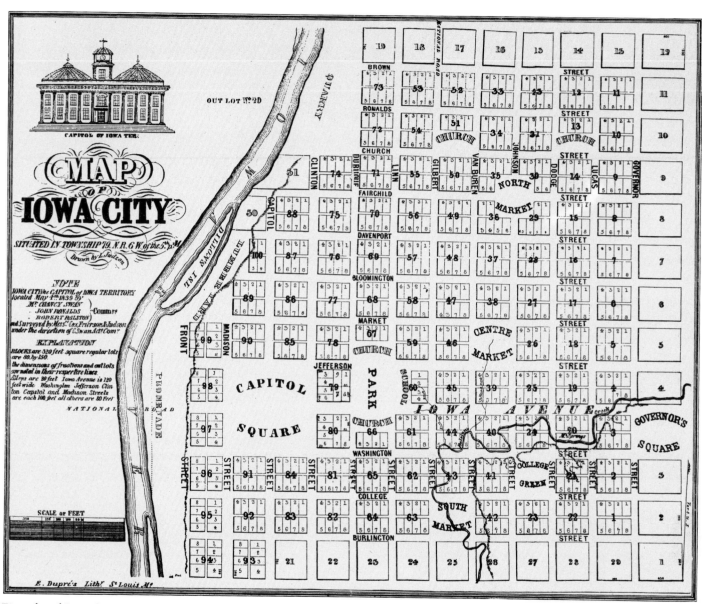

First plat of Iowa City, 1839, including an early design for the capitol.

OPPOSITE
The capitol, c. 1853. This daguerreotype by Isaac Wetherby is the earliest known photographic image of the capitol.

ments, Iowa City was the commercial center of Johnson County. Steamboats chugged up the river from St. Louis and the four-horse coaches of the Western Stage Company maintained daily schedules to and from Davenport, Fort Des Moines, Cedar Rapids, and Fairfield. But after the first locomotive of the Mississippi and Missouri Railroad (later the Rock Island) arrived in Iowa City at midnight on December 31, 1855, the years of the steamboat and stage coach were numbered. Within the limits of the town were a courthouse (described as "elegant" by a gazetteer of the time), a jail, a schoolhouse (there were three by 1858), the Asylum for the Blind, and the State Institution for the Deaf and Dumb. In addition, Iowa City had two weekly newspapers, five churches, a philharmonic society, and such reform groups as the Sons of Temperance and the Anti–Chewing Tobacco Society. Public lectures were frequent and so, in the summer, were camp meetings. But the focus of the city was the capitol. From the start the capitol gave Iowa City its reason for being, and ever since it has provided it with a special ambience.

The Capitol

On July 4, 1840, the cornerstone of the capitol building was laid, and three hundred settlers celebrated with a dinner followed by a frontier dance. But the celebration was premature, for the building's progress was plagued with troubles. The architect, John F. Rague, quit just days after the celebration, leaving incomplete plans for Chauncey Swan and his successors to follow. Then the quarry from which the building's limestone was cut was exhausted, and stones from the new quarry, located near North Liberty, had to be floated

down the Iowa River on rafts. Still, by the fall of 1842 the roof was on and four rooms were ready for Iowa Territory's Fifth Legislative Assembly.

Yet the building was far from complete. Because of problems with funding, the plans had to be continually revised. The west portico was eliminated from the plan (it was added, finally, in the 1920s), and plain cornices were substituted for elaborate ones. The reverse spiral staircase went only from the first floor to the second, not, as originally planned, from the basement to the dome.

Work proceeded in fits and starts through the rest of the 1840s and into the 1850s. The cupola was eventually finished, chimneys were built, and steps were added to the east portico. In 1851 funds were made available for stairs, a fence, and work on the grounds. By 1854 the capitol's interior contained the Senate and House chambers on the second floor, and on the first floor there were rooms for the state supreme court and the offices of the governor, the state auditor, and the state treasurer. By the mid-1850s the westward expansion of the state's population dictated that the capital be located more centrally. In 1855 the General Assembly voted to locate it in Des Moines, and the state constitution of 1857 stipulated that Des Moines should be the permanent capital. The actual move took place in November 1857, with the wagon drivers almost losing the road in a snow storm. Immediately thereafter, the still-unfinished capitol building was transferred to the University.

Establishing the University

The birth of the University occurred on February 25, 1847. On that date the First General Assembly of the State of Iowa passed a bill authorizing a state university, and Governor Ansel Briggs signed it immediately. At the time, the state was only fifty-nine days old, and the widely scattered population still numbered only about one hundred thousand.

Even though other states in the Midwest had succeeded in starting public universities, it was a courageous undertaking for Iowa. The example offered by private colleges in the state was not encouraging. Most quickly failed, including in Iowa City the Iowa Seminary (1840), Iowa City College (1843–47), and Iowa City University (1845–c. 1847). Of the fifty-eight private institutions chartered between 1838 and 1850, only a handful were in existence in 1880, and only Clarke, Loras, Iowa Wesleyan, and Iowa College (now Grinnell) showed promise of surviving. Of course, a state university, with its access to public funds, had a far better chance of survival. But because there were so few high schools in the state that prepared students adequately for college-level work— perhaps four or five—if the university was to prosper, it

would have to offer its own precollege work. Proponents argued that this was a necessary investment, because Iowa badly needed teachers for its schools and professional people for its economic and cultural development. The main impetus for a university, therefore, was practical. In fact, even before the school had a president the legislature created a professorship for an expert in teacher training.

What undoubtedly gave the members of the First General Assembly confidence as they voted to establish the institution was the belief that they already had funds for its operation. One of the first acts of the territorial legislature after it was organized in 1838 had been to petition Congress for a grant of land that could be sold and the proceeds used to endow "a literary institution." The territory of Wisconsin had already received such a grant, as had other territories in the Old Northwest. (These grants preceded the grants authorized by the Morrill Land Grant Act of 1862 to create and maintain colleges, such as Iowa State at Ames, for the agricultural and mechanical arts.) In 1840 Congress had responded by giving Iowa Territory the equivalent of two townships (46,080 acres) of federal land with the understanding that they would be turned over to the state of Iowa as soon as it came into being. In the 1847 bill, consequently, the First General Assembly not only constituted the University but also, following the injunction of Congress, passed on to it the donated federal land.

In the same bill the legislature broke other ground. It located the proposed university in Iowa City "with such branches as public convenience may require," and it promised the university the state buildings and grounds as soon as the capital should move to a more central location in the state. Moreover, it created a board of trustees of fifteen members to be appointed by the legislature. To

An act to locate and establish a State University

Sec 1 Be it enacted by the General Assembly of the State of Iowa. That there shall be established at Iowa City, the present seat of government of the State of Iowa, an institution to be called the "State University of Iowa" with such branches as in the opinion of the general Assembly the public convenience may hereafter require

Sec 2 The public buildings at Iowa City, together with the ten acres of land on which the same are situated be and the same are hereby granted for the use of said University provided that the sessions of the General Assembly and the officers of the officers of State shall be held in the present Capitol until otherwise provided for by law

Sec 3 The two townships of land granted by act of Congress of July 20th 1840 for the support of a University be and the same are hereby donated to the said State University to be and constitute a permanent fund the interest of which shall be applied exclusively to the support of said University and such branches as the General assembly shall establish

Sec 4 That for the control of said University and for the better management of the same there shall be appointed by the General assembly

First page of the act that established the University, passed by the First General Assembly on February 25, 1847.

this board it gave authority to select and sell the land donated by Congress and to use the interest on the proceeds for the operation of the new institution. The legislators could go home in February 1848 confident that they had prepared the way for an institution that would be invaluable in the development of what was still a frontier state.

Troubles, however, lay just ahead, and the university did not open its doors for eight years. One cause of the delay was the wrangling over whether Iowa City should be the site for all the divisions of the university. The mention of "branches" in the original bill encouraged other towns to think that they might share in the funds from the sale of the land. They dreamed up all kinds of claims in support of other sites. A representative from Jasper County, for example, argued that a branch of the university should be in a quiet rural area because it is "well known" that cities like Iowa City "are productive of influences to which parents, as a general thing, would not desire to have their children exposed." The lobbying was so vigorous that the legislature finally approved branches in Fairfield and Dubuque and normal schools (teacher training schools) in Andrew (Governor Briggs's hometown in Jackson County), Oskaloosa, and Mount Pleasant. It also converted the College of Physicians and Surgeons of the Upper Mississippi at Keokuk into the Medical Department of the University. The legislature granted no funds, however, for any of these proposed branches. All of them except the medical school at Keokuk died aborning or were killed when the new state constitution of 1857 stipulated that the university was to be in one place and that that place was to be Iowa City. The key arguments for consolidating the university, as put forth by State Superintendent of Public Instruction Thomas Hart Benton, Jr., Governor James W. Grimes, and others were that there was too little money for more

than one institution and that Iowa City, having lost the capital to Des Moines, deserved the university as a consolation prize (it also got the state historical society). Undoubtedly they realized, too, that if the university could move into the vacated capitol in Iowa City, the legislature would not have to cover the cost of a new building.

A second cause of the delay was a lack of money. Despite the grant of over 46,000 acres from Congress, the trustees, who were empowered to select and sell the land, were so shortsighted or so under the thumb of the legislature that even by the late 1850s the interest on the endowment was not enough to cover the operation of the institution. In the first place, the trustees selected primarily timberland, apparently not realizing that prairie land would be much more profitable. Second, they were forced to sell much of what they had selected for far less than it was worth. They started out well enough in June 1851 by setting a minimum price of $5 an acre and shortly thereafter boosting that figure to $10 an acre. But then pressure from squatters and new land-hungry settlers and speculators caused the General Assembly to force the trustees to put the land on the open market, where it averaged only $3.52 an acre. Matters were not helped when in January 1855 five of the trustees bought over 11,000 acres at $3.20 an acre for themselves. No fraud was revealed, but the attorney general did void their purchases. In any event, when the school finally opened in 1855, the interest on the endowment still amounted to less than $3,000. From all sources there was little more than enough money to hire a president and a small faculty and to rent the Mechanics' Academy, just off Iowa Avenue, to house the institution.

Delay occurred, too, because the trustees had difficulty in persuading anyone to accept the presidency. It was

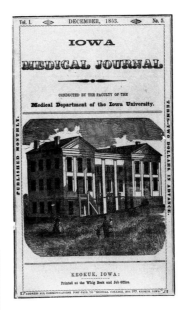

A page from the minutes of the Board of Trustees, showing lands belonging to the University, 1856.

Title page, Iowa Medical Journal, *showing the Keokuk medical college, 1853. Founded in 1850 and closed in 1899, the Keokuk Medical College was never officially part of the University, because Iowa's 1857 constitution prohibited branch campuses. Medical degrees were nonetheless granted by the University to those who had completed the Keokuk program until the University's own medical department was established in 1870. Early diplomas were inscribed "Doctorem in Arte Medica" by "Universitatus Iowaensis, Keokukii." The structure pictured was advertised as being both "neat" and "tasty."*

hardly an attractive position. The president, in addition to administering the affairs of the University under the close supervision of the trustees, was expected, among other things, to assemble a faculty, develop a curriculum, teach a class that met every weekday, see that the faculty and students attended daily chapel, excuse absentees or mete out punishment to those not excused, oversee the maintenance of the property, keep peace among the faculty and students, and build up the student body by speaking throughout the state. For all this he would re-

ceive two thousand dollars a year. Three men promptly turned down the offer, though one made a trip to Iowa City. Prodded by an exasperated governor and legislature, the board in the spring of 1855 hired Abel Beach, a professor of ancient languages, and Alexander Johnston, a professor of mathematics, to offer sixteen-week courses. In addition, E. M. Guffin was hired to supervise the necessary preparatory work. Fifty students attended. During those weeks the board finally found a president— or chancellor, as they chose to call him. On the recommendation of James Hall of Albany, New York, whom they had hired as a professor of natural history (though it is not clear that he ever served), the board offered the position to Amos Dean, the head of the Albany Law School. He accepted on the condition that he keep his Albany position and not have to move to Iowa.

The Curious Administration of Amos Dean

Amos Dean served as the University's chancellor from 1855 to 1859, but it was part-time service, since he simply added the new post to a list that included teaching at the Albany Law College (which he had helped to found), lecturing in history at the Dudley Observatory in Albany, and serving as a trustee of the State Normal School of New York (now the State University of New York at Albany). A dedicated educator, Dean was a highly methodical man who rose at five each morning to review his lecture notes, lectured from nine until eleven, and filled the rest of the day before dinner with administrative duties. After dinner, he wrote until ten-thirty and then retired. Among other works, he published *Bryant & Stratton's Commercial Law* and *The History of Civilization*, a seven-volume masterwork that took him thirty years to complete. Although he made only three trips to Iowa, his impact on education in the state was notable, for he not only acted as the head of the University but also served with the famous educator Horace Mann on a commission that recommended a unified system of education for Iowa extending from the first grade to the University.

For the University, Dean devised an organization composed of three "departments" (not to be confused with present-day departments): the Collegiate Department, the University proper; the Normal Department, the teacher-training division; and the Preparatory Department, the division for students deemed inadequately trained for college work in grammar, Greek and Latin, arithmetic and algebra, and the "rudiments" of natural philosophy (science). Only the Collegiate Department was empowered to confer degrees: the B.A. for four years of study in, primarily, the languages and philosophy, and the B.S. for two years of work in mathematics and the sciences. Dean's second circular for potential students, however, explained that only two courses in each area would be immediately available, since the University was more solicitous of future growth than "present perfection." The circular clearly implied that the chancellor was not unaware of the legislature's desire that the University serve the state in practical as well as cultural ways. Students preparing for "the common pursuits of life" were not to be held to Greek and Latin but could concentrate on the sciences and their practical applications.

The University officially opened in September 1855 for a two-semester academic year of forty weeks. The faculty included H. S. Welton as professor of languages and Alexander Johnston as professor of mathematics in the Collegiate Department, John Van Valkenburg as head of the Normal Department, and E. M. Guffin as principal of the Preparatory Department. The following year Dean added J. M. Stone as professor of natural philosophy (Physics). Dean himself served, nominally at least, as professor of history. In the first year 124 students enrolled, 83 "gentlemen" and 41 "ladies." Of these, 65 registered for some or all of their work in the Preparatory Department, and 40 in the Normal Department. Only 25 were full-time students in the Collegiate Department. Of the total of 124, moreover, 113 came from Iowa City, and

6 more from such nearby towns as Clear Creek and So-
lon. To the embarrassment of its supporters, the University almost immediately became known as the Johnson
County High School.

To be admitted to the Collegiate Department, male
students normally had to be at least fifteen, and female
students fourteen. The daily schedule included chapel at
7:45 A.M. and classes from 8:45 until 5:00 in fall and
spring and 4:00 in winter, with a period for lunch. At
the end of a semester, students were expected to participate in public exercises, usually declamations or readings
of personal essays, though at the end of the first semester
in February 1857 four lady students offered a "Collo-
quy" on the subject of "Home Education and Home Influences." Chancellor Dean opened a small library in 1857
and a museum of natural history in 1858. Both were
housed on the north side of the second floor of the capitol building, which the University had just taken over.

Under Amos Dean (the "President in absentia," as he
was called) the University managed to hold its own for
three years and then almost expired. In the new state
constitution of 1857, the legislature, still irritated with
the dilatoriness if not the untrustworthiness of the first
board of trustees, put the trustees under the new Board
of Education, which was to control all public education in
the state. This board then promptly reduced the number
of trustees from fifteen to seven, reappointing only one
of the original fifteen. When the new trustees took over,
they were appalled at the University's financial state. Because of the panic of 1857, conditions would have been
bad enough anyway, but poor judgment by the first
trustees had escalated the situation into a crisis. On
the recommendation of the chancellor, the new trustees
closed the Collegiate and Preparatory departments for
1858–59 and, later, for 1859–60 to allow time for funds

*Amos Dean (1803–68), first
president of the University,
1855–59.*

to accumulate and for the buildings to be properly prepared for University use. They also hoped that students
could become qualified in other institutions to enter the
Collegiate Department and that the Preparatory Department could be dispensed with. Pursuant to these ends,
they fired all the faculty except the chancellor and D.
Franklin Wells, who held the special professorship created by the legislature in the Normal Department. They
insisted, however, that the chancellor take up his residence in Iowa City. In response Dean resigned. In his behalf it should be added that he had accepted only $500
(for traveling expenses), though the trustees owed him
considerably more. The new trustees also voted to ex-
clude women from the Collegiate Department, but this
action provoked such strong opposition that it was not
enforced. A year later the Board of Education rescinded
the action. Thus the University of Iowa has been able
to claim that it has never in practice excluded women.

Before they were dismissed, the faculty memorialized
the legislature, requesting funds to repair and renovate
the capitol building, to erect a new structure as a board-

ing hall for out-of-town students, and to provide books and scientific apparatus. They pointed out that Iowa's library of 500 volumes compared most unfavorably with Ohio State's 4,000 volumes, Indiana's 5,000 volumes, and Michigan's 6,000 volumes, not to mention the collections at Harvard and Yale and at foreign universities. The legislature remained unstirred by the plea for books, but it did provide $13,000 in 1858 and $10,000 in 1860 to renovate the Old Capitol and to construct a boarding hall. It is a good guess that in funding a boarding hall they wanted to overcome the impression that they had created nothing more than an advanced school for residents of Johnson County.

Clinton Street, 1854. When Isaac Wetherby made this daguerreotype of Iowa City, sidewalks were rare, hogs rooted in the streets, and horses were routinely pastured on Capitol Square, even though an ordinance passed soon after the city was incorporated in 1853 prohibited "horses, jacks, mules, swine and cattle, except milch cows, from the first of April to November first, running at large within the limits of Iowa City."

Terrell's Dam and Mill. In 1843 Walter Terrell, one of Iowa City's early settlers, built a dam on the Iowa River. The following year he added a mill, the only one for miles around. It was not unusual in the 1840s and 1850s to see as many as fifty wagons lined up, waiting to have grain ground.

Wetherby's Gallery, 1860s. Isaac A. Wetherby, Iowa City's first photographer, operated this studio and gallery on South Clinton Street. Photo portraits were made on the top floor, where skylights provided illumination for the long exposures then necessary.

Hutchinson-Kuhl house. Said to be constructed with limestone rejected for use in Old Capitol, the Hutchinson-Kuhl house, located on present-day Park Road, is the oldest house still standing in Iowa City. Robert Hutchinson, a carpenter and joiner from New Hampshire, built it as a farmhouse shortly after 1840. He later helped erect the First Presbyterian Church (Old Brick) and the Mechanics' Academy, a building he eventually purchased and rented to the University. In 1927 dormers were added and other changes made to the house by its owner at the time, Ernest P. Kuhl, a professor of English. The property was sold to the University in 1977 and is now the home of the University of Iowa Press.

Abel Beach, professor of ancient languages. Along with Beach, Alexander Johnston, professor of mathematics, and E. M. Guffin, principal of the Preparatory Department, constituted the full faculty for a sixteen-week term that opened on March 15, 1855.

Dexter Edson Smith (1839–1928). Smith, the University's first graduate, led an unusually varied life. A few years after he received his B.S. in 1858, Smith joined the Oneida Community in Oneida, New York, a utopian community whose members believed in mutual criticism, complex marriage (everyone married to everyone else), and male continence. In 1881 Smith moved to Santa Ana, California, where he became a prominent citrus farmer and civic activist, and was involved in the development of Orange County, outside of Los Angeles.

Normal Department textbooks, first circular, 1855. When the General Assembly established the University in February 1847, it also created a professorship for the training of public-school teachers. Thus, when the trustees of the new University gathered in 1855 to select the first faculty, they appointed John Van Valkenburg to head the Normal School even before they had named a president for the institution. Popular with the legislature, the Normal Department, as it was later called, was never highly esteemed by faculty members in other areas; they referred to it as the "trundle bed school."

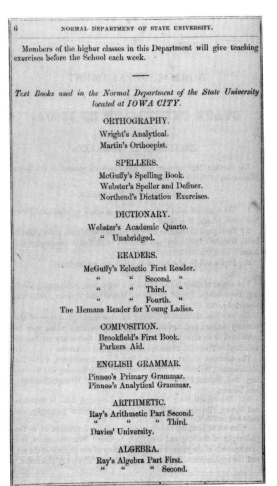

6   NORMAL DEPARTMENT OF STATE UNIVERSITY.

Members of the higher classes in this Department will give teaching exercises before the School each week.

Text Books used in the Normal Department of the State University located at IOWA CITY.

ORTHOGRAPHY.
Wright's Analytical.
Martin's Orthoepist.

SPELLERS.
McGuffy's Spelling Book.
Webster's Speller and Definer.
Northend's Dictation Exercises.

DICTIONARY.
Webster's Academic Quarto.
"   Unabridged.

READERS.
McGuffy's Eclectic First Reader.
"   "   Second. "
"   "   Third. "
"   "   Fourth. "
The Hemans Reader for Young Ladies.

COMPOSITION.
Brookfield's First Book.
Parkers Aid.

ENGLISH GRAMMAR.
Pinneo's Primary Grammar.
Pinneo's Analytical Grammar.

ARITHMETIC.
Ray's Arithmetic Part Second.
"   "   "   Third.
Davies' University.

ALGEBRA.
Ray's Algebra Part First.
"   "   "   Second.

NORMAL DEPARTMENT OF STATE UNIVERSITY.   7

GEOMETRY.
Davies' Legendre.

SURVEYING.
Davies' Surveying.

GEOGRAPHY.
Monteith's 1st. Lessons.
"   Youths Manual.
McNally's complete.
Mitchell's Series of large outline Maps.

HISTORY.
History of United States by Emma Willard.
Universal History.   "   "

PHILOSOPHY.
Parker's Philosophy.

ANATOMY, PHYSIOLOGY AND HYGIENE.
Human and comparative Anatomy, Physiology and Hygiene, by Eunice P. Cutter, and Cutter's Anatomical Charts.
Anatomy, Physiology and Hygiene, by Calvin Cutter, M. D.

ASTRONOMY AND GLOBES.—McIntire.

BOTANY.
Wood's Class Book of Botany.

CHEMISTRY.
Foster's First Principles of Chemistry, and Chemical apparatus.
Chemistry for beginners ; by Mrs. A. H. Lincoln Phelps.
Lectures on Chemistry, by A. H. Lincoln Phelps.

BOOK KEEPING.
Fulton & Eastman, Single and Double Entry.
"   "   Single and double entry with blanks.

POLITICAL ECONOMY.
Political Grammar, by Edward Mansfield.
Exposition of the Constitution of the United States, by James Bayard.

LIBRARY AND APPARATUS.
A well selected Library, consisting mostly of works on Education, belongs to the school, also a well-assorted Apparatus, for the illustration of the principles of natural philosophy, chemistry, mathematics, &c.

Mechanics' Academy. The first classes of the brand-new State University of Iowa met in the spring of 1855 in the Mechanics' Academy, near the corner of Iowa Avenue and Linn Street, where a wing of Seashore Hall now stands. Erected in 1842 by the Mechanics' Mutual Aid Association, the building initially housed a private school, followed in 1853 by the first public school established in Iowa City. The University trustees rented it in 1855 for $250 a year. In 1858 the University left it for Old Capitol, but two years later the Normal Department moved back. In 1861, when the legend "Iowa State Normal School" appeared over the door, the trustees ordered its removal, insisting that teacher training was to remain a subdivision of the University. In 1866 the trustees traded other property for it and turned it into a men's dormitory. Students called it the Syn Trap because many of the residents belonged to the Syntrapazones (table companions), a dining cooperative that sported the motto Vita sine grub, more est. *Five years later its interior was remodeled again, this time for a twenty-bed hospital for the use of the new Medical Department and some of the town doctors. A two-story addition on the east side housed the hospital's amphitheater. Though not a Catholic institution, the hospital was under the care and su-pervision of the Sisters of Mercy. When the building was razed in 1897 to make room for a larger and more modern hospital, canes and gavels were made out of its timbers. The canes were sent to members of the legislature, the gavels to presidents of various Iowa colleges. Its original cornerstone is embedded in the wall of the east entrance hall of the present Medical Laboratories Building.*

TWO

The College Years,
1859–1878

The east entrance to campus,
c. 1875.

After a two-year interlude when only the Normal Department remained in session, the full University reopened in the fall of 1860. Over the following eighteen years it endured a veritable parade of administrators: four presidents and two acting presidents, with one of the latter serving two terms. Despite the inevitable pulling and hauling, the institution developed from what was little more than a high school into a respectable four-year college, with law and medicine as professional addenda.

The Hiatus

Fortunately for the University, the Board of Trustees appointed in 1857 and chaired by Thomas Hart Benton, Jr., was a vigorous one that looked upon the University's closing in 1858 as a temporary suspension. The trustees kept the Normal Department in session while preparing for the reopening of the Collegiate Department. To head the Normal Department they retained the energetic and ambitious D. Franklin Wells and Lavinia Davis, "an accomplished female assistant." To direct the model school they found Mrs. M. A. McGonegal, who turned out to be so popular that her chief problem was holding down the enrollment, not building it up. Enrollment in the Normal Department itself also proved heartening: sixty-three in 1858–59 and eighty-nine in 1859–60, representing eleven counties. In addition, the trustees appointed Theodore S. Parvin to put the cabinet of natural history in order and to build up the library. Finances, of course, were the most bothersome problem. Only about $1,240 was in the hands of the treasurer from the interest on the University lands. But by diverting some of the funds previously appropriated for a residence hall and by obtaining new appropriations, the trustees managed to repair the roof on Old Capitol and to prepare rooms for the Normal Department and its model school. As much as their funds would allow, they continued to renovate Old Capitol and to buy furniture and equipment. In October 1859 they voted to reopen the University the following September, and in the meantime they appointed a president and a small faculty. They made the Normal Department a separate organization under the control of its principal. Once on the job the president and faculty added a Preparatory Department, with its principal, E. M. Guffin, receiving each student's tuition or matriculation fee (five dollars a term) as his compensation. Furthermore, to give all parts of the state a stake in the University, four students from each county (two in the Collegiate Department and two in the Normal) were admitted free. Before the 1860–61 school year was out, 172 students had been admitted. (At this time students could enter at any time during the school year.)

Years later, Benton wrote that if the board had foreseen that this would turn out to be a period "unprecedented in American history, and unexampled in the general prostration of the commercial and production interests of the country, . . . it is not probable that the University would have been opened."

Early Presidents

In seeking presidents for their institution, the Board of Trustees followed the tradition begun in the Middle Ages of placing learning in the hands of the clergy. One suspects, however, that the trustees were not as concerned with maintaining a tradition as they were with assuring parents that even in a state-supported school their sons and daughters would be under the influence of strong Christian leaders. In any event, their appointees

Silas Totten (1804–73), second president, 1859–62.

Oliver M. Spencer (1829–95), third president, 1862–67.

Nathan R. Leonard (1832–1917), acting president, 1867–68 and 1870–71.

James Black (1826–90), fourth president, 1868–70.

were clearly men of religious conviction. Several might also have provided a measure of intellectual leadership if they had had a chance, but during this period all of them were overworked, underpaid, and kept on short tether by the trustees or, after 1870, by the regents. Besides, only one of them stayed on campus longer than five years, and he was ultimately fired. Taken individually, the four presidents and two acting presidents from 1860 to 1878 were not known throughout the country as distinguished educators, but as a group they managed to guide the University on its early faltering steps rather well. Under their direction the University shook off its reputation as a high school for Johnson County residents and developed one as a superior midwestern college.

The first of this group was Silas Totten (1859–62), an Episcopalian rector who had been president of Trinity College in Hartford, Connecticut, for eleven years and who had taught at the College of William and Mary, also for eleven years. His was the dubious privilege of starting up the University for a second time and of doing this in the backwash of the panic of 1857 and the outbreak of the Civil War. To his credit, he put together a small but capable faculty and devised a departmental organization for the collegiate division that was neatly balanced between languages, philosophy, and history on the one hand and mathematics and the sciences on the other. Totten might have proved to be the leader Iowa needed, but word got out that he was a Southern sympathizer. In the summer of 1862 his son Richard had the bad judgment to denounce the North publicly. He was chased by an Iowa City mob, and Totten found it prudent to return to the pulpit. The Board of Trustees, all of them Unionists, later referred to his presidency as a "season of unprecedented embarrassment and discouragement."

Oliver M. Spencer (1862–67), a Methodist minister, was dignified and intelligent and much concerned that the students lead upstanding Christian lives. In addition to carrying out his presidential tasks, he taught chemistry and physics creditably, and partly because land sales were picking up, he was able to reassure the trustees that the University really had a future. Unfortunately, he was not temperamentally suited to the rough-and-tumble of a university on the edge of the prairie, and he spent much of his time in Washington seeking the job he finally obtained as United States consul in Genoa. Hoping to persuade him to return, the Trustees granted him a fifteen-month leave of absence. But once he left the campus in 1866, President Spencer never returned. After a tour of duty in Genoa, he became a consul in Australia and wrote for such magazines as *Harper's Monthly* and the *Atlantic Monthly*.

Nathan Leonard, a member of the faculty, served twice as acting president (1867–68 and 1870–71). Since he was an able administrator, some held that the trustees should give him an honorary doctorate of divinity and keep him on as president. Instead, on both occasions they sought out men trained as ministers. In 1868 they chose the Presbyterian minister James Black (1868–70), the first president to be formally inaugurated. In many respects the choice of Black was a good one. He had a shrewd understanding of what the University might realistically accomplish, especially in the sciences and their practical applications. He set it on track as a university, too, by approving the creation of departments of law and medicine. He proved to be too ardent a Democrat for the political tastes of the trustees, however, and too friendly with John P. Irish, the Democratic leader in Johnson County. Soon fed up with what he considered to be irrelevant attacks, Black quit in disgust in December 1870. Leonard again had to step in.

Shortly afterward, the Board of Regents (newly constituted in 1870) appointed George Thacher (1871–77),

George Thacher (1817–78), fifth president, 1871–77.

Christian W. Slagle (1821–82), acting president, 1877–78.

a Congregational minister and a graduate of Yale, who came with a reputation for outstanding oratory and teaching. Almost immediately he began dismantling the University's fast-developing program in the sciences and substituting for it the classical curriculum of the eastern schools, which stressed philosophy, philology, and ancient languages. This move aggravated the dissension that already existed in the faculty between the classicists and the scientists, and in time the quarrels and bickering helped to undermine Thacher's health to the point that he was unable to keep the faculty and students under control. In the spring of 1877 the regents concluded that it was necessary to replace him. But instead of telling him so, they sent him a letter the day before spring commencement, declaring his position vacant. At the end of the commencement services President Thacher read the letter to the assembled graduates and relatives. There was great distress for the sick man. The newspapers of the state, even those that admitted that the president was no longer fit to continue in office, blasted the regents for clumsiness, if not cruelty. On the same day that they agreed to fire Thacher, the regents appointed one of their own members, Christian W. Slagle (1877–78), as acting president. A Fairfield attorney of broad interests, Slagle might have given the University a unified direction, but he accepted the position only with the understanding that he would be relieved of the responsibility as soon as the board could make a more permanent appointment.

Unimpressive as their administrations were individually, as a group these early presidents, with the help of the trustees, managed to persuade the legislature that the University was the state's rightful responsibility, to win agreement that high-school-level education was not part of the University's function, and to fend off those who opposed the inclusion in the University of departments of law and medicine. On the campus they maintained

rather remarkable discipline, given the great unrest in the country as a whole. On the whole, theirs was not an insignificant set of accomplishments for administrators whose terms were so short.

Finances

To obtain an understanding of the life of the University from 1859 to 1878, the work of the six administrators can be viewed as a unit, since the major problems remained largely the same throughout the period. Finances were the most worrisome of them. In the early 1860s times were so hard that the already-modest salaries had to be reduced, the faculty had to teach unduly heavy class loads, and even the grass on the east lawn of Old Capitol had to be cut and sold for hay. One of the difficulties was the widespread impression, already mentioned, that the University was rich because it had the endowment resulting from the sale of federal land. At no time, however, did the interest provide enough for the normal operation of the school. Another harmful impression was that in granting land to the University, Congress acknowledged that it was responsible for taking care of the school financially. The idea was, of course, preposterous, but it was a convenient one for those state legislators who were reluctant to grant the University state funds. By 1872 the legislators had made only five ad hoc grants to the University, none of them for more than $25,000. Then in 1872 President Thacher persuaded them to appropriate $52,300 for improvements and increases in salaries. There was literally dancing in the Iowa City streets. More important, though, the legislature in 1878 by making the first annual appropriation to the University, for $20,000, at long last acknowledged that the state university was indeed a ward of the state. There were hard times ahead, but at least University administrators would no longer have to argue for the appropriateness of state appropriations for the state university.

Buildings and Grounds

With money so tight, funds for new buildings were especially hard to come by. Again a widespread impression had to be overcome, in this case that by turning over the Old Capitol to the University the legislature had taken care of the space problem for the foreseeable future. When it had become convinced, however, that without a dormitory the University would remain nothing more than a local school, the legislature in 1858 granted $10,000 for a "boarding hall" and in 1860 an additional $5,000 from the sale of the saline lands. (These were lands adjoining twelve salt springs that Congress had given the state in 1852 and that totaled over 46,000 acres in seven counties, chiefly Lucas and Appanoose.) On the same two occasions the legislature also granted $3,000 and $5,000 for renovating the interior of the capitol building. The new "boarding hall," called South Hall because it was located just south of Old Capitol, opened for students in 1863. It served as a residence hall for only three years, however, because in 1866 the students were moved out to make room for academic offices and classrooms. As a substitute, the trustees bought the Mechanics' Academy, which they had been renting, and turned it into a low-cost dormitory. (Five years later the students would be moved out of it, too, when a hospital building was needed.) In the mid-1860s new appropriations and gifts made North Hall possible. About the same time, an iron fence was put around the Old Capitol grounds to keep out the hogs and other

livestock, and in the mid-1870s a small observatory was built at the head of Clinton Street, where the president's house now stands. It would take a wizard to chart how the various administrations found space at one time or another for classrooms, offices for administrators, faculty offices, laboratories, the library, the museum, the chapel, meeting rooms for the literary societies, a place for the janitor and his dog (or pig), the new Law Department and its library, and the new Medical Department with its operating room and repository for cadavers.

The Preparatory Department

A second major problem confronting all six presidents was the position of the University in the state educational system. Would it be solely concerned with the top of the educational pyramid or did it have to assume some responsibility for the middle level—the high school level—as well? The fact that there were so few high schools in the state capable of training students for college-level work forced the hand of these early administrations. Following the lead of President Dean, President Totten in 1860 created a Preparatory Department for inadequately trained students. Some 40 percent of the students immediately registered in that department. President Spencer, however, believing that preparatory work was not part of a University's obligation, eliminated the Preparatory Department—but quickly restored it when the faculty of the Collegiate Department complained that half the students in their classes were not equipped for college-level work. He did, however, recommend to the board that the preparatory program be reduced from three years to two. To qualify for it, students had to demonstrate that they could read,

An 1869 engraving of the campus, showing South Hall, Old Capitol, and North Hall. While the University's catalog *promised that "no pains will be spared to make the grounds attractive," they were not quite so pristine as this engraving* *suggests. About this time the Board of Trustees authorized the University's janitor, Herman Rupine, to "purchase . . .* *a dog at a cost not exceeding the sum of five dollars to assist him in keeping the yard clear of stock."*

had some mastery of penmanship, and possessed at least a good grade-school command of grammar, arithmetic, and geography. In 1869 President Black dropped the first year of this preparatory program and added a subfreshman year to the collegiate curriculum, making the latter a five-year program, three years for general study and two for specialized study in either the sciences or languages and literature. In the catalogue the term "Introductory" replaced "Preparatory." Shortly after, the Iowa City School Board voted to discontinue its high school because it cost too much, and besides, Iowa City students could obtain the necessary training at the Iowa City Academy or the University. This action provoked an indignant protest in the Iowa City *State Press* and an even more vigorous response from Gustavus Hinrichs of the University faculty, whose career at the University is discussed in the next section. Three days later the Iowa City School Board rescinded its action. Slowly, as the result of public concern, the pendulum swung toward the elimination of what was really high school work. In 1878, in authorizing the first annual appropriation, the General Assembly stipulated that no part of it should be used for the Preparatory Department. The following year the regents dropped that department and agreed that the University would accept graduates from high schools or private academies accredited by the University itself, provided that they had demonstrated a competence in high-school-level mathematics, English, science, history, German, and Latin or advanced science. The effect was salutary. In Iowa City alone some three hundred students registered in the public high school or private academies instead of trying to jam into University classes before they were ready. The University had finally established itself as the top level of the state's educational system.

The Classical versus the Practical

The issue that faced Chancellor Dean about whether undergraduate work should be primarily classical or practical in its orientation continued through the several administrations from 1860 to 1878. Should it serve the cause of learning and stress ancient languages and literature and abstract reasoning, or should it serve the immediate needs of the people of the state and stress teacher training and the practical application of the sciences? Building on Chancellor Dean's plan, President Totten tried to maintain a balance. He established a three-year bachelor of science program and a four-year bachelor of arts program and retained the two-year non-degree normal program. In the sciences he appointed Professor James Lillie and in the languages Professor Oliver Spencer, but these two gentlemen promptly asked for and were granted the privilege of exchanging chairs. He also appointed Nathan R. Leonard in mathematics and astronomy, and Theodore S. Parvin in natural history, and continued Professor D. Franklin Wells as principal of the Normal Department. He himself took over the chair of intellectual and moral philosophy and rhetoric. Following what he called the German and Scottish plan, Totten created six "departments" in the collegiate division, three in letters and three in the sciences. Each department was controlled by a single professor, who set the standards for the department and who was responsible for all of the instruction in it. Students could enter the work of a department at any level for which they were prepared and could confine their study to three, two, or even one of the departments. Thus, for example, students of a practical bent could escape requirements in Greek and Latin and other classical subjects.

President Spencer also tried to maintain the balance

between the classical and the practical, but he gave the total program more cohesion by taking away the independence of the various professors in the collegiate division and making each of them—and the students—responsible to the division. Unknowingly, he precipitated a major swing toward the sciences by appointing a dynamic and headstrong graduate of the University of Copenhagen by the name of Gustavus D. Hinrichs as a professor of modern languages and then reassigning him to physics and chemistry. The effect of Professor Hinrichs on the University was extraordinary. His laboratory method of teaching chemistry and physics soon began to attract students from other fields, and his papers on the order of elements began to win him—and the University—not only national but international attention, though not always agreement. It was principally his reputation that persuaded the trustees and the legislature to provide an appropriation for North Hall, in which the whole first floor was to be laboratory space. They even sent him to visit the four best laboratories in the country so that he could make Iowa's just as good, or even better. President Spencer, also a scientist, encouraged Hinrichs, and so did Presidents Leonard and Black. Hinrichs's influence peaked at the beginning of the 1870s when he was granted a second assistant professor and when all students were required to take physical science. His star began to fall, however, when Yale-trained George Thacher became president in 1871 and started to push classical studies at the expense of theoretical and applied science.

Thacher was evidently not against change per se, for during his administration the University added courses in military tactics and homeopathic medicine, a homeopathic hospital, and an astronomical observatory. The social sciences were strengthened by the addition of Leonard F. Parker in history and Stephen N. Fellows in political and moral science. Thacher even dismayed his friends among the classicists by appointing Gilbert L. Pinkham to a chair of English language and literature, thereby making possible courses in Chaucer and Shakespeare, writers the classicists considered much too recent to be proper subjects for advanced study. Thacher, however, strongly opposed laboratory science and civil engineering as too practical to be appropriate for a university curriculum. First he cut Hinrichs's laboratory budget, thereby making an implacable enemy of the fiery Dane. Then he withheld support for equipment in the newly established Department of Civil Engineering, headed by Philetus H. Philbrick, an able and articulate engineer. Lacking sufficient equipment, Philbrick had to give up the new department and return with some bitterness to his original chair of civil engineering in the Collegiate Department.

By the spring of 1877 the regents had become convinced that Thacher's biases and his clearly failing health had made him unfit to govern the University, and on June 21 they declared the office of president vacant. With Thacher's departure went the last president to promote cultural elitism at the expense of the theoretical and practical sciences. However, even under the new acting president, Christian W. Slagle, Hinrichs failed to regain his former influence. Always unpredictable, he shifted his interest to meteorology and got into a dispute with Professor Leonard over who should teach astronomy. Both were reprimanded by the regents. Slagle restored something of a balance between the classical and the practical by reorganizing the Collegiate Department into a Faculty of Letters and a Faculty of Science. The change did not eliminate the issue, but at least it drained the altercation of some of its ferocity.

Gustavus Hinrichs (bottom row, center) and his laboratory class on the steps of North Hall, c. 1874. In the late 1860s and early 1870s, all Iowa freshmen and subfreshmen took a yearlong course in physical science. Professor Hinrichs and his two assistants ran the classes, which met on the first floor of North Hall. The floor was divided into four large rooms, the largest of which (30 by 60 feet) was the student laboratory. According to an 1869 issue of the University Reporter, "Neatness and almost perfect order was observed. We saw much new apparatus purchased by Prof. H. when east last summer: a new analytical balance, a series of models of crystals and glass, and a collection of finely crystallized minerals." In following years appeared a "goniometer for measuring the angle of crystals, a Rhumkorff induction coil, Hofmann's apparatus for the decomposition of water and a Holtz electrical machine capable of producing electricity without friction." Hinrichs's rules for this "temple of science" were BE QUIET, BE CAREFUL, BE CERTAIN.

Law and Medicine

There was strong opposition to the inclusion of professional schools in the University in its early days, for it was felt by many that taxes should not be used to pay for the training of a privileged class. The first venture into professional training came in September 1868 when the University took over the Iowa Law School of Des Moines, which had been founded three years before by Iowa Supreme Court justices George C. Wright and Chester C. Cole and conducted by them with William G. Hammond. These men became the law faculty in Iowa City, with Hammond as the resident professor and chancellor. Initially the Law Department was granted $7,600, with $2,000 of this designated for a library. For quarters, it was assigned a section partitioned off on the second floor of Old Capitol. More than thirty students enrolled the first year.

The Medical Department was begun in the fall of 1870, with eight women in the first class of thirty-seven. It was squeezed into South Hall, where Dr. W. F. Peck performed operations and then sent his patients to rooming houses in Iowa City. This department was quite distinct from the medical school at Keokuk, whose graduates received their degrees from the University until 1870. Friends of the Keokuk school attempted to block the creation of the Iowa City school and even managed to push a bill to abolish it through the Iowa Senate, but it was indefinitely postponed in the House of Representatives.

The Grave-Robbing Incident

Hardly had the University's Medical Department started before it became involved in a case of grave-robbing that threatened its existence. For instruction in anatomy, the department so badly needed cadavers that several people took things into their own hands. In December 1870, Dominique Bradley, the janitor of the Medical Department, and two students lifted the body of a woman newly buried in Iowa City's Oakland Cemetery and carried it to the medical laboratory in the basement of South Hall. In the uproar that followed, suspicion centered on the Medical Department after Bradley's notebook was found at the grave site. Because it was New Year's weekend, law officers were slow in beginning a search. Before they did, John P. Irish, the local Democratic leader, arranged for two students to cart off the body and conceal it in a haystack three miles west of town. He then made a deal with the relatives that the body would be returned if no charges were filed. When the body was brought back, however, it showed plainly that dissection had already begun. Warrants were issued against the janitor, the professor of anatomy, two students, and Irish. Even as late as the following summer the affair raged in the newspapers, but although the janitor confessed, no indictments were returned. Dr. J. M. Boucher, the professor of anatomy, resigned, and the Republicans attacked Irish more vigorously than ever. The upshot of the affair was that the General Assembly made it possible for the Medical Department to obtain the unclaimed dead from the state prisons. Soon the Mechanics' Academy, in another of its transformations, became a hospital under the direction of the Sisters of Mercy.

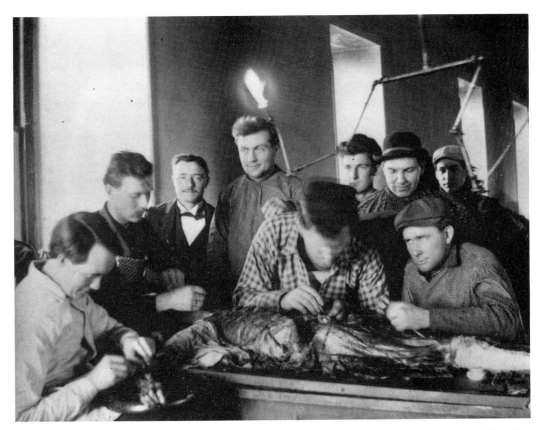

Anatomy students in the basement of South Hall, 1880s.

John P. Irish (1843–1923). Irish was one of the University's most active supporters in the 1860s and 1870s; he was especially popular with the students, partly because of his role in the grave-robbing incident. Born in Iowa in 1843, he became the editor of the State Press *at the age of twenty-one and made it one of the best-known Democratic papers in the state. Elected to the Iowa House of Representatives in 1867, 1869, and 1871, he campaigned vigorously for funds for the University and for the establishment of the departments of law and medicine. In 1868 he was appointed to the Board of Trustees. He had served only two of his six years on the board, however, when the Republicans, in order to get rid of him, changed the Board of Trustees to the Board of Regents and saw to it that he was not appointed to the new governing body.*

The Demise of the Normal Department

The Normal Department had continued to operate between 1858 and 1860 when the rest of the University was shut down, and its enrollment regularly exceeded that of the Collegiate Department. In many respects it had been the darling of the legislators, because they had looked to it to train teachers for the hundreds of schools that were opening throughout the state. In 1866, however, when Professor D. Franklin Wells, who considered the Normal Department his personal fiefdom, refused to allow it to become part of the Collegiate Department, he was dismissed by the Board of Trustees. The Normal Department then merged with the Collegiate Department, and in 1872 a chair of didactics was established and subsequently assigned to Professor Stephen N. Fellows. The creation of this chair constituted the first recognition in the United States that the training of teachers was appropriate collegiate work.

The Civil War

In the eighteen years from 1860 to 1878, student enrollment rose, though not steadily, from 173 in 1860–61 to 612 in 1877–78. During the Civil War some classes had to be canceled, but the war seems not to have hurt the University's overall registration. Understandably, though, the tone of the campus changed. The rattle of the drums of the provost marshal on Clinton Street broke into its normal quiet. Students in the Military Department trained with real guns, and war news was as avidly sought by students as it was by townspeople. On April 19, 1865, a memorial service for Abraham Lincoln took place on the east steps of Old Capitol, and many of the faculty and students joined others through-out the North in wearing mourning crepe for thirty days after the assassination. Between 1861 and 1865, 124 students entered the Union ranks. Of these, three were killed—Israel M. Ritter, George A. Remley, and Samuel Kirkwood Clark—and many were wounded. At least three others who had previously been students were killed. After the war, the regents granted free tuition to all Iowa soldiers who had served three years in the Union army or who had received honorable discharges because of wounds or other disabilities. Fifty-five, many of them wounded, took advantage of this offer. The legend is that there were seven empty sleeves in one class alone.

Student Life

Coming as they did from the homes of farmers, mechanics, and small businessmen, most of the students of the 1860s and 1870s were the first in their families to go to college. Those who did not live in Iowa City brought their belongings in a carpetbag or, if they planned to rent an unfurnished room, borrowed a horse and wagon to cart not only their clothes and books but also a wood stove and a few pieces of furniture. Often the president himself or a member of the faculty—or the janitor—helped them find rooms. Expenses averaged about $2.50 a month for a room, $2.50 to $4.00 a week for board, and $20 a year for washing. Tuition for undergraduates consisted of a $5 matriculation fee each term for incidental expenses. This was waived for Union veterans, as mentioned above, or for orphans of Union soldiers. Also, the practice was continued of waiving the fee of two collegiate students from each county plus two more students in the Normal Department so long as that department was in existence. Since professional schools

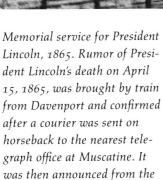

Announcement of a benefit for soldiers' families, 1863. Of the eighty-three men in Company D of the Forty-fourth Iowa Infantry Regiment in the Civil War, forty were students from the University.

Memorial service for President Lincoln, 1865. Rumor of President Lincoln's death on April 15, 1865, was brought by train from Davenport and confirmed after a courier was sent on horseback to the nearest telegraph office at Muscatine. It was then announced from the pulpits of the city's churches on the morning of Sunday, April 16. Bells tolled in mourning for three days and nights. On the day of the memorial service, April 19, Iowa City townspeople, students, and faculty gathered at Old Capitol to hear a eulogy delivered by former Iowa governor Samuel Kirkwood. Ironically, less than two weeks before, every window of Old Capitol and South Hall had been illuminated with candles to mark the surrender of Confederate General Robert E. Lee at Appomattox.

were expected to pay their own way, tuition for those in law and medicine was $20 a course or $80 a term. To meet even these costs, over a third of the students had to work at least part-time, the women doing housework or clerking, and the men doing everything from lighting and extinguishing the street lamps to taking care of their landlady's horse and buggy. When they could, students organized cooperatives, such as the Syntrapazone Club in the Mechanics' Academy. The only restriction the University placed on housing was that men and women students could not rent rooms in the same house.

In dress, the students were a good deal less than nobby, to use their word. In their calicoes and ginghams and rough woolens, they were probably less well-dressed than the townspeople. Many of the men had beards and chewed tobacco and smoked cigars. The University forbade smoking and spitting in the halls and classrooms but imposed no other restrictions on the use of tobacco. It did, however, outlaw drinking and loafing in saloons and billiard parlors. There is no record of any student being hauled up for sexual misconduct. Men and women were permitted to sit together in laboratories and classes—except in, of all places, penmanship classes in the Preparatory Department. On the whole, therefore, the ways of the campus reflected those of the families from which the students came: conservative, religious, friendly but often shy in mixed company, sometimes rowdy (especially the law students), and in morals extraordinarily decent—or at least discreet.

For some students the required daily chapel and Sunday church service were not enough to meet their religious needs, and so they organized Tuesday prayer meetings and assisted in conducting the daily noonday businessmen's prayer meeting in Iowa City. When the town's YMCA folded in 1870, the students organized a campus Christian Association, with Stephen N. Fellows as president. This, in turn, gave way to a campus YMCA

and YWCA. If the students knew about the writings of Darwin, Huxley, and Tyndall and the speeches of Robert Ingersoll, there is little evidence that such writers undermined their belief in God or in material progress as a demonstration of God's plan for his people.

At one point the trustees, apparently thinking that the students might not be combining a strong body with a sound mind, established a requirement in gymnastics, but they soon abandoned the idea. The students themselves did a fair amount of walking, especially those who lived on the outskirts of town. For recreation, some paddled on the river or took hikes on its banks as far north as Butler's bridge. In 1867 there was a rage for riding velocipedes of every variety from four wheelers to unicycles. In the spring of 1873 there was a craze for quoits. Also in the 1870s various organized groups on the campus began playing each other in baseball—not a game for the tender-handed, for no one wore gloves. In the fall of 1872 a sophomore team challenged the rest of the University and lost by the whopping score of 45 to 22. In 1876 the *University Reporter* (an eight-page monthly paper published by the students) noted that an Iowa team had played a team from Cornell College in Mount Vernon. Pickup football games began after a student subscription yielded enough money for a ball. There was no set number of players, and there were few rules. Again, the players used no protective equipment. Probably the roughest games were between the "Laws" and the "Medics," a rivalry immortalized in the stiff little jingle,

> Lawyer Charlie is my name,
> Playing football is my game
> When I go out, some fun to see
> Medics are the lads for me.

Enough stories of pranks survive to suggest that the student body had its quota of clowns. The president seems to have been a favorite butt of practical jokes. Once, for example, when President Spencer was on one of his trips to Washington seeking a United States consulate, the students put a sign on the bulletin board announcing him as "Strayed or Stolen." Another time they put plaster of paris in the keyhole of the door to President Leonard's office. The most elaborate affair was a burlesque of the faculty produced in the Coldren Opera House at the corner of Clinton and College streets. Featured was a George Thrasher (President George Thacher). The faculty seems to have become steamed up after such events, but there is no record of any punishment being assessed.

Unlike what happened at many other American colleges and universities, there was little town-and-gown squabbling in Iowa City. So many of the students came from the town or boarded in it that an unusual identity of interests developed. Besides, townspeople were constantly being invited to University affairs, and the University faculty frequently spoke in Iowa City churches or lectured at public meetings. On occasion the town put up money to help with University building construction and other activities. Differences arose, of course, but there is no record of any great hostility. The fact that so many of the presidents and faculty members during these days were ministers undoubtedly gave the University a sanction in the town that it would otherwise not have had.

Literary Societies

Outside the classrooms the intellectual life of the campus centered around the four main literary societies. The first of these, organized in 1861, was the Zetagathian Society for men. This was followed a year later by the Erodelphian Society and in 1863 by the Hesperian Society, both of them women's groups, and by the Irving Institute for men in 1864. All of these soci-

eties, and others that followed their pattern, had lofty purposes that boiled down to a desire to advance the learning, morals, and literary and rhetorical skills of their members. When the Zetagathians began, they had to meet by the light of two tallow candles. They bought notebooks for their secretary through an assessment of ten cents a head. In a short time the societies so impressed the trustees that the board allocated substantial funds for fixing up two rather handsome meeting rooms on the third floor of South Hall, one for the Zetagathians and Hesperians, and the other for the Irving Institute and the Erodelphians. The women's societies met in the afternoon and the men's in the evening. A typical meeting included the reading of an essay, one or two declamations, and a debate involving six or twelve of the members on such propositions as "Roman Catholicism Is Incompatible with Free Institutions," "Land Grants to the Railroads Are Injurious to the Country," "The Classics Are as Important as Science," and "A Woman Has the Right to Marry for Money." Several times a year each society sponsored a special public meeting in the chapel or in Iowa City's Metropolitan Hall, where attendance would sometimes exceed a thousand. Gradually the dues went up, and before the end of the 1870s the Zetagathians were able to buy a four-hundred-dollar piano. There was little faculty control of these groups, for normally none was needed. The societies were probably the most important extracurricular activity on campus, because they gave the students a chance to socialize as well as to hone their literary and forensic skills against the day when they would be asked to take over responsibilities in public life. Out of these societies there developed first an interest in state and interstate oratorical contests and eventually the intercollegiate debating team coached by Professor A. Craig Baird. Another legacy was Iowa's unusually strong Speech Department, now the Department of Communication Studies.

Members of the Erodelphian Society, 1883. "You belonged to the 'literary societies' or you didn't belong at SUI in those days," said a student in 1890. One of the four literary groups sharing two rooms on the third floor of South Hall, the Erodelphian Society was founded October 6, 1862, "for the purpose," said the constitution drafted by its twenty-two members, "of improving ourselves in intellectual and literary attainments." One motto of the group was "We gather light to scatter."

Zetagathian Society program, 1865.

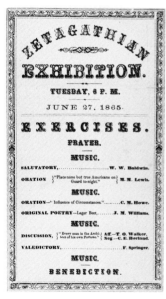

Meeting room of the Erodelphian Society and the Irving Institute on the third floor of South Hall, 1890.

The campus in winter, showing South Hall, Old Capitol (then called Central), and North Hall, c. 1870. In the spring of 1868 the Board of Trustees re-solved that "the Council of Iowa City be requested to take the necessary steps for the re-moval of all obstructions, in-cluding agricultural imple-ments, from the fence and sidewalks immediately around the University grounds." The next year brought an order for removal of theater posters from the same area, and tradi-tion has it that University stu-dents with axes chopped down the billboards advertising for-bidden entertainment.

South Hall, after a hailstorm, c. 1890. Although ground was broken due south of Old Capitol for South Hall in June 1858, the legislature released the funds for its completion so slowly that it did not open until September 1861. The three-story structure quickly became the all-purpose building on the campus. For a few years it was a men's dormitory, with its ten chimneys on each side providing vents for stoves and fireplaces. By 1864 classrooms and faculty offices had crowded out the bedrooms, including the apartment on the first floor used by Theodore S. Parvin, a professor of natural history, and his wife and family. In the late 1860s the third floor was renovated for the four earliest literary societies, and the second floor for liberal arts classrooms and faculty offices. In 1870 the Medical Department moved in, sharing the first floor with the registrar and the basement with the janitor. That year, gas lights replaced kerosene lamps and candles, and by the early 1880s steam radiators had made stoves unnecessary.

Library and chapel in North Hall, 1870s. Soon after North Hall was completed in 1866, the State Press *of Iowa City called it "the most barnlike public structure we ever saw; it looks like a cross between a dog kennel and a country church." The Iowa City Re-publican, however, thought the chapel on the second floor "the finest audience room in Iowa. . . . Its spacious dimensions, frescoed walls, stained glass windows, with emblematic representations, make up a hall that is a great credit to the state that has erected it."*

Chemical laboratories were in the basement, lecture rooms and the student laboratory occupied the first floor, and the library and chapel shared the large upper chamber seen here. Until 1879 all students were required to appear for morning chapel exercises. Attendance decreased markedly after that time. In the fall of 1883 the Vidette-Reporter *noted, "If you see a solitary senior wander into chapel, you may know he has come upstairs to size up the freshmen."*

Faculty of the Collegiate Department, 1874. In the front row from left to right are Amos Currier (Latin and literature), Celia A. M. Currier (instructor in Latin), George Thacher (president, moral philosophy), Elizabeth Griffith (instructor in mathematics), and Stephen Fellows (didactics). In the back row from left to right are Samuel Calvin (natural science and curator of the University cabinet), Gustavus Hinrichs (physical science and director of the laboratory), Nathan Leonard (mathematics and astronomy), Leonard Parker (civil engineering), two unidentified assistants, and Philetus Philbrick (civil engineering). At this time women were hired to teach as instructors but were not considered regular faculty.

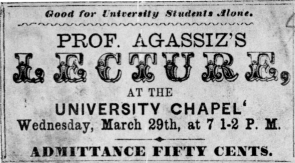

Ticket to Professor Louis Agassiz's lecture in Iowa City, 1864. The date on this ticket is wrong, but yes, Louis Agassiz, the celebrated Harvard naturalist, lectured in Iowa City on March 2, 1864. Agassiz spoke on the "Coral Reefs of Iowa City." Coralville, Iowa City's neighboring town, is named for these fossil reefs. They give the stone used in Old Capitol its pinkish tint.

Theodore S. Parvin (1817–1901). Lawyer, historian, university professor, and public-spirited citizen, Parvin should be better remembered than he is. He came to Iowa in 1838 as the private secretary of Robert Lucas, the first governor of Iowa Territory, and was immediately certified to practice law in the territorial courts. As district prosecutor he took part in the first term of court held in Johnson County, with the judge sitting in a one-story cabin and the grand jury assembled on the ground outside. He was the territorial librarian, a probate judge, and the clerk of the United States district court from 1847 to 1857. In 1859 he was appointed curator and librarian of the University, in 1860 professor of natural history, and in 1868 professor of history. In 1870 one of the first acts of the new Board of Regents was to eliminate the chair of history in order to remove Parvin. There was no clear reason for the action other than that Parvin was a Democrat, for he was immensely popular with the students and was one of the hardest workers on the faculty. Parvin was among the first curators of the State Historical Society of Iowa, as well as a secretary of the society and the editor of the Annals of Iowa. *He was also a founder and president of the Iowa State Teachers Association.*

Phoebe Sudlow (1831–1922). In 1878 Phoebe Sudlow became the first "lady professor" at the University when she was hired to teach English language and literature. She was the superintendent of public schools in Davenport, Iowa, from 1874 to 1878, the first woman to serve in such a position anywhere in the country. When she was appointed principal of School No. 3 in Davenport, she argued that women who did work equal to that of men should receive equal pay—and the school board agreed. She was the first woman to be elected president of the Iowa State Teachers Association, triumphing over both Amos N. Currier and Henry Sabin in 1876. Because of illness she was forced to retire from the University in 1881, but in 1888 she returned to the Davenport school system for one year as principal of School No. 1. One of her pupils was eleven-year-old John G. Bowman, who later became president of the University of Iowa.

Gustavus D. Hinrichs (1836–1923). Hinrichs joined the Iowa faculty in September 1862. He first taught both modern languages and the physical sciences in general but soon began to concentrate his efforts on physics and chemistry. He was a man of incredible energy, meeting classes from 8 A.M. to 1 P.M. daily, writing textbooks, giving public lectures, laboring continually to make his laboratories in North Hall the best of their kind in America, campaigning for more science classes in the public schools, crusading internationally for his theory of the order of elements, and even directing instrumental music for chapel services. Thanks largely to his efforts, by 1870 all students were required to take physical science and to do some work in the laboratory. Hinrichs was so domineering and self-centered, however, that he antagonized his colleagues on the faculty and therefore found little support when President Thacher cut back his science program in favor of more traditional work in philosophy and letters. In 1875 Hinrichs turned to meteorology and organized the Iowa weather reporting service. Ultimately, President Pickard found his incessant needling so troublesome that he brought charges against him before the Board of Regents. After hearing the case, the board dismissed Hinrichs from the collegiate faculty but retained him at half salary on the medical and pharmaceutical faculties. In March 1886 the board dismissed him completely. He then accepted the chair of chemistry in the St. Louis College of Pharmacy, and from St. Louis for many years he kept up a stream of intemperate attacks on the University and its administrators in pamphlets and in the press. A gifted scientist, Hinrichs was defeated by his own irritability and his belief that the world was against him. At his best, however, he provided undergraduates with an almost religious faith in the value of the physical sciences.

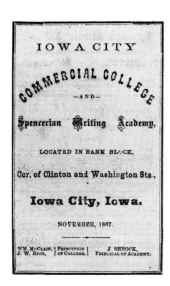

Advertisement for Iowa City Commercial College and Spencerian Writing Academy, 1867. After the Civil War, students preparing themselves for business careers would combine a course of study at the University with study at Iowa City business colleges. The first business school in Iowa City was the Spencerian Writing Academy, which opened in 1865, followed shortly by the Iowa City Commercial College. In 1870 William C. McClain bought and merged them into a single institution. Three years later he divided the school into two sections, the Iowa City Academy and the Iowa City Commercial College. The former benefited greatly when the regents eliminated the University's Preparatory Department in the summer of 1879. After McClain's death, F. E. Williams and J. H. Williams continued the school until 1905. Later schools included Elizabeth Irish's Business College (1897–1940) and Brown's Business Institute (1924–34).

First Observatory. This photograph, appearing in an 1899 album belonging to Pharmacy graduate John M. Lindley (class of 1889, state senator, 1915–19), bears the following inscription: "Old Observatory at head of Clinton St., overlooking the Iowa River. Here we looked thro the telescope at the rings of Saturn." The second of the University's observatories stood on the west slope of the Pentacrest just below where Jessup Hall now stands. It was removed in 1916 to the west side of the river after a runaway truck knocked it several feet off its foundation.

Law class, 1879. The graduating class of 1879 included Alexander Clark, Jr. (back row, to right of left pillar), of Muscatine, the first black law graduate, and Moung Edwin of Burma, the first foreign student (second figure to right of Clark). Alexander Clark, Sr., followed his son to Iowa and received his law degree in 1884. He was appointed minister to Liberia in 1890.

Law library in Old Capitol, c. 1900. Law classes were held in the former House chamber in Old Capitol, and the library was in the old Senate chamber. From the outset, instruction in law at Iowa was partly by the case method, which entailed the professor's offering commentary on recent legal decisions in addition to a lecture on theory. While in time this became an accepted method of legal instruction, it was highly controversial into the late 1880s.

Mary Humphrey Haddock, law graduate and 1875 class valedictorian. In 1873 the Iowa Code was amended to strike out "white" and "male" as qualifications for admission to the bar. Mary Humphrey Haddock, from Tipton, was the first woman admitted to practice before the United States circuit and district courts. In 1865 she married William J. Haddock, secretary of the executive committee of the Board of Regents, and served for a time as assistant secretary.

Medical faculty, 1871. In 1871, the University's first Medical Department faculty included, standing, left to right: G. Hinrichs (chemistry), J. C. Shrader (diseases of women and children), W. S. Robertson (theory and practice), W. D. Middleton (physiology and microscopic anatomy), and E. F. Clapp (anatomy); seated, left to right: P. J. Farnsworth (materia medica), W. F. Peck (surgery), and J. F. Dillon (medical jurisprudence). Faculty members in medicine did not receive salaries from the University at this time. Their compensation for teaching came from student fees, often supplemented by income from private practice. For many years, all of the professional schools were expected to be self-supporting.

MEDICAL DEPARTMENT.

Programme of Lectures for the Regular Term---Session of 1875-6.

TIME:	Monday.	Tuesday.	Wednesday.	Thursday.	Friday.	Saturday.
9 A. M.	Chemistry.	Chemistry.	Chemistry.	MATERIA MEDICA.	Obstetrics and Dis. of Women.	Chemical Analysis.
10 A. M.	OBSTETRICS & DIS. of WOMEN.	Anatomy.	MATERIA MEDICA.	OBSTETRICS & DIS. of WOMEN.	Anatomy.	
11 A. M.	Theory & Practice	Surgery.	EYE AND EAR.	Theory & Practice	Surgery.	
1:30 P. M.	MEDICAL CLINIC.	CLINIC DIS. of CHILDE'N	EYE and EAR CLINIC	CLINIC DIS. OF WOMEN.	Surg. Clinic.	
2:30 P. M	Anatomy.			Anatomy.		
3 P. M.		Surgery.			Matr. Medica.	
3:30 P. M.	Physiology.		Physiology.	Theory & Practice		

The Lectures in Medical Jurisprudence, Insanity and Dentistry will be announced from time to time during the session.

Medical Department course schedule, 1875–76. To register for classes, students in medicine paid tuition (in this year, twenty dollars) and secured tickets from the professors whose lectures they wanted to attend. Classroom lectures, rather than bedside teaching, were the rule, and very little laboratory work was required. Prior to 1881, an M.D. degree at Iowa required two years of course work, from 1881 to 1896 it took three years, and ever since it has taken four years. By 1890 the University of Iowa had graduated 550 doctors, 40 of them women.

Students from the class of 1866. The following account of social life on campus is from Celia Currier, wife of the acting president and herself a Latin instructor in the Collegiate Department from 1869 to 1874: "Student social affairs were very limited in the early years. For several years there was a Friday night gathering in the chapel known popularly as 'The Walkaround,' but which I find referred to more respectfully in my diary as the Student Social. A line of settees was ranged round the walls and a few placed back to back in the center, the rest stacked in the lobby. There was no ceremony—no receiving line. As soon as a few were assembled the line of march started. For the whole blessed evening the company circled around the room in couples, dropping down at intervals to rest. Sometimes somebody played the cabinet organ which led the morning devotions."

Campus advertisement, 1870s.

St. James Hotel, 1880s. From 1872 until 1914 the St. James was Iowa City's finest hotel. A four-story brick building with a mansard roof, the St. James was located at the corner of Iowa Avenue and Clinton Street, where Iowa Book and Supply now stands. It had forty rooms, and according to the advertisements it ran in the Vidette-Reporter, *everything was first class. In 1914 the St. James became the Iowa Student Union, with rooms for students. It burned on Good Friday in 1916.*

Bill of fare for the first alumni banquet, St. James Hotel, 1875. Starting in 1866, one day of commencement week was set aside for the alumni. In 1875 came the first alumni banquet, an event which became so popular that in 1885 the Vidette-Reporter *labeled it the "crowning feature of Commencement Week."*

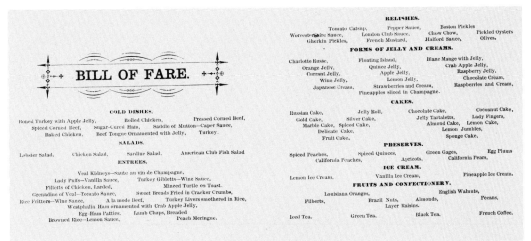

BY T. W. TOWNSEND.

North.   Iowa City

Views of Iowa City and Vicinity,

An 1870s stereograph of Clinton Street between Washington Street and Iowa Avenue. On the far corner of the block stood the St. James Hotel, and on the near end was a hardware store, with Townsend's photo gallery upstairs. Next to the hotel was the post office and Mrs. J. G. Fink's, which in addition to cigars, tobacco, and related supplies, sold ammunition and stationery. Eight of the city's seventeen law firms and five of its seventeen shoe stores were in the block, as well as the offices of the Iowa City Republican, Nixon & Doe Undertakers, Robinson Bros. Dry-Goods, and the Johnson County Savings Bank. The city was said at the time to be "provided with good substantial sidewalks, all usually in good condition."

THREE

The Emerging University,
1878–1916

*Ladies' gymnasium, 1904.
When Schaeffer Hall opened in
1902, the women's athletic facilities were a single basement
room that students called "The
Crypt."*

The narrative of the six administrations between 1878 and 1916 is one of accelerating growth. Unlike the seven earlier administrations, these enjoyed regular appropriations for salaries and equipment and eventually the income from a millage tax that made more handsome buildings possible. The organization of the institution as a whole and the curriculums of the various colleges assumed a modern form. Student enrollment jumped almost sixfold, from 561 to 3,286, and the faculty from 45 to 192, nearly one-quarter of them full professors. By 1916 no one could any longer refer disparagingly to the University of Iowa as an undergraduate college and certainly not as the Johnson County High School.

Josiah L. Pickard

Josiah L. Pickard was the first public schoolman to be appointed president of the University. A graduate of Bowdoin College, he came to Iowa City after serving as superintendent of schools for the state of Wisconsin for five years and for the city of Chicago for thirteen years. The experience enabled him to strengthen the ties between the public schools and the University. It was during his administration, for example, that the University began to accept without examination the graduates of high schools with approved academic programs. Pickard also supported an extension of the Bachelor of Science program from two to four years, and the Bachelor of Law program from one year to two. Undergraduates could substitute French or German for the Greek requirement and could add carefully monitored elective courses in their junior and senior years. In the professional area the University added departments of dentistry and pharmacy.

Physical signs of progress on the campus included new buildings for medicine and science (Calvin Hall). New chairs with arms to hold notebooks pleased the students, and everyone rejoiced in the introduction of steam heating in the major buildings and running water in the toilets. The administration also tidied up the slope west of Old Capitol, installed gas lamps between Old Capitol and North and South Halls, and issued uniforms to the band.

Political and personal problems, however, bedeviled President Pickard from the start and ultimately led to doubts about his competence. Not all of the troubles were of his own making. He inherited a collegiate faculty still split in educational philosophy between the classicists and the pragmatists. Even the separation of the factions into a Faculty of Letters and a Faculty of Science just before he took office failed to quell the squabbles over preeminence. The faculty members were still fuming over charges in the legislature that they did not work hard enough and over a request from the regents that they spend at least four hours a day in the classroom. Once he became president, Pickard, too, was immediately exposed to the needling of Gustavus Hinrichs, who by this time was clearly paranoid. Pickard put up with the barbs until he realized how badly they were corroding relationships throughout the University and then requested that the regents fire Hinrichs. At first they responded by firing him from the Collegiate Department but not from the Medical and Pharmacy Departments, in which he also taught. When Hinrichs continued to be insufferable, the regents in 1886 took the final step and fired him outright. In the meantime, stories about unrest on the campus began to spread around the state, stories prompted not only by Hinrichs's criticisms but also by rumors of rowdiness among the law students and dissension between students in the Medical Department and those in the Homeopathic Medical Department. A bill

Josiah L. Pickard (1824–1914), sixth president, 1878–87.

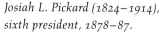

Pamphlet circulated by Gustavus Hinrichs, 1892. Other pamphlets bore such titles as "Regents of the University—How They Elect and Reward Themselves in Darkest America," "Rotten to the Core Is the Management of the State University of Iowa," and "The Whitewash of the Legislative Investigating Committee—Rubbed Off in a Few Spots by Dr. Gustavus Hinrichs."

Buildings and grounds, 1895. A view south from Old Capitol (before the west portico was added), showing portions of South Hall and the Old Medical Building.

was introduced in the legislature to reorganize the University, fire the regents, and dismiss some of the faculty. Fortunately for the University, it was not passed.

Off one hook, the University was soon impaled on another. In the early spring of 1887 the running fight in the state between the prohibitionists and the liquor interests focused on the University campus when, in class and out, several of the ranking professors became quite intemperate in their defense of temperance. Apparently the liquor interests put so much pressure on the regents that Stephen N. Fellows (mental and moral science and didactics), Leonard F. Parker (history and comparative philology), and Nathan R. Leonard (chemistry and twice acting president) were dismissed, though his friends always claimed that Parker was railroaded.

In 1887 Pickard resigned rather suddenly, giving as a reason the need to spend more time with his ailing wife. A student of history, Pickard continued to interest himself in the work of the state historical society, in 1881 serving as its president. He contributed a number of articles to the *Iowa Historical Record* and wrote a history of the University, which today is interesting particularly for his impressions of the campus. "A square of four blocks constituted the site of the University" in 1878, he wrote. "The eastern half with its grove of native oaks, like the groves of Academus suited to study, was kept in excellent order. The western half was too 'litterary' in character to be attractive. Unsightly outbuildings with fire-wood thrown carelessly about, and piles of ashes indicated that the refinement of the east had not then reached the west."

Charles A. Schaeffer

Charles A. Schaeffer was selected as the University's seventh president from a group that included Edmund J. James, later president of the University of Illinois, and David Starr Jordan, later president of Stanford University. Raised in a scholarly eastern family, he had been schooled at Pennsylvania, Harvard, Göttingen, the Berlin School of Mines, and in Paris before being appointed to the chemistry staff at Cornell University. At Cornell he also served as dean of the faculty. Schaeffer arrived on campus in the wake of the firing of Professors Leonard, Fellows, and Parker to find tempers running high and morale low. He seems to have been undaunted by the situation, however, and announced in his inaugural address his desire to make Iowa one of the leading universities in the country. His plan was comprehensive. First he wanted an able faculty ("All else is accessory"). Then he wanted larger buildings and better-equipped laboratories, more books and periodicals for the library, additions to the collections in the museum, and increased financial aid. He took neither side in the controversy between the faculties of science and letters, arguing that the University should provide excellent training in both areas.

Hardly had he begun his campaign to achieve these ends when the legislature, as a result of continuing public clamor over the dismissals, launched an investigation of the University that lasted from May to July 1888. Composed of both senators and representatives, the investigating committee heard testimony from over two hundred individuals. The committee called on President Schaeffer to testify also, though he had played no part in any of the dismissals. He used his time before the committee to demonstrate by facts and figures how strong the University really was. Largely because of his presentation and his forthrightness about what he planned to do, the University was cleared of virtually all the charges against it.

Chiefly, though, Schaeffer spent his first years in office rebuilding fences. He worked closely with the faculty, attending many of their meetings and helping them individually. At the suggestion of his wife, Schaeffer threw open their handsome home for a day during commencement week for a reception for the faculty and everyone else connected with the institution. He won over Iowa Citians so fully that the city deeded a small park to the University, the square block now occupied by Van Allen Hall. Most important for the welfare of the institution, he established cordial relations with the regents and legislators and the governors who served during the years of his administration (William Larrabee, Horace Boies, and Frank D. Jackson). After considerable prodding, he persuaded the legislature to grant the University the proceeds from a tax levy for new buildings. He wanted a fifth of a mill levy but got only half of that. Nevertheless, the grant was a major breakthrough.

President Schaeffer prepared the way for the modern university brought into being by his successors. Following his belief that a great faculty was essential for a great university, he added such outstanding scholars and scientists as Isaac A. Loos (political science), Franklin H. Potter (Latin), Elbert W. Rockwood (chemistry), Benjamin F. Shambaugh (political science), Bohumil Shimek (botany), Wilbur J. Teeters (chemistry and pharmacology), William C. Wilcox (history), and Charles Bundy Wilson (German). Of all his appointments, the most fortunate for the University was that of Carl E. Seashore in philosophy and psychology. Before he retired for the second time in 1946, Seashore had been graduate dean for thirty-three years and had become the dominant force in

creating for Iowa a reputation of being willing to experiment. With a growing faculty, the University could offer a wider variety of courses, and that in turn led to a diminution of required courses in favor of electives. The semester-hour system, an innovation that required students to attend a particular class only three days a week, was introduced in 1892. In addition, more graduate courses were introduced; in 1897–98 sixty-six students were working toward the master's degree.

A vigorous and indefatigable man (some said he looked more like a boilermaker than a scholar), Schaeffer campaigned for the University throughout the state, kept in touch with individual students and faculty members, ran his own errands, wrote all his letters and speeches in longhand, and still found time to help his wife raise a family of four, serve on the vestry of the Episcopal church, and play a mean game of whist. Both the leaders and the citizens of the state were confident that the University would be strongly led for years to come. Schaeffer's sudden death in September 1898 came, therefore, as an enormous shock to everyone. Shortly before he died he had turned the first spadeful of earth for what he hoped would eventually be a splendid new home for the Collegiate Department. Appropriately, the building was eventually named Schaeffer Hall.

Scientific Expeditions

Iowa's program in the natural sciences gained national prominence in the 1890s. Large numbers of students were attracted by the young and energetic faculty and the chance to work in the field as well as the classroom. Expeditions led by members of the Iowa faculty went to the Laysan Islands, the Rocky Mountains, the Arctic, and the Bahamas.

*The faculty on the east steps of
Old Capitol, c. 1894.*

*Charles A. Schaeffer (1843–
98), seventh president,
1887–98.*

"Seasick," Bahamas expedition, 1893.

"The Party in Working Clothes," Bahamas expedition, 1893.

One of the most successful expeditions left Baltimore for the Bahamas in May 1893 aboard the *Emily Johnson*, a two-masted schooner chartered by the University and captained by Charles B. Flowers. The ship was rigged with dredging gear capable of raising specimens from as deep as three hundred fathoms, and it was fitted with a library and a laboratory below deck for study and identification. A party of twenty-one students and faculty were aboard, seven of whom were women. Zoology professor Charles C. Nutting, who led the group, explained the presence, surprising for those times, of so many women: "The ladies had proved their ability to work shoulder to shoulder with the men in the classroom and the laboratory. . . . It would be inconsistent to debar ladies who had shown ability in biological work from advantages which were offered men." The party covered five thousand miles in eighty-three days, with stops in the Florida Keys, Cuba, and the Dry Tortugas. According to an account written by William Larrabee, Jr. (son of the Iowa governor), the expedition was both delightful and rewarding, but, Larrabee cautioned, "the idea entertained by many persons that, like the measles, a single attack of seasickness exempts [one] from further visitation, is without any foundation in fact."

So strong was the University's reputation for sending out educationally important expeditions—twenty-five took the field between 1895 and 1900 alone—that the naturalist Alexander Agassiz remarked that Iowa was "doing more in the way of original exploration than any other educational institution in America."

Amos N. Currier

After Charles Schaeffer's death, Amos Noyes Currier, a professor of Latin and the dean of the collegiate faculty, performed capably as acting president while a search for a new president went forward. After graduating from Dartmouth College in 1856, Currier had come to Iowa to visit an uncle, but during his stay he was persuaded to join the faculty of the recently established Central College at Pella as a professor of ancient languages. In 1861 he enlisted in the Union army, and was wounded and taken prisoner at the battle of Shiloh. It was later said of him that "Dean Currier is never without his Grand Army button and takes a seat with the veterans of the Civil War on Decoration Day instead of with the faculty."

In 1865 he rejoined the Central College faculty, and in 1867 he came to the University of Iowa as a professor of Latin and Greek. He served the University for forty years as teacher, dean of liberal arts, librarian (he worked without extra pay and organized the University's first card catalog), and acting president until President George

E. MacLean took over. Currier was the first president of the Iowa chapter of Phi Beta Kappa. In the faculty tussle over the curriculum, Currier argued forthrightly against expanding the curriculum to include laboratory science and modern languages. He was a skilled mediator as well, and it was said, "If you have differences, let Currier present them."

George E. MacLean

A scholar and educational philosopher, George E. MacLean figuratively as well as literally brought the University into the twentieth century. His background for doing this was impressive: a doctor of divinity degree from Yale, seven years as a Presbyterian minister, a doctor of philosophy degree from the University of Leipzig, eleven years as head of the Department of English Language and Literature at the University of Minnesota, and four years as chancellor of the University of Nebraska.

In his inaugural address MacLean set the goals for what he called the New University. It must, he said, be the crown of the public school system. Its faculty must be investigators as well as teachers and must be willing to take a stand and make any sacrifice for truth. More, they not only must be investigators themselves but also must train others how to be investigators. In turn, the University must grant them the academic freedom to teach and to publish the results of their research. After calling for a partnership of regents, faculty, alumni, students, schoolmen, the press, and the people of the state in a new venture, he ended by urging that they all work together to shape a new era of expansion.

Given MacLean's interest in research, it followed that he would make graduate study the centerpiece of his pro-

Amos N. Currier (1832–1909), acting president, 1898–99.

George E. MacLean (1850–1938), eighth president, 1899–1911.

gram. Enrollment in master's degree programs had been climbing, and work leading to a doctoral degree had started just the year before under the direction of a committee headed by Laenas G. Weld of the mathematics department. As recommended by President MacLean, the regents established a Graduate College in June 1900 with Weld as dean. In 1901, when the college first admitted students, seventy-eight enrolled. By the end of the MacLean administration, with Carl Seashore as dean, the number had jumped to 231, and Iowa was thirteenth among all the universities in the country in the percentage of its student body engaged in graduate study—and tied for first with Wisconsin among state universities. The faculty kept pace, too. When MacLean took office, only 26 percent of the professorial staff had doctoral degrees. Twelve years later when he resigned, over 50 percent had the Ph.D. degree. Seven research bulletins got their start during MacLean's years as well.

President MacLean was especially pleased by the six-year degree programs that combined work in the liberal arts with work in law, applied science (engineering), medicine, or dentistry, upon completion of which students were awarded both baccalaureate and graduate degrees. Setting the academic year at nine months for all colleges made such cooperation possible. Moreover, assigning faculty members to courses in more than one college helped the smaller and newer colleges to expand their offerings. The new emphasis upon graduate work, plus a general tightening of standards for both students and faculty, resulted in Iowa's election to the Association of American Universities, the most prestigious organization of research universities in the country.

To relieve the faculty of much of the paperwork it had been saddled with, he added, with the approval of the governing board, a registrar (Bertha Bell Quaintance), an examiner (Forest C. Ensign), and a secretary for himself.

The board itself hired a superintendent of the physical campus (Gilbert Ellsworth). For the women students, MacLean added a dean of women (Alice Young) and for the freshmen especially he instituted a student advisory system under which each faculty member advised ten to twelve students, keeping an especially close eye on those feeling homesick or out of place.

Needless to say, the bustle President MacLean created did not please everyone. He upset many of the faculty members by being more of an administrator and less of a faculty colleague than previous presidents had been. His effusive manner also seemed insincere to some. He was the first president not to teach regularly, and he expected faculty members to come to his office for conferences. President Schaeffer had always gone to theirs. More seriously, certain faculty members (abetted by some students and alumni) began complaining about his leadership, accusing him of favoritism, unfulfilled promises, and undue support for athletics. Alfred V. Sims (a professor of civil engineering) and Launcelot W. Andrews (head of the Department of Chemistry) were among those particularly opposed to the president, but a large segment of the faculty was distressed that enrollment had fallen off for three successive years. In June 1904, after yet another investigation, the Board of Regents exonerated the president and asked Sims and Andrews to resign—and invited any other dissatisfied faculty to do the same. As if to validate the action of the regents, enrollment climbed to 2500 by 1908–09.

In 1909 the General Assembly passed legislation proposed by Senator William Whipple of Vinton that called for supplanting the University's Board of Regents with a Board of Education that would govern all three of the state's institutions of higher education. It was to have nine members, with no more than five from one political party and no more than one alumnus per school. Once

<table>
<tr><td colspan="2">GOVERNING BOARDS OF THE UNIVERSITY</td></tr>
<tr><td>Board of Trustees</td><td>1847–1870</td></tr>
<tr><td>Board of Regents</td><td>1870–1909</td></tr>
<tr><td>Board of Education</td><td>1909–1955</td></tr>
<tr><td>Board of Regents</td><td>1955–present</td></tr>
</table>

organized, the new board quickly set about attempting to coordinate affairs. Among other things, it established a single accounting system, a single high school inspector to represent all three institutions, and uniform entrance requirements. Then, in January 1911, the board lowered the boom. It asked for the resignation of President MacLean and President Albert B. Storms of Iowa State College at Ames. The explanation to the General Assembly was that neither official was dealing capably with the situation on his campus. Undoubtedly the complaints in 1904, along with those resulting from a 1910 report critical of the medical school, affected the thinking of the board, though the Iowa City *Republican* maintained that the underlying reason was that MacLean placed too much stress on the cultural work of the University. The board, according to the *Republican*, wanted more emphasis on studies that would benefit the state in practical ways. Whatever the reasons and whatever substance they possessed, President MacLean had to resign.

In retrospect, MacLean emerges as one of the University's most influential presidents, and the first to be recognized as a national figure in higher education. In his attempts to bring his New University into existence, he undoubtedly broke with practices and attitudes that the faculty had become accustomed to. Nevertheless, MacLean was the architect of the University of the twentieth century.

The Expanding University

In its organization during the MacLean years the University lost most of what now seems its quaintness. The Collegiate Department became the College of Liberal Arts, and the departments of law, medicine, homeopathic medicine, dentistry, and pharmacy all became colleges. So did the School of Applied Science (engineering), but not without a tussle. In 1903 Professors Weld and Sims persuaded the legislature to create a School of Applied Science, with Weld as its director. The next year they persuaded the president to include in his askings $50,000 for an engineering building and $10,000 for a dam and powerhouse on the Iowa River. The request almost backfired, however, because a small committee of the legislature recommended instead that all work in engineering be transferred to Ames. But after the full legislature was invited to Iowa City by the Iowa City Commercial Club, and after Weld and Sims once more made their pitch, the legislature voted the funds for the engineering program. As a logical consequence, the School of Applied Science in 1905 separated from the College of Liberal Arts and became the College of Applied Science.

The MacLean years also saw the creation of a School of Political and Social Science and Commerce, a School of Education, a Training School for Nurses, and a School of Music affiliated with the University. The Iowa Lakeside Laboratory at Lake Okoboji and a School of Library Training became parts of a newly constituted summer session. By 1911 the number of museums, including departmental museums, climbed to nine, and the number of volumes in the library to 75,000 (not including some 15,000 in the College of Law's collection).

The Flexner Report

In 1909, under the aegis of the Carnegie Foundation for the Advancement of Teaching, Abraham Flexner visited medical schools in the United States and Canada, and in 1910 he published a report that brought humiliation, dismay, and fury to scores of schools. Certainly it did so to Iowa. Flexner praised Iowa's work in the basic sciences, but in the clinical area he found the hospital facilities inadequate and the teaching disorganized and not wholly modern. "President MacLean," Flexner wrote, "witnessed my unavailing efforts to find anyone—nurse or physician—who could describe the system on which the bedside teaching was conducted." The protest in Iowa City was so great that the head of the Carnegie Foundation sent Flexner back to the campus accompanied by Dr. R. H. Whitehead, dean of the University of Virginia Medical School. Supported by Whitehead, Flexner refused to amend his original judgment, though he did spell out his reasons more fully, one of which was that the dean of the medical college lived in Dubuque and the head of surgery in Sioux City. The faculty, still incensed, supported their dean and placed much of the blame on the president for not giving full cooperation, particularly in fiscal matters. They were further agitated when Des Moines doctors began a campaign to get the medical school moved to the capital, where more "material" (sick people) could be found. The president and the medical staff had good reason to join forces, and this they did in persuading Dr. Campbell P. Howard of McGill University to become head of Internal Medicine for a salary of $5,000. In their campaign to obtain Dr. Howard, they even enlisted the help of the internationally renowned Sir William Osler. This was the first step in the medical college's dramatic climb upward.

John G. Bowman

At thirty-four, John G. Bowman was not only the youngest man to be appointed president of the University, he was also the first native Iowan and the first alumnus. Born in Davenport, he had earned both his B.A. and M.A. degrees at Iowa. After a stint of teaching English, first at Iowa and then at Columbia University, he became the secretary of the Carnegie Foundation for the Advancement of Teaching (1907–11) and then president at Iowa for the next three years. Particularly interested in the life of the undergraduates, he improved the advisory system and strongly supported the drive for a student union.

During President Bowman's administration the Board of Education stubbed its toe by proposing to the legislature that all work in engineering be consolidated at Ames and all work in home economics at Iowa City. So the fight that had first erupted over the site of engineering in 1904 had to be fought all over again in 1912. The opposition on the part of the faculty, alumni, and students at both schools was so immediate and so strident that the legislature demanded that the board rescind its action.

Possessed of a curious blend of the romantic and the practical, Bowman never got along particularly well with the Board of Education, and when in March 1914 he discovered that the board had fired a member of the faculty without consulting him, he resigned without warning. The resignation was unsettling not only because it had occurred so suddenly but also because Bowman was the second president in three years to leave after a rift with the board. Bowman became director of the American College of Surgeons (1915–21) and then chancellor of the University of Pittsburgh (1921–45). During his first years at Pittsburgh he seriously cut into the Department

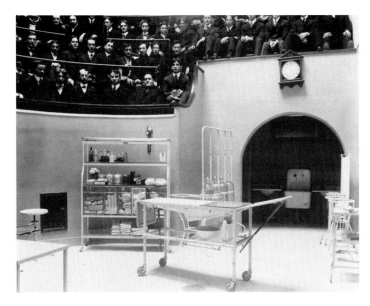

Operating theater in University Hospital, 1905. When University Hospital was built in 1898 on the site of the old Mechanics' Academy, it provided Iowa with its first modern facilities for clinical teaching. Local private practitioners, fearing unfair competition, protested its exclusive use by the University faculty. However, practice was not formally limited to members of the hospital staff until 1913. Besides the operating rooms, at this time the hospital included a section for administrative offices, wards and private rooms, and the two-hundred-seat amphitheater shown here. Later known as East Hall and now as Seashore Hall, the building acquired a southeast wing in 1908, a northwest wing in 1912, and a northeast wing in 1914, by which time the hospital had 240 beds. In 1928 the new hospital on the west side of the river was dedicated, and the older building has since served numerous other University departments, such as psychology, the College of Education and the Extension Division (now Continuing Education).

John G. Bowman (1877–1962),
ninth president, 1911–14.

of English at Iowa by attracting away from it Percival Hunt, an outstanding teacher of Shakespeare and English composition, and three younger professors of exceptional promise.

Thomas H. Macbride

Thomas H. Macbride was Iowa's Man for All Seasons. An eminent scientist, an inspiring teacher, a scholar of language and literature, a brilliant public speaker, an ardent conservationist, and a courtly gentleman, he brought to the presidency a respect that it had never before enjoyed. His years as president were a period of quiet and good will in the interval between the stress of the Bowman and Jessup administrations.

Macbride came to Iowa in the mid-1850s, when his family migrated from Tennessee. Later he wrote about the spirit of these pioneers in his book *In Cabins and Sod-Houses.* He attended Lenox College in Hopkinton, Iowa, where by great good fortune he met Samuel Calvin, already a distinguished geologist. Having earned a B.A. degree at Monmouth College and an M.A. from the University of Bonn, he taught mathematics and modern languages at Lenox from 1870 to 1878. During the summers he accompanied Calvin on field trips, and from those trips he developed what amounted to a passion for the flora of the country. In 1878 he followed Calvin to the University of Iowa, accepting a position as assistant professor of natural science at a salary of $1,200. It was soon understood by the undergraduates that one took Macbride's course in basic botany if it could possibly be squeezed in. For Macbride taught not only the nature of plant life but also, through it, the beauty of nature and the marvel of life itself. Although Macbride became a world authority on slime moulds, he never accepted the notion that there is a dichotomy between research and teaching and always believed that one of his two main functions was "to arouse and awaken" his students in a way they would never forget.

Macbride remained at Iowa for thirty-eight years, acting as professor and head of the Department of Botany from 1884 to 1914. During parts of that period he also served as secretary of the faculty and as director of University Extension. He helped found and strongly supported the Iowa Lakeside Laboratory at Lake Okoboji and campaigned for a state park system. Today Macbride Hall and Lake Macbride keep his name familiar even among those who know nothing about the man.

Construction

Perhaps the most significant event for the physical development of the campus between 1878 and 1916 occurred in the 1890s, when President Schaeffer persuaded the legislature, after considerable prodding, to grant the University the proceeds from a tax levy of a tenth of a mill for new buildings. Schaeffer was the first president to develop a comprehensive building program, though a good part of it was not realized during his administration. From his list he was never to see a library building, a museum, a gymnasium, a hospital, and a classroom building that would break the dreary straight line of Dental, North, Central (Old Capitol), South, and Medical. The buildings that did go up during his term were a dental building, a chemical laboratory (later Electrical Engineering), a homeopathic medicine building and homeopathic hospital, and Close Hall, which, though used by the students, was built with pri-

Thomas H. Macbride (1848–1934), tenth president, 1914–16, at the Iowa Lakeside Laboratory, c. 1914.

vate funds. One setback to the physical plant occurred in June 1897 when North Hall was struck by lightning. Although the building was only partly gutted, the library on the top floor lost three-fourths of its 33,000 volumes.

When President MacLean took office, the Hall of Liberal Arts (later Schaeffer Hall) was being built. Before it was opened in 1902, however, another fire destroyed the Medical Building and South Hall, leaving the University severely short of laboratory and classroom space. MacLean acted quickly to remedy the situation. With the support of the board and the legislature, he authorized the construction of medical laboratories (now part of the Biology Building) on Jefferson Street, closer to the University's hospital (now Seashore Hall), the completion of the Men's Gymnasium (Old Armory, since demolished) and the moving of Calvin Hall from its old foundations to a site across Jefferson Street to make way for the new Hall of Natural Science (Macbride Hall). Other building projects in the MacLean era included a law building (Gilmore Hall), a physics building (MacLean Hall), a wing of the University Hospital, and a central power plant and dam across the river. The president's house at 102 Church Street was completed in 1909. Two bathhouses were projected along the river but were never built. All told, $1.5 million was spent on construction during the MacLean years, many times the amount spent during all the previous administrations combined. In addition, MacLean sought the advice of the Olmsted brothers, sons of the famous landscape architect Frederick Law Olmsted, on how the campus could be further extended. Their advice was to increase the University's landholdings by obtaining seventy acres on the west side of the river. Although this land was not obtained during MacLean's administration, enough was purchased on the east side for the campus to grow from thirteen to forty acres.

The physical campus continued to expand during the Bowman and Macbride administrations, especially with buildings for students: Currier Hall, a dormitory for women, was completed in 1913, and the Women's Gymnasium (now Halsey Gymnasium) in 1915. In addition, in 1912 President Bowman persuaded the board to remodel and refurbish the old Unitarian Church building on the northeast corner of Iowa Avenue and Clinton Street as a student union.

Student Life

Until the turn of the century, student life remained much the same as it was in the 1860s and 1870s. There were still no dormitories, which meant students had no natural meeting ground outside of the classroom, and trying to locate a reasonably priced place to eat and sleep was still a problem. "My first requirement was a room with heat and light in a comfortable locality within reasonable walking distance of the University," wrote engineering student Charles Perry Chase of Clinton about his arrival on campus in 1886. "Rooms were hard to find. You furnished your own fuel and boiled all water before speaking to it. There was no electricity and kerosene lamps were needed, for the city gas pressure might fail. Board was fair and reasonable. Once I tried a club, at $1.90 per week with milk and $1.80 without. The meals were filling, if not balanced, but dad came out, took one meal, and said 'move'! There were three choices for a bath—a sponge, the river, or the barber shop."

The literary societies were still in command of social life, but their influence was waning, partly because of the growth of fraternities and sororities. The first Greek let-

Removal of the Old Oak, 1897. President Schaeffer stands at the far right, holding an umbrella, while workmen remove the last of the original bur oaks on the campus in preparation for a new liberal arts building. Although he died shortly after this picture was taken, it was Schaeffer who urged the legislature to provide for an ambitious University building program that would greatly expand the campus in the years that followed.

Commencement Dance, June 10, 1896. A hop was held at 9 P.M. at Smith's Armory, located at the southwest corner of Linn and College streets. Tickets cost $2.50, and everybody had dance cards.

ter society, or fraternity, appeared at Iowa in 1867, the first panhellenic meeting took place in 1887, and the first chapter house (Beta Theta Pi) was occupied in 1898. In 1900 there were six fraternities and three sororities at Iowa, and by 1916 there were eight of each. President MacLean strongly supported most student societies, since he believed that such organizations helped cultivate the students' social nature. The president had belonged to a fraternity himself and thought them of value as a rule but hedged by saying, "I favor a good fraternity and oppose a bad one."

After 1900, student life began to change considerably. Not only were fraternities and sororities increasingly popular, but movies, vaudeville, and the automobile arrived in Iowa City. Construction of the Armory on Washington Street in 1904 provided a place on campus for dances. While these diversions did eventually kill off the literary societies, the Forensic League maintained the popularity of debate. When E. K. Brown won the championship of the Northern Oratorical League in Chicago in 1902, his train was met by a huge crowd, and he was carried in triumph to the president's horse-drawn cab.

Athletics

In 1882 a number of sports-minded students got together to form an athletic association, and in the years to come, sports played an increasingly important part in university life. Baseball, first played at Iowa around 1870, was considered the roughest sport. The first gymnastics exhibition was held in 1886 at the Opera House. It featured routines on the parallel and horizontal bars and pommel horse, Indian-club swinging, and numbers by the University band. The first official gymnastics team was founded in 1909.

Athletics became even more important at the University during the Schaeffer and MacLean administrations, since both presidents, believing a healthy body to be the foundation for a healthy intellect, strongly supported student athletics. Schaeffer saw to the construction of Iowa Field, located along the Iowa River, which had facilities, when it was not flooded, for baseball, track, and football. In 1891 Close Hall was completed as the first YMCA and YWCA center west of the Mississippi River. It had space for a variety of physical-education activities and was considered especially attractive because of its bathing facilities, no small consideration in those days. Close Hall was also the site, in 1893, of the first basketball game ever played in Iowa. Benjamin F. Shambaugh, soon to be a professor of political science, played forward for one of the teams.

The first Iowa Field Day took place on May 10, 1890, and according to the *Vidette-Reporter*, the cheer "Hi! Hi! Hi! S.U.I.! Giddy, giddy, uni, S.U.I." echoed repeatedly during track events. Jeremiah Slattery, later to become a surgeon in Chicago, was the star that day. When President Schaeffer's daughter presented him with his medals, it is said she had to avert her eyes—Slattery wore a track suit with short pants, a daring costume for that day.

Football at Iowa had a rocky beginning. In the early 1890s the game had only just evolved into something resembling the modern game, though forward passes would not be legal until 1906. Padding was minimal and the action brutal. Nationwide, the game had become so violent that in 1897 Georgia passed a law prohibiting football altogether. Other states seriously considered similar legislation. At Iowa there was also the problem of finding men willing to play. In 1893, for example, the *Vidette-Reporter* ran an announcement that "men who are heavy and strong can have places on the team for the asking." But by 1899 and 1900 there were enough heavy and strong men (the team averaged about 175 pounds per man) to make Iowa the best team west of the Mississippi and one of the best in the country, what with all-American S. Clyde Williams as quarterback.

Basketball became an official intercollegiate sport in 1903, but at Iowa intramural basketball remained more popular than intercollegiate games. In 1902, in fact, the last intercollegiate game of the season had to be canceled for lack of support. In 1906, to put basketball on a paying basis, dances were held after the games, and the *Daily Iowan* reported that "this will probably be a feature of basketball games in the future."

In 1900 the University joined the Western Intercollegiate Athletic Conference, or "Big Nine," and a few years later also joined, and then dropped out of, the Missouri Valley Conference. That year Iowa also hired its first director of athletics, Alden A. Knipe. When this position was first proposed in 1899, Amos N. Currier (then acting president) said, "A director of athletics is most essential and should be as much a part of a well equipped institution as a professor of language." Knipe, who also coached the football team, had been an all-American at the University of Pennsylvania, where he had earned an M.D. An accomplished singer, he also led the University's cho-

A group of engineers with the "Mechanical Rooter" on the sidelines of Iowa Field, 1901.

ral group. He was all these things and was only in his midtwenties.

By 1903 physical training had become compulsory for women, but it was not required of men until 1910. The first swimming class was held at the Iowa River in May 1906, and a year later the Board of Regents appropriated $50 for a swimming float, landing, springboard, and safety line. In 1915 the first indoor pools were built, one in the new women's gymnasium and one in an addition to the Armory, next to Iowa Field. Wrestling became an official University sport in 1913.

Student Newspapers

The first student newspaper at the University of Iowa was the *University Reporter*, a sixteen-page monthly that printed its first issue in 1868. In 1881 it merged with its two-year-old rival, the *Vidette*, and became the *Vidette-Reporter*, a four-page paper that appeared three times a week and cost three cents a copy. The next paper to appear was the *S.U.I. Quill*, a weekly. It started in 1891 and lasted until 1901, when it and the *Vidette-Reporter* merged and became the *Daily Iowan*, which is still the student newspaper at Iowa. The class of 1892 assembled the first edition of the *Hawkeye*, the student yearbook, and it appeared in 1891. In 1910 *Haw-*

Haw-Hawkeye, the first campus humor magazine, appeared and then disappeared after only one issue.

For most of the nineteenth century, the various student newspapers were modest in size—usually eight pages long, with a good half of that taken up by advertisements. A typical issue reported mostly University news: what the literary societies were doing, what well-known person had spoken at the University, and what sporting events had taken place. One of the newspapers' perennial topics was the library. Hardly a month went by without some mention either of noise in the library or of students writing in the margins of library books. The young journalists also commented on the relative popularity of course offerings. With typical overstatement, one issue of the *Vidette-Reporter* said: "In ninety-nine cases out of a hundred, no branch of the college course is approached by the student with a sense of greater misgiving than that of psychology or mental science."

On October 25, 1883, the *Vidette-Reporter* covered the appearance of Buffalo Bill in Iowa City, and the same issue ran ads advising readers, "Don't Forget Sawyer the Clothier," and warning that "Tomorrow you may break your leg. Take out an accident policy before it is too late. W. E. Atwater, Agent." Another ad proclaimed the wonders of the Magnetion Appliance Company's magnetic kidney belt, which would cure an astonishing number of ailments, among them nervous debility and lumbago. In years to come, medical and law department notes were a regular feature, as were alumni notes and personal essays with titles such as "Good Manners," "Mental Harmony," and "Moral Chemist." There were also more prosaic personal notes. In February 1893 the *Vidette-Reporter* informed interested parties that "B. J. Sweat, '96, is confined to his room by sickness."

First issue of the Daily Iowan, *September 21, 1901.*

Campus north of Old Capitol, c. 1900. Nothing shown here is still standing, at least where it was when this photograph was taken. North Hall (left) was demolished in 1949, and Old Dental (center) in 1975, Calvin Hall (right) was moved across the street in 1905, and the last of the old oaks in the center of the picture came down in 1936.

Around the turn of the century, however, this was half of the campus. Calvin Hall (originally Science Hall) was the most impressive of the group. When it was completed in 1885 the Burlington Hawkeye *remarked, "It presents the nearest approach to elegance to be found in any of the university buildings."*

The executive committee of the Board of Regents, 1892. From left to right, William J. Haddock, secretary, Albert W. Swalm, D. N. Richardson, and Howard A. Burrell. It was largely a committee of editors. Swalm was the editor of the Oskaloosa Herald, Richardson *of the* Davenport Democrat, *and Burrell of the* Washington Press.

From the time it was established in 1847 by the act creating the University, the Board of Trustees (or Regents) set general policy for the University. In the early years, however, board members also assumed direct authority over administrative and even curricular matters. They would interview candidates for faculty positions and on occasion hire a professor without consulting the president. Commit-

tees of the board would visit classes and report in writing on the deportment of the students. Thus in 1887 a committee of the board found students of Professors Macbride, Weld, and Currier to be attentive and responsive but reported that certain students of Professor Leonard F. Parker tittered and those of Professor Andrew A. Veblen whispered and seemed listless. As the University grew and became more complex, the board began to delegate the execution of its policies to its executive committee, which was awarded legal status by the state legislature in 1870. In turn, the executive committee delegated much of its work to its secretary, a practice that gave a longtime secretary such as William Haddock enormous power.

William J. Haddock (1832–1906). Haddock graduated from the University of Iowa in 1861 and was elected secretary of the Board of Trustees (later the Board of Regents) in 1864. He held the post for thirty-eight years. In that office he did the work of the registrar; collected students' tuition; oversaw buildings and grounds; supervised janitors, firemen, and other employees; and served as a lobbyist for the University before the state appropriations committees. It is probably no exaggeration to say that he could make or break a president, for a later officer of the board wrote that "the old geezer" practically ran the University for a while and "had more influence with the Regents than the President did."

BELOW

Beaumont Apple, B.S. 1894, and an 1893 absence excuse for him. Apple, from Panora, Iowa, enrolled at the University of Iowa in 1890. In the 1892 Hawkeye, the University's first yearbook, there appears this remark in a section called the Children's Corner: "Dear Corner:—I am a student at the State University of Iowa, and the people call me 'freshie.' I advise all good little boys who wish to become great and good men to come and stay with 'Prexie' Schaeffer. We all call him 'Prexie.' Your little friend, Beanie Apple." Note that Apple's absence form, for October 23 and 24, 1893, was signed by the president himself. In those days, according to the University catalog, absence was considered "one of the most serious evils incident to the practical working of the university." Apple's schedule card shows that he took a scientific course of study. He ultimately graduated with a degree in electrical engineering and was a member of the Delta Tau Delta fraternity.

"Ladies Band," c. 1895.

Close Hall, home of the YMCA and YWCA, c. 1900. Mrs. Helen S. Close contributed $10,000 when the fundraising drive for the new YM-YWCA stalled, and in gratitude the building was named for her and her late husband. When Close Hall was dedicated in 1890, so many people came to admire it that the floors sagged alarmingly, and the building was instantly condemned. After repairs, it reopened and became home to the YM-YWCA. On January 16, 1896, Close Hall was the site of the first basketball game between two college teams of five men on a side. Iowa lost to the University of Chicago, 15–12. After 1924 Close Hall served the Journalism Department, the University printing service, and the **Daily Iowan.** On New Year's Day in 1940 the building caught fire, and firemen rushed to the scene. President Gilmore, holding a faculty reception at his house, allegedly said, "Why don't they mind their own business?" Close Hall was demolished in stages between 1968 and 1970.

The Class of 1906, ready for
battle. Class scraps were common at the University until
the 1920s. Hostilities would
typically begin with the sophomores taunting the freshmen
by prominently displaying a
crude effigy of a baby or a
milk bottle somewhere on the
campus. While the rivalries
were basically harmless, some
got out of hand, as in 1898,
when twenty-three sopho-
mores were suspended for a
term after kidnapping a
freshman.

Faculty production of Hamlet, May 25, 1894. Amos N. Currier (professor of Latin and dean of the faculty) and Charles C. Nutting (zoology) are the gravediggers in this production presented to "an invited few" at the opera house. Also in the cast were Launcelot W. Andrews (chemistry) as Hamlet, Edward E. Hale (English) as Horatio, Bohumil Shimek (botany) as Claudius, Thomas H. Macbride (botany) as Polonius, and, as Rosencrantz and Guildenstern, Charles B. Wilson (modern languages) and Marvin H. Dey (class of 1887, Iowa City civil engineer and banker). For Ophelia the faculty had to borrow a sophomore, Redelia Gilchrist of Iowa City.

Engineering students, 1883. Together Elwyn N. Brown (peering through the transit) and George H. Bremner represent half of the graduating class in civil engineering for 1883. The other two graduates were Fred Ogle and Bohumil Shimek. The latter became famous as a professor of botany at Iowa. Taking notes at right is Laenas G. Weld, who later became a professor of mathematics and astronomy.

Waiting for battalion review, 1896. The fountain just south of Calvin Hall was a popular spot to watch spring military drills and listen to the band. In 1874 the regents established a Department of Military Science and Tactics and made military training with government equipment compulsory. There were two or three drills a week, with credit given toward graduation requirements. In the spring and fall terms in the 1880s, the drill convened on Monday, Wednesday, and Friday from four to five P.M. and included every male student in the Collegiate Department. In winter, seniors also had to attend weekly lectures on a wide variety of military topics. According to Charles Perry

Chase, an engineering student in the 1880s, "Military drill was popular and was accepted without question; and the raw uncouth freshmen of September were erect, peppy, keen-eyed boys, full of snap as a new whip, when the competitive drills came in the spring, with the girls there to watch them."

S.U.I. Battalion Band on the steps of Old Capitol, 1890s. The first official University band was founded in 1881. The band was in the military department until it became part of the School of Fine Arts in 1936.

Medical students, class of 1897, with plenty to indicate that medicine was not their only thought.

Old Medical Building (left) and South Hall, 1890s. Constructed to house the Medical Department in 1882, the facilities in Old Medical included dissecting rooms, faculty offices, an anatomy chamber, lecture rooms, a 257-seat amphitheater, and an elevator exactly like the one installed in Chicago's Rush Medical Center by Reedy Elevator Works. Walter L. Bierring, an early graduate and faculty member of the College of Medicine, remembered that "many a lecture had to stop in the midst of an interesting part in order to permit Billy [Green, the janitor] and his creaking elevator to pass from the basement to dissecting room, and back again."

William (Billy) Green, 1890s. When Dominique Bradley was fired because of his part in snatching a body for the Anatomy Department in December 1870, Billy Green became the janitor for the Medical Department. In that position he not only kept the quarters clean but also served as a general assistant in all the medical departments, was in charge of anatomical material, and attended the clinics regularly. According to Dr. John T. McClintock, Green kept well posted on all the Medical Department's affairs, "but when questioned he always replied in a soft whispering voice 'I don't know.'" For nearly a decade his name was listed along with the faculty in the Medical Department's annual announcements.

Superintendent of Nurses Jennie Cottell and the first graduating class of the School of Nursing, 1900. The School of Nursing was organized in 1898 when the hospital (now Seashore Hall) was completed. One of the students, Emma Randall, remembered that during that first year the nurses were "fined 50 cents if we left pins in our clothing when we sent it to the laundry, and we were not allowed to talk in the halls or to read our mail when on duty. Neither were we permitted to talk with the patients." The first graduating class consisted of five members. Upon completion of the course, students were awarded a diploma that made them eligible to take the examination for nurses registration given by the State Board of Examiners.

Dental Clinic, 1895. In Iowa in the nineteenth century, dentistry was more handicraft than science—not for nothing were dentists called "tooth carpenters." The University's first lecturer on dentistry, P. T. Smith, joined the faculty of the Medical Department in 1870. In 1882 the state legislature finally passed laws regulating dentists and established the University's Dental Department. In 1895 the department moved from basement rooms in South Hall into a new brick building north of North Hall.

Homeopathic Hospital, c. 1900. The Homeopathic Medical Department had been established by the regents in 1887 in connection with, yet separate from, the Medical Department. Homeopaths, in contrast to "allopaths," prescribed medicine on the basis of symptoms, without recourse to a diagnosis of the underlying disease. The Homeopathic Hospital was built in 1894 at the corner of Jefferson and Dubuque streets. It was designed to accommodate two hundred students and fifty-four patients. It served as an annex to the University Hospital from 1919, when the homeopathic department closed, until 1929, when the building was demolished after a fire.

Pharmaceutical manufacturing laboratory, East Hall Annex, c. 1910. Shortly after the turn of the century, the University's College of Pharmacy took charge of dispensing all the drugs and medicines used by the University Hospital, something no other college in the United States had done before. It was also the first in the country to establish a pharmaceutical laboratory for the manufacture of products used by hospital patients. The manufacturing laboratory became a highly successful venture both educationally and financially. Not only medicines but also such products as food flavors, baking powder, cleansing fluids, liquid soaps, and insecticides were manufactured for use in the University hospitals and in departments throughout the campus. During World War I, after the British blockade cut off shipments of aspirin (patented by the Bayer Company of Germany), the laboratory manufactured aspirin for use in the University's hospitals.

East Hall Annex, 1905. When it was built in 1890 to house the Chemistry Department, and soon the Pharmacy Department, most students considered the East Hall Annex, two blocks from Old Capitol, to be much too far away from campus. In later years the building held some of the library's overflow and served as the home of the Electrical Engineering Department. To the left of the building is the old Homeopathic Hospital and, to the right, the Mechanics' Academy.

Geology classroom in Calvin Hall, c. 1895. From 1884 to 1905 Calvin Hall was the campus center for studies in the natural sciences. The Geology Department, chaired by Samuel Calvin, occupied the first floor; the Biology Department, chaired by Thomas Macbride, was on the second; and the third floor housed the Museum of Natural History. These early days of natural science at Iowa are remembered in a 1932 interview with Bohumil Shimek, a colleague of Calvin and Macbride. "Those two men worked together for years and years," Shimek said. "They consulted each other on all important matters. When professor Calvin needed invigorating, Dr. Macbride was there to do it. When Dr. Macbride needed calming, professor Calvin was there." In an effort to carry out the plan of laboratory study outlined by Gustavus Hinrichs in the 1870s, both Calvin and Macbride used personal funds to supply their students with microscopes and books. Before Calvin Hall was built, some laboratory work took place in a small room in the northwest corner of Old Capitol, where two microscopes (called "Kentucky squirrel guns" by students) were kept. The use of these instruments required discretion, for as Shimek explained, many of the more classically oriented faculty members objected to such practical methods of study.

Samuel Calvin (the bearded man in the center of the picture) with a geology class at the state quarry near North Liberty, 1899. Samuel Calvin, one of the most distinguished scholars and teachers in the University's history, taught geology from 1874 to 1911. The students doing fieldwork in predenim days were most likely enrolled in General and Practical Geology, a class that met daily for lectures at 10 A.M. In addition to his work in geology, Calvin was a keen amateur photographer. He amassed a collection of over 7,000 photographs, many recording University life.

Frank Russell (1868–1903). After receiving his B.S. from Iowa in 1892, Frank Russell set off for the Arctic in August of that year to collect specimens for Iowa's growing Museum of Natural History. Although the Board of Regents had encouraged Russell to make the trip, they were not forthcoming with funds, and it was President Schaeffer who stepped in personally with $2,050 to finance the expedition. Traveling by dogsled and snowshoes into the far reaches of Canada's Northwest Territories, Russell gathered everything from the hides of endangered musk-oxen to weather data and studied the artifacts and culture of Eskimos and Indians. The con-ditions of his life as a naturalist were not always comfortable. He wrote that at times he had been "awakened by the bitter cold, which sometimes gave me the impression my feet were certainly frozen." Of his first winter in the Arctic, passed at a Hudson's Bay Company post, he reported: "The winter passed slowly; the temperature several times reached sixty below zero." After his return in 1894, Russell went on to receive his B.S., M.S., and Ph.D. degrees in anthropology at Harvard, where he taught while also working as an ethnologist for the Smithsonian Institution. Russell died of tuberculosis at the age of thirty-five, never having recovered from the injuries to his health incurred while in the Arctic.

The Laysan Expedition, left to right: Horace Young (student, expedition cook), Clarence Albrecht (student), Homer Dill (expedition leader), and Charles Corwin (scene painter from the Field Museum), 1911. This important expedition, undertaken by the University in 1911, was led by Homer R. Dill, the University's chief taxidermist and later the curator of the Museum of Natural History. The Laysan Islands, largely uninhabitable islands at the extreme western end of the Hawaiian archipelago, were home to an impressive array of birds, and it was Dill's hope to secure examples of all the species and with them (and the appropriate fauna) to build a cyclorama for display at Iowa's museum. He succeeded, but it was not easy. Dill and his assistants arrived at the island just after a band of Japanese poachers had killed some 200,000 of the island's birds for their feathers. The island was littered with the carcasses of these birds, and insects swarmed everywhere. Dill reported: "Never have I seen so many flies in one small area. Our laboratory is so full of them that we were obliged to suspend work to reduce their numbers." In spite of this, Dill and company brought back thirty-six large cases of specimens. Charles Corwin completed a mural painting measuring 12 by 138 feet as a background for the bird display. When the cyclorama was opened to the public in 1914, William T. Hornaday, one of the world's great naturalists and director of the Bronx Zoo, reported that "the largest and by far the most spectacular of all the world's habitat groups of birds is to be seen at the museum of the University of Iowa, in Iowa City." The cyclorama is still located in Bird Hall on the third floor of Macbride Hall.

Bohumil Shimek (1861–1937). Shimek was born in Shueyville, close by Iowa City. He earned a degree in civil engineering from the University of Iowa in 1883 and worked as the Johnson County surveyor for two years before becoming a science teacher at Iowa City High School. He went to the University of Nebraska as an instructor in zoology in 1888, but he returned to Iowa City two years later as an instructor of botany. Shimek taught at Iowa for the next forty-seven years, during which time he was also curator of the herbarium (1895–1937), director of the Iowa Lakeside Laboratory three times, and president of the Iowa Society of Engi-

neers, the Iowa Academy of Sciences, and in 1915 the National Bohemian Alliance. A fierce Czechoslovakian partisan, Shimek was decorated in the late 1920s for his achievements in behalf of his parents' homeland. He was a great teacher, said one student, "because he was an ecologist, not merely a plant ecologist. He knew animal life as he did plants; he did not collect fungi and remain incurious to the scuttling insect life which the overturned log revealed. He taught us the bird calls as we tramped and showed us the all but invisible snail shells in whose lines we read the story of the wind deposition of the loess."

The Iowa Lakeside Laboratory, 1915. The laboratory, on West Okoboji Lake, was founded in 1909. Thomas Macbride had dreamed of such a field center since the 1890s, when Bohumil Shimek, Samuel Calvin, and he had made several field trips to explore the region, the geology and botany of which was unusually rich and varied. When a five-acre tract of land on Miller's Bay was put up for sale in 1908, Macbride secured the option. With the help of the Alumni Association, the University purchased the property, which included an eight-room cottage, a two-room cottage, a boathouse, an electric light plant, and a water-pumping station. The alumni group also raised money to construct a building that housed laboratories, a 125-seat lecture hall, study rooms, and space for a library.

When he established the Iowa Lakeside Laboratory,

Macbride envisioned a place where all Iowa naturalists would be welcome. Accordingly, in the early years faculty and students from Coe, Buena Vista, Cornell, Morningside, Parsons, Drake, Iowa State, Iowa Wesleyan, and other colleges and universities across the state studied there. Students came at the rate of thirty a year to study nature firsthand with such faculty members as Macbride, Bohumil Shimek, Robert B. Wylie, and Samuel Calvin. Macbride also hoped the laboratory could grow larger, and it has, now encompassing 140 acres. In 1932 the University deeded the field station to the state of Iowa, and in 1947 the Lakeside Laboratory was made a separate regents institution that would serve all three state universities. Richard V. Bovbjerg, a professor of zoology, has been its director since 1964.

Academic procession on Iowa Avenue, 1899. Over three thousand students, faculty, and townspeople turned out on the cool and windy afternoon of September 28, 1899, to participate in the inauguration of George MacLean as president of the University of Iowa. Those involved assembled at Close Hall on the corner of Iowa Avenue and Dubuque Street and are shown here on their way to Old Capitol, where the ceremony took place. An editorial in the Vi-dette-Reporter, *the student newspaper, reflected in its own patois something of the enthusiastic reaction to MacLean's inaugural address: "Every man and woman who heard him yesterday is his personal friend today. . . . He is going to be more than popular. He is going to be a personal friend. Here's to 'Prexie' MacLean. He's all right."*

Architectural drawings of Schaeffer Hall, east elevation and section, 1898. In October 1897 the Board of Regents announced a competition for the design of the new Collegiate Building. Instructions to the architects specified that the building must be fireproof and must cost no more than $150,000 but otherwise gave wide latitude in matters of design. Perhaps too wide, for at the close of the competition Secretary William Haddock wrote, "The twenty-two samples of architecture examined by the board were very miscellaneous. Some with high peaked roofs and steeples and they were called French Renaissance. Others had no visible roof at all and that was pure Greek Renaissance. Others were called after other nations, but all were renascent I think in fixing on the central building as a model, that what the board wanted was a good square turn of Iowa Renaissance for a change." Seeking a design more harmonious with Old Capitol, the board asked eight of the original twenty-three architects to resubmit plans and hired as the judge Henry Van Brundt of Kansas City, one of the architects of the 1893 Chicago World's Fair. Van Brundt chose a scheme in the grand style of the exhibition by the Des Moines firm of Proudfoot, Bird, and Rawson. More important, he recommended that the regents locate the Collegiate Building (now Schaeffer Hall) east of the established axis then running north and south from Old Capitol. Evidence suggests that this was part of his plan to group four architecturally similar buildings around Old Capitol, forming what would come to be called the Pentacrest. Slowed by a dispute between the architects and the contractor, construction of Schaeffer Hall took nearly four years. When the doors opened on January 23, 1902, students and faculty found a new library, classroom and office space, and an auditorium large enough to permit university-wide gatherings.

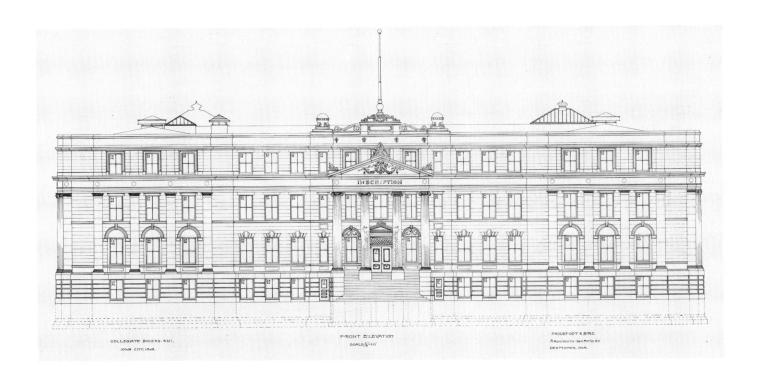

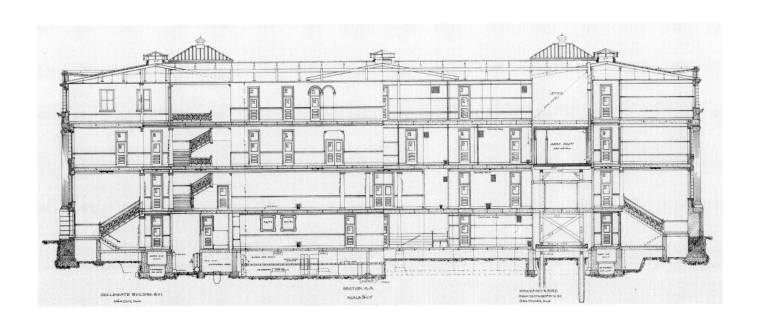

Librarian J. W. Rich, seated, after North Hall library fire, June 1897. After the library was moved to the third floor of North Hall in 1882, the University repeatedly asked the legislature for funds for a fireproof building. When North Hall did catch fire, not only was three-fourths of the library's collection destroyed, but a fireman, Lycurgus Leek, lost his life when the roof collapsed. Even after the fire, the legislature, widely blamed for having been foolishly frugal, still did not provide funds for a new library building but instead appropriated only enough for repairing and refurnishing North Hall and for restoring the 8,821 books that had been saved.

RIGHT

Remains of the Medical Building and South Hall, 1901. The alarm sounded at 2:45 on Sunday morning, March 10, 1901. The University's medical building was on fire, and nearly all of Iowa City was awakened when the laboratory chemicals exploded. Within an hour the Medical Building was little more than a brick shell, and a strong wind had spread the fire to South Hall as well. So intense was the heat from South Hall that the Hall of Liberal Arts (Schaeffer Hall), which was then under construction, suffered five hundred dollars worth of damage to its windows. "If it had not been for the rain and sleet," said the Vidette-Reporter, *"the livery barn and Kirkwood hotel*

[across Washington Street] would very probably have gone the way of the two university buildings." The Medical Department lost its library, fourteen cadavers, "many specimens of morbid anatomy," ten thousand dollars worth of microscopes, many lecture notes, and, of course, all of its classrooms. The Engineering Department in South Hall fared better. "From half past three until six in the morning a constant protecting stream of water was kept playing on the big 100,000 pound cement-and-iron testing-machine in the basement, which prevented it from being ruined," reported

the Iowa Alumnus. *Most of the Engineering Department's library and instruments were rescued, as were the elaborate furnishings of the literary societies, then located on the building's third floor. Total damage from the fire was estimated at $100,000. There was no insurance. While there was sadness, "already on that Sunday morning the vision was clear," wrote Dr. Walter L. Bierring of the College of Medicine. "Phoenix-like, there would rise from the ashes a greater medical school than ever before."*

building over the new foundation. The turning movement was accomplished by 'cutting' the rollers, and the adjustment of the rollers was so nicely done that the double movement landed the building almost exactly on the required spot." The process took six months, during which time the building—all three stories and 6,000 tons of it—was kept perfectly level, and classes continued to meet inside the entire time.

Moving Calvin Hall. In 1904 ground was broken for the new Hall of Natural Science (now Macbride Hall). Before it could be completed, however, it was necessary to move the old Science Hall (now Calvin Hall) out of the way, 105 feet across Jefferson Street. The nineteenth-century college was literally making way for the twentieth-century "New University" under President MacLean. In a letter to the president of the University of Oklahoma in 1905, Maclean said, "The overwhelming majority of universities have hodge podge buildings which are dropped here and there like ostrich eggs in the sand. . . . At great cost, we are rescuing this university from these defects."

The moving project, undertaken by the L. P. Freistedt Company of Chicago, required roughly 1,000 screw jacks to lift the building, twenty-seven railroad cars of timber to serve as cribbing, and about 700 rollers, each six inches in diameter and four feet long. "One of the most interesting features of the movement," according to the November 1905 Iowa Alumnus, "was that of turning the building on its axis as it moved forward. In order to pass another building [Old Dental] a one-eighth turn was necessary, and a back turn was necessary in order to bring the

President MacLean at the ceremonies for the laying of the cornerstone of the new Physics Building, 1908. When first occupied in the fall of 1912, the Physics Building provided space for mathematics, electrical engineering, and the fine arts, along with lecture rooms and laboratories for physics. The wooden structure behind the construction site is the "Sheep Shed," built by the engineering faculty and students over the foundation of South Hall after the 1901 fire. Inside were classrooms, drafting rooms, and a few offices, and in the basement there was machinery for metal- and woodworking. Long considered an eyesore, the building was razed during the construction of the new Physics Building.

During excavation for the Physics Building (now MacLean Hall), a cistern filled with human bones was uncovered. Work ceased immediately and the discovery was reported to President MacLean. After determining that the bones were refuse from South Hall's anatomical laboratory, MacLean arranged for the secret removal of the bones under cover of darkness. Afterwards MacLean enjoyed retelling the tale, and would always end: "And that was the only order I gave during my administration which was not countermanded by the State Board of Education."

The campus from the west bank of the Iowa River, 1908. The university buildings are, from left to right, Calvin Hall (after it was moved across Jef- *ferson Street), Old Dental, North Hall (with Macbride Hall behind), Old Capitol (the small brick buildings nearby are the first armory and the* *privy), Schaeffer Hall, the Engineering Building, and, at the far right, the octagonal smokestack of the power plant on Madison Street. Nearer* *the riverbank are the baseball diamond and the Men's Gymnasium.*

The Emerging University, 1878–1916

Postcard view of the President's house, c. 1910. In his Jottings, written more than two decades after he resigned as president of the University of Iowa, George MacLean remembered, "I advocated the building of a President's House, not only to entertain properly distinguished guests of the University but to develop the spirit of a family in the faculty circle and among the students. It might be said that the President's House was built to match the colonial furniture which had come to us as heirlooms." But not all visitors approved. One observed that it was "a pity that the new house was furnished with old furniture."

Steam laboratory, 1910. Since 1873, the University's engineering courses had been taught at a variety of locations, some of them rather makeshift. When Charles Perry Chase arrived on campus to study engineering in the fall of 1886, he was directed to the first Armory, north of Old Capitol, and this is what he found: "The armory was on the first floor, the engineering department on the second floor, and a heating plant in the basement. What a shock that bare room was. It was 30 by 60 feet, with cracked walls, dirty windows, and an old pine floor. In one corner were field instruments and equipment; on the west side was a blackboard. The windows on the east side looked out across the campus to Clinton Street and the view included the Indian

standing stoically in front of Wieneke's cigar store. The room was equipped with a half dozen crude drawing tables, school desks for the drawing and art classes, and a couple of filing cases. The only object of beauty was a girl who sat in front of me."

The School of Applied Sciences (later the College of Engineering) was formed in 1903, and two years later a building was completed to provide modern facilities. The steam shop was built in 1908, and later additions included a materials testing lab, an engine shop,

and classrooms with private work stations for individual instruction.

often elaborate reflections of national as well as campus issues, had become too expensive for the students. But MECCA week continued with a banquet, exhibits, the annual search for the MECCA stone, and (still) pranks aimed at the law students. The Law Jubilee, after gaining a reputation for rowdiness and bad taste, was put to rest with a military funeral on the steps of Old Capitol and was replaced by the altogether more dignified Supreme Court Day, devoted to law students arguing cases in moot court before visiting Iowa Supreme Court justices.

Engineers' parade, Washington Street, 1919. After Iowa City Catholics complained about the Engineering students' appropriating St. Patrick as their patron saint, the name of the annual St. Patrick's Day celebration was changed in 1913 to "Meccasacius." (Spelled backwards, these were the initial letters of State University of Iowa, College of Applied Science, and then the five branches of study: Architectural, Chemical, Civil, Electrical, and Mechanical.) This was usually shortened to MECCA. For the first parade in 1910 there were twenty-one floats, including a complete section of railroad track mounted on a wagon, giant calculus and physics "texts," and a group labeled the "newest developments in the field of engineering for biscuit making," consisting of a concrete mixer run by a gas engine and a wheelbarrow, a mortar board, and a hoe. The notorious rivalry between the colleges of applied science and law apparently began early on the day of the first celebration with a rumor that some law students planned to break up the parade. Armed with poles for defense, a group of engineering students escorted the floats in front of about five thousand spectators. Beginning in 1917, the law students scheduled an evening of satirical skits and musical numbers each year in tandem with the engineering students' celebration, but the Law Jubilee, if anything, simply fired up the law students' interest in disrupting the engineers' activities even more.

In 1926 both the engineers' parade and the Law Jubilee were discontinued. The MECCA floats, which were

Law library, Gilmore Hall, 1910. Long crowded into inadequate chambers in Old Capitol, the College of Law moved to a new building in February 1910. When what is now Gilmore Hall opened, the law librarian, Merton Leroy

Ferson (LL.B., 1901), had four assistants to help him meet the needs of the school's 211 students and twelve faculty. Ferson also taught law and later became head of the George Washington University Law School.

Home Economics class, c. 1915. In 1914–15 the Home Economics Department had three faculty members, and the courses they offered included work on textiles, foods, sanita-

tion, the house, the selection and making of clothes, dietetics, and household management. The department started out in North Hall in 1913.

Senior Frolic, 1912. For the senior class's annual commencement week frolic on June 11, 1912, the students marched from Old Capitol up Clinton Street past the President's House, downhill on Dubuque Street, and across the bridge to City Park. Soon after their arrival they competed in a 25-yard dash, a three-legged race, a potato race, a barrel rolling race, an obstacle race, and a human wheelbarrow race. Graduating seniors from the various colleges also performed

"stunts." The first commencement frolic took place in 1909. Reporting on it, the Iowa Alumnus *mentions "a weird performance in which most of [the seniors] joined hands and circled about a few who with due ceremony and incantation proceeded to burn notebooks and 'wash their hands' of certain courses which had been inflicted upon them in the University." For the first few years of the frolic's history, crowds of up to four thousand were not uncommon.*

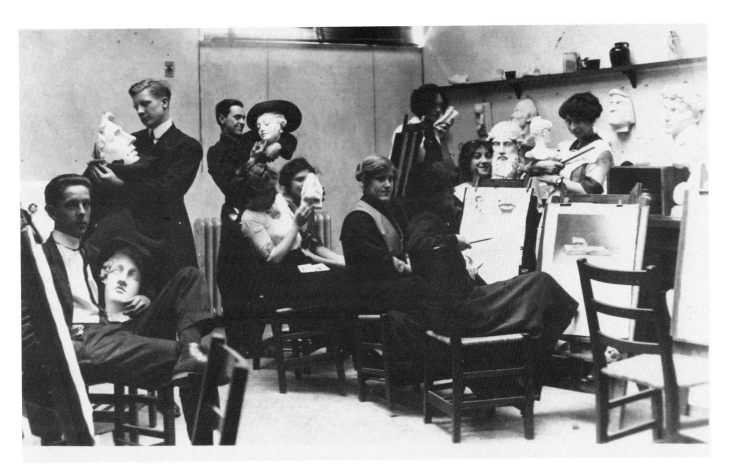

*Drawing students get close to
their subjects during a class in
the Physics Building (now
MacLean Hall), c. 1915.*

*May Fete in City Park, 1916.
With the help of a local steed,
well-curried for the occasion,
Phoebus Apollo and a girl-
friend make a breathtaking
arrival.*

*Billiard parlor on Iowa Ave-
nue, c. 1915.*

Skating on the Iowa River, c. 1890. Skating on the river was popular, but it was not without danger, and in 1889 the student newspaper urged caution: "We want to call the attention of students to the danger of skating on the river. Scarcely a day passes that the [Iowa City] Republican does not record a cold bath for someone. Almost every year the treacherous Iowa claims some poor fellow's life, and it is about time for collection again."

University Book-Store, c. 1915. So much a part of university life was the bookstore that advertisements from the time said simply that it was "on the corner."

Interurban crossing the Iowa River, 1904. The Cedar Rapids and Iowa City Interurban made its inaugural run on August 13, 1904. The cars averaged an hour in covering the twenty-seven miles between the two cities, with fifteen intermediate stops. There were fourteen runs a day, so scheduled that, when necessary, one car could make them all. The first car left Iowa City at 5:15 each morning and the last at 1:10 the next morning. The depot in Iowa City was at the corner of Clinton and College streets. From there the car went down the hill, under the east stands of Iowa Field (until they were torn down after Iowa Stadium opened in 1929), and across the river. Ridership peaked in 1947, when 534,476 passengers used the interurban, but only six years later, on May 30, 1953, the "Galloping Goose" made its last run. The CRANDIC is now a successful freight line. In the background is the Folsom house, later the site of Westlawn.

Svendi Hall, c. 1890. Originally a hotel on the northwest corner of Jefferson and Dubuque streets, Svendi Hall in the 1860s became St. Agatha's Seminary, a boarding and day school for girls. St. Agatha's closed in 1911, at which point Svendi Hall became a dormitory for University women. In 1927 the building was bought by Albert Burkley, who remodeled the structure into twenty-seven apartments.

Currier Hall dorm room, with members of the Currier orchestra, 1918. In the early years of the century, housing for University women was so scarce that on May 9, 1908, nearly eight hundred rallied for a women's building. Four years later, ground was broken for Currier Hall, named to honor equally the contributions to the University of Amos Noyes Currier and Celia Moore Currier. Finished in 1913, Currier was occupied by 168 women, among them the dean of women, who kept a watchful eye on dormitory life. A year later, English instructor Florence Livingston Joy wrote in the Iowa Alumnus: *"At Currier Hall were warmth and jollity and sympathy and friendship—nourished and sheltered in something that very nearly approached the snug security of home." She also observed that "the Currier Hall girl is no angel of perfection. I suspect she consumes fudge in larger quantities than the family physician would advise."*

Sigma Chi initiation, Washington and Clinton streets, c. 1910.

Spring baseball game, 1896. This season the University of Iowa team had twelve players. It won five games and lost three. The team belonged to the Iowa Intercollegiate Baseball League, which included the Iowa Agricultural College (now Iowa State University), Cornell College, and Iowa College (now Grinnell)—serious rivals all—and also played semiprofessional and professional teams from Cedar Rapids, Rock Island, and Davenport. Game scores decreased in the 1880s when players began to wear gloves and pitchers were allowed to raise their arms higher than elbow level.

T. P. Findley (left), a top sprinter for Iowa from 1888 to 1890, toes the line against a "professional racer" at the fairgrounds track (near the present site of Iowa City High School), c. 1889. The results of the race are unknown.

Track and field meet, May 12, 1894. Curtis Dey won the high jump at this Home Field Meet at the old fairgrounds (where City High School now stands) with a jump of 5 feet, 6½ inches. That same day W. T. Chantland won the pole vault by clearing nine feet. Judges of the finish that day (at left) were C. C. Nutting, Launcelot Andrews, and Lt. Vodges, a military instructor.

John Van Fleet Crum, 1895. Born in 1872, Crum graduated from the University's law school in 1895, the same year he concluded his amazing thirty-seven-race winning streak in the 100- and 220-yard dash at intercollegiate and invitational meets around the country. After graduation, Crum practiced law in Bedford, Iowa, and marketed a liniment called John V. Crum's Rub Out. When he died from a burst appendix in 1897, a friend said of him: "John Crum was as clean in his life as his mother believed him to be."

Henry Kallenberg, the basketball coach, and his team, 1893–94. In the fall of 1891, Henry Kallenberg received a letter from James Naismith containing a typed set of rules for a game Naismith had just invented. The game was called basketball. Because of Kallenberg's friendship with Naismith, Iowa City was the site of the first basketball game played west of the Mississippi. The game began at 8:30 P.M. on April 26, 1893, in Close Hall and was preceded by a gymnastics exhibition. Admission was fifteen cents. The Vi-dette-Reporter said that "the game is perhaps not as interesting as Rugby, yet it is a very pleasant indoor game." Kallenberg worked his way through the University by serving as the physical director of the YM-YWCA, and he also found time to teach the game to the Sioux Indians in 1896. He earned his M.D. at Northwestern in 1900 and had a nationally prominent career in physical education. The basketball team that surrounds Kallenberg in this photograph was comprised of University students and one town boy (right front).

Women's fencing, c. 1890. When the University's first fencing club was organized in 1887, it had fifty members.

Fencing was part of Iowa's second annual gymnastics exhibition that same year.

Women's field hockey, Iowa Field, c. 1910. This sport, which was sometimes known as English hockey or field ball, became part of the course offering in women's physical education in 1907.

Football team, 1898. Third from the right in the back row is S. Clyde Williams, known in his day as the "most brilliant field general in college football." Five feet seven inches tall and only 155 pounds, he led Iowa to records of 8-0-1 in 1899 and 7-0-1 in 1900. During those two years Iowa outscored its opponents 532–17. Williams was also captain of the baseball team in his senior year and later played professionally in the American Association. He earned his degree in dentistry but practiced for only a few years before being named head football coach at Ames in 1907. Football was first played at Iowa around 1872, but it was not until the late 1880s, when "Rugby rules" were adopted, that the game began to resemble what we see today. Then as now, it was a rough and dangerous sport. Rule 13 of the 1889 handbook stated: "No tripping, hacking, pushing, or retaining with the hands, charging from behind, striking with the fists, or unnecessary roughness shall be allowed. Projecting nails and iron plates on shoes are prohibited."

CROSS COUNTRY RUN IOWA CITY NOV. 25 1911 Kant.

Cross-country race, Centennial Bridge on Iowa Avenue, November 25, 1911. The Daily Iowan called this event the "annual Big Eight Meet," but this was not the Big 8 Conference of today. Included among the fifty-four runners were participants from Ames, Wisconsin, Minnesota, Purdue, Nebraska, Indiana, Northwestern, the University of Chicago, and Iowa (note that there were nine teams in the Big Eight Conference). The Iowa team finished sixth that day, and a Wisconsin runner won individual honors with a time of 29 minutes, 43.2 seconds, which the DI said was "considered exceptionally fast for the course, which was ankle deep in mud."

FOUR

A One-Man Operation, 1916–1934

*President Walter A. Jessup
with the campus planning
committee, c. 1930; left to
right: Arthur A. Smith (superintendent of buildings and
grounds), Arthur H. Holt (civil
engineering), Walter A. Jessup
(president), Clement C. Williams (dean of the College of
Engineering), Rufus H. Fitzgerald (director of the School
of Fine Arts), Frederick G. Hig-
bee (engineering), George L.
Horner (university architect),
and Byron J. Lambert (civil
engineering).*

What Iowa needed after an educational architect such as MacLean was a contractor to turn the plans for the New University that MacLean visualized into reality. Walter A. Jessup was just such a man. Frequently called a master builder, he thrived on difficulties and crises. Although his policies cannot be solely credited for the fact that enrollment tripled during his presidency and the University's academic program and public services expanded correspondingly, his strong hand on affairs kept the University on a steady course—even when it was thrown out of the Western Conference!

Walter A. Jessup

Walter Jessup's speeches and writings exhibit him as a serious man totally committed to the University. He possessed little humor and no whimsey. Even at social gatherings he would go off into a corner with Dean Packer or another of his lieutenants and talk shop. But he was determined to see Iowa become one of the top institutions in the country. Toward that end, a colleague once recalled, he kept a mental file of every governor, every legislator, every board member, and every civic leader who might be of use to the University, and he maintained close touch with as many as he could. Invaluable for this purpose was a remarkable memory for names and faces, and a forthright approach in conversation. Arthur M. Schlesinger, Sr., who was head of the Department of History from 1919 to 1924, described Jessup in his autobiography, *In Retrospect*, as "a stocky, square-jawed man who looked and acted more like a business executive or banker than a university president." Jessup's main priority, Schlesinger added, was the budget. The life of the University, Jessup believed,

depended on the budget, and therefore anything that threatened the budget could not be tolerated. In short, there was never any question when Jessup was president about who was in charge. As one member of his staff put it, "When Jessup takes snuff, you better sneeze."

Jessup's background was Education with a capital E. He grew up in Indiana where he served as a teacher and administrator in the public schools while he earned his B.A. at Earlham and his M.A. at Hanover. For his Ph.D. he went to Teachers' College, Columbia University. After graduating from Columbia in 1911, he became head of the College of Education at Indiana University. Even then he was recognized nationally as an authority on education. In 1912, on the invitation of President Bowman, he accepted the directorship of the School of Education at Iowa, and a year later, when the school became a college, he became its first dean. When President MacBride retired in 1916, Jessup was quickly selected as his successor. Long afterward, Bowman said that his greatest achievement at Iowa was to discover Walter Jessup. President Jessup left the University of Iowa in 1934 to accept the presidency of the Carnegie Foundation for the Advancement of Teaching. He died in New York City on July 5, 1944.

World War I

Jessup hardly had time to get used to the presidential chair before the United States declared war on Germany on April 6, 1917, and the University was caught up in the frenzy of nationwide war activities. He immediately offered the facilities of the University to the federal government. The eight colleges in the University began to expand their curriculums to include one hour of academic credit for five hours weekly of military drill

Walter A. Jessup (1877–1944), fourteenth president, 1916–34.

and to add some kind of military instruction other than the drill. A voluntary company of graduate students was formed, and the College of Applied Science added instruction in such subjects as range work, map sketching, and field fortification. In June 1918, the Colleges of Medicine and Dentistry and the School of Nursing began the academic year's work in the summer session so that students could speed up their progress toward graduation. At the request of the government, the University took in 165 enlisted men for short courses in blacksmithing, concrete work, radio operation, and auto mechanics. The College of Pharmacy continued the instruction it had begun during the Spanish-American War in theoretical hospital corps work. The Physics Department turned over equipment to the Bureau of Standards for testing purposes, the College of Dentistry offered free dental service to Iowans who had been rejected by the armed services because of tooth defects, and the Chemistry Department produced, among other things, a "cootie" repellent that made sleep easier for soldiers abroad who slept in treated pajamas. President Jessup offered the army the use of the University's wireless station, but in April 1917 the government placed a ban on all radio experiments. Antennas were lowered, transmitters sealed, and receiving apparatus dismantled. Unaccountably, the ban was not lifted until October 1919.

Both the faculty and the student body supported the war effort with distinction. Fifty-three of the faculty were in the armed forces, thirty-eight of them as officers. Many other faculty members served with the Red Cross or the YMCA or in other civilian capacities. Professor Stephen H. Bush of the Department of Romance Languages, for example, served in the French Foreign Legion and was twice cited by the French government for bravery. Dean Carl E. Seashore was a member of the Na-

A One-Man Operation, 1916–1934

Student Army Training Corps (SATC) units march past the campus on Clinton Street during closing drills in 1918.

Rifle drill in Old Armory, 1920. Colonel Morton C. Mumma, "the best shot in America," according to the 1921 Iowa Hawkeye, ran Iowa's military department from 1909 to 1912 and from 1919 to 1928. Not surprisingly, Iowa's rifle teams were also quite good, routinely finishing near the top in intercollegiate competition.

Quadrangle and Armory, 1921. Both the Quadrangle and the Armory were intended for military use, but neither was completed before World War I ended.

tional Research Council, and with the help of others in the psychology program he developed the "Pitch Range Audiometer" as well as standardized diagnostic tests to help screen volunteers to be wireless operators. Professor George W. Stewart, also a member of the National Research Council, worked with some of his colleagues on the problem of locating enemy aircraft. Professor Charles Bundy Wilson and others in the German Department translated foreign-language publications so that they could be examined for violations of the Espionage Act and the Trading with the Enemy Act. And Professors H. G. Plum, G. G. Benjamin, and Louis Pelzer of the History Department lectured to soldiers training at Camp Dodge near Des Moines.

The University was active in other ways, too. President Jessup campaigned vigorously throughout the state on Liberty Loan drives, and Virgil M. Hancher, the senior-class president in 1917–18, organized a strong campus campaign. The young women in Currier "adopted" two French orphans, and the College of Law turned over one of its rooms for use by the Red Cross and the School of Nursing, and another for instruction in telegraphy. With such special activities taking place, the faculty tried resolutely to keep the regular academic program on schedule, and the administration attempted to keep within its budget by such economies as reducing the heat in most buildings on weekends. But sometimes improvisation was necessary. A senior engineering student, William H. Brush, was called for service just before completing all of his work for the bachelor's degree in civil engineering. So that he would not have to leave Iowa City without the degree, William G. Raymond, dean of the College of Applied Science, invited him to dinner together with President Jessup and the engineering faculty. During the evening at Raymond's home, the president conferred the degree on Brush. On another occasion, Jessup, Raymond,

Colonel Morton C. Mumma (the professor of military science and tactics), and other necessary officials journeyed to Fort Snelling near Minneapolis, where they held a miniature commencement for the Iowa seniors in the officer candidate school at the fort.

Nothing, however, disrupted the University's academic program as much as the Student Army Training Corps (SATC). Authorized by Congress in the summer of 1918, the program went into effect in October of that year on 550 campuses throughout the nation. Headed by military personnel (often young officers without field experience), the SATC was designed to prepare officers for the army by combining military and academic instruction. Desperately in need of officers, the War Department actually pleaded with young men who were in, or who were eligible for, college not to enlist but to join the SATC. Derisively, men in active service interpreted the acronym as Saturday Afternoon Tea Club.

Almost fifteen hundred "citizen soldiers" swarmed onto the Iowa campus, taking over the men's and women's gyms, the Armory, Close Hall, and portions of the Engineering, Law, Dentistry, and Natural Science buildings. They occupied tents on the tennis courts, too, until the weather became so cold that they had to move to the unfinished Children's Hospital. To improve the situation, the War Department provided funds for the construction of wooden barracks on the west side, but President Jessup held off construction until he obtained state funds that, when combined with the federal money, would make a permanent brick dormitory possible. The trainees referred to the building they would never occupy as "Jessup's Folly," but the building—the Quadrangle—still stands and is in daily use.

After being sworn in, the trainees were divided into companies by professional schools, age groupings, and college-year status. Interestingly, the Iowa program was one of the few that included several blacks. Among these was Duke Slater, who would become an all-American tackle on Iowa's championship team in the early 1920s.

The kindest thing one can say about the SATC is that in its two-month life it had too little time to succeed. Neither the military nor the academic training was adequate. Military affairs included mass calisthenics, policing of barracks, close-order drill, bayonet practice, and, of course, preparation for inspection. Inspection was a snap for those who had no guns and for whom a latrine was a hole in the ground. Except for a course on Issues of the War taught by University personnel, academic instruction was superficial. It consisted chiefly of courses on military mapping and surveying, military sanitation and hygiene, and military law and practice taught by instructors who were new to their subjects and who were unaided by textbooks. There was a study hall of sorts in the Natural Science Building, but there was nothing to study. In fact, the hardest task of the trainees was to find ways of filling the time. So much for their dreams of getting a college education paid for by the government.

Crowded together as they were, the trainees and the regular student body were especially hard hit by the national epidemic of Spanish influenza that broke out a month after the corps arrived. The campus was promptly quarantined, and even faculty members were halted at bayonet point and not allowed on campus without proper credentials. Almost a thousand patients filled the Isolation Hospital, the General and Children's hospitals, the Law Building, the gymnasiums, and several of the fraternity houses. The corpsmen who were not ill had to take turns helping in the mess halls and hospitals, and standing guard on campus with guns that had bayonets but no ammunition. Many of the faculty were pressed into service to help, especially those in medicine, nursing, and home economics. By Armistice Day, November 11, the epidemic had run its course, but thirty-one men and seven women had died, either from the flu or from pneumonia brought on by the flu.

After the Armistice, the SATC remained until almost Christmas, though the men had little to do after the daily inspection except to raise minor havoc. Later, they recalled loafing at Racine's Cigar Store or Whetstone's Drug Store, tormenting those they considered misfits and singing such songs as this parody of "Smiles":

> The styles that Eve wore in the garden
> Are the styles that appeal to me.

The regular faculty considered the period of the SATC to be an academic disaster. A faculty report declared that the program was ill-conceived and "jerkily" administered. There was general relief on campus when the program came to an end.

Not counting the 1,480 men in the SATC, roughly 1,500 Iowa students and alumni were in the service. Seventy-nine of them died. On their return to the campus, honorably discharged veterans were allowed to register in the Colleges of Liberal Arts and Applied Science without paying the twenty-dollar tuition, and returning veterans in professional colleges had their tuition reduced by the same amount. Faculty members who had been in the service were welcomed back to their former positions.

After the War

In the postwar years, enrollment boomed, jumping from slightly more than four thousand in 1918–19 to more than six thousand in 1921–22. The conviction had grown in Iowa and nationwide that a college education was necessary to success in business and industry and government. A good college education, it was said repeatedly, is a prerequisite for achievement in "the real world"—or as some students engagingly put it, "in the after life." Growth characterized every aspect of the University: administration, faculty, student activities, and public service. Fortunately, President Jessup, far from being cowed by it all, prospered from the challenge, and so did the University.

With the positions that had been vacated by retirements during the war and the additional appropriations he was able to obtain from the legislature, Jessup began to put together a faculty that won national attention. He especially sought scholars and scientists who had already begun to make names for themselves in their specialties, persons like Edward W. Chittenden in theoretical mathematics, Emil Witschi in endocrinology, Craig Baird in British and American oratory, and Hardin Craig in Shakespearean studies. Soon Iowa began to develop a reputation for skillful recruiting, one that it still retains. It also became known as an exciting place to work because Jessup was willing to permit outstanding faculty members the broad freedom they needed to do what they did best. Jessup's influence on the makeup of the faculty continued long after he left Iowa City. In 1944 Henry C. Shull, president of the Board of Education, wrote in the Iowa *News Bulletin* that 95 out of 158 full professors then listed in the University catalog had been appointed by Jessup.

Undergraduate education at Iowa during the Jessup era became better organized and more rigorous. Course numbers in the catalog, for example, became regularized across department lines. A requirement in public speaking was added to the two-year requirement in composition and literature. Superior students were excused from one of the two years of required English. Honors programs became available, first in English and then in history. To bring freshmen and senior faculty together in its

large courses in European and American history, the History Department shifted to an instructional system that combined lectures by senior professors and discussion groups led by instructors. Military training was required of all physically fit male freshmen and sophomores in the liberal arts, engineering, and pharmacy. Engineering, Dentistry, and Medicine had their own Reserve Officers' Training Corps (ROTC) units. Perhaps most important of all, the grade point average necessary for graduation was raised from 1.5 to 2.0.

A number of organizational changes took place. In 1927 the program in museum training under Professor Homer Dill was separated from zoology, and at long last, psychology was separated from philosophy. Psychology had not only developed into a discipline of its own but was also a useful adjunct of such subjects as art, commerce, education, child welfare, music, physical education, and psychiatry. New programs of study included one in general science that required at least forty semester hours of work distributed among the science departments, and one in the social sciences that required at least fifty semester hours in the several social science departments.

The School of Journalism

In 1915 the liberal arts faculty's decision to create schools within the college resulted in some of the University's strongest and most innovative programs. The first of these programs, the School of Journalism, was carved out of the Department of English in 1923. Charles H. Weller was its director, and on his staff at the beginning were William S. Maulsby, George Gallup, Loren D. Upton, and Frank Hicks. The school was located in Close Hall, with overflow classes meeting across

Journalism class taught by George Gallup, standing at left, Daily Iowan *editorial room, 1924. Gallup (1901–84) served as managing editor (1921–22) and editor (1922–23) of the* Daily Iowan *and then joined the faculty of the* School of Journalism. His time here was short because, in his words, "In 1924 I got interested in the research side of media, and did some readership surveys." He became director of research at Young & Rubicam, a famous New York advertising agency. Before too long, Gallup's name came to be synonymous with public opinion polls. Among the Daily Iowan's *editors after Gallup were Loren Hickerson (director of Alumni Services, 1947–68), James Zabel (voice of Hawkeye* sports for WHO radio, Des Moines), Dorothy Klein (of the Dottie Ray Show on KXIC), Gary Gerlach (publisher of the Des Moines Register *for many years), and Dwight Jensen (director of the Office of Public Information from 1981 to 1986).*

Dubuque Street in the Electrical Engineering Building. When Professor Weller died in 1927 he was succeeded by Frank Luther Mott, who would become one of the two or three most distinguished professors of journalism in the country. One of Mott's first accomplishments was to help settle a fight with Iowa State by agreeing that Iowa State should stress technical journalism and Iowa, journalistic writing. The two schools also agreed to cooperate in working with newspapers in the state.

Classes in journalism soon became so popular that Mott instituted not only aptitude tests but also a semester "testing" course in reporting, both of which a student had to pass satisfactorily before being allowed to major in journalism or work on the *Daily Iowan*. Readers of the *DI* immediately profited. Professor Mott also instituted a short-story course, with remarkable results. Among his students who sold stories to such journals as the *American Mercury* and the *Saturday Evening Post* were Bruce Gould, who later, with his wife, Beatrice Blackmar, edited the *Ladies' Home Journal*, and Marquis Childs, later a nationally syndicated columnist. Possibly even more remarkable was that in the depression year of 1932, two thirds of the graduating journalism students found jobs.

In 1922 the *Daily Iowan*, with George Gallup as its editor-in-chief, became a full-fledged daily receiving United Press wire service and with its own presses in a red brick building between Close and Unity halls on Iowa Avenue. The first edition from the new plant was a forty-page issue of eight thousand copies, a near record for college newspapers. Not all of the campus publications, however, were so successful. The *Hawkeye*, the yearbook put out by the junior class, embarrassed the University by defaulting on its bill to a printer, and the *Iowa Alumnus* folded and was replaced by the *University of Iowa News Bulletin*, edited by Fred Pownall, a journalist of great good humor and common sense. The

Iowa Literary Magazine gave way to *Hawk Wings*, which in turn collapsed. Other publications included *Frivol*, the humor magazine, the *Journal of Business* (originally called the *Organizer*), and the *Philological Quarterly*, a distinguished scholarly journal founded in 1922 by Hardin Craig, chairman of the Department of English, and taken over in 1928 by Baldwin Maxwell.

To provide greater stability for all such publications, the administration in June 1924 created the Iowa Board of Publications, which oversaw their editorial policies and, more particularly, their financial condition. A few fly-by-night journals eluded the new board. One such was a razz sheet put out by the Sigma Delta Chi journalism fraternity and called *Pooh, Pooh-Hooey*. Very shortly President Jessup lost his patience with its wit, reprimanded the editors, and made the Department of Journalism responsible for its contents. Soon the cry of the *Pooh, Pooh-Hooey* was heard no longer in the land.

The School of Religion

The School of Religion was established in 1925, though classes did not begin until 1927. As planned with the help of Rev. O. D. Foster, university secretary of the Council of Church Boards of Education, the school was a unique experiment sponsored by the University and the major religious bodies of the state. Its purpose was to give students insight into the nature and meaning of religion and to provide training for those wishing to become religious leaders. The Protestant, Catholic, and Jewish faiths each funded a professorship, with support for the school's administration coming initially from the Rockefeller Foundation. For director of the school, the trustees were fortunate in obtaining Rev. M. Willard Lampe from the Board of Christian Education of the Presbyterian church. Dr. Lampe headed the school from 1927 until he retired in 1953. Besides Lampe, the original faculty consisted of Professors H. G. Takkenberg, a Catholic; Maurice H. Farbridge, a Jew; and Charles A. Hawley, a Protestant. Not all religious groups in the state enthusiastically supported the new school. The Unitarians, for example, protested that liberal religion was not sufficiently recognized, and on at least one occasion the Catholic bishop of Davenport withdrew his approval. But support was strong enough for the school to prosper and to offer such courses as Christian Ethics, Comparative Religion, and the History of Religion. By accepting credits from such departments as English, philosophy, and psychology, the faculty of the school integrated their work with what was being taught in more established areas. Ultimately the school came to serve the state more generally by broadcasting over radio station WSUI. Two programs became regulars: "Religious News of the World" and Professor Marcus Bach's "Little-Known Religious Groups." Because of Bach's flair for the dramatic, the latter program became enormously popular throughout eastern Iowa. Today the School of Religion remains a highly successful venture in bridging the gulf between church and state without doing violence to the First Amendment.

Religion faculty, 1929. Clockwise from upper left, they are M. Willard Lampe, Charles A. Hawley, William P. Shannahan, and Maurice H. Farbridge.

The School of Fine Arts

The School of Fine Arts, which included as sections Music, Graphic and Plastic Arts, the History of Fine Arts, and Dramatic Art, was established in the fall of 1929 under the direction of Rufus H. Fitzgerald, who was also the director of the Iowa Memorial Union. During its early years, Music had an anomalous position in the University. It was associated with the in-

Painting class, MacLean Hall, 1925.

stitution, but instruction consisted of private lessons. Fees from these lessons paid the salaries of the instructors, and proceeds from concerts paid the expenses of the glee club, the choral societies, the orchestra, and the band. With the coming of Philip Greeley Clapp in 1919, music was accorded formal University support, and its instructors became members of the faculty. Professor Clapp quickly organized a large chorus and symphony orchestra, and, with the enthusiastic support of President Jessup and Dean Seashore, he began the unheard-of practice of awarding undergraduate and graduate credit for performance in voice and instrumental music. By the time Music became a department of the School of Fine Arts, it was sponsoring three symphony concerts a year, a variety of choral presentations, and one or more operas. Spring music festivals for high school students helped attract superior young musicians to the University. A hard driver, Professor Clapp gave national prominence to the work in music at Iowa.

Work in art started at Iowa in 1909 when Charles A. Cumming was brought to the campus to establish a Department of Graphic and Plastic Arts. Art became a unit in the short-lived College of Fine Arts, which existed from 1911 to 1915. As a department in the College of Liberal Arts, it outlived the arts college and began awarding bachelor's degrees in liberal arts in 1915–16. Special courses were devised for home economics and predental students, and Professor Norman C. Meier of the Department of Psychology offered a course in the psychology of art. After Professor Cumming died in 1927, Professor Roy C. Flickinger became head of the department. Although student enrollment and the arts faculty continued to grow during the Jessup administration, its best days were yet to come.

Even during the war years, dramatics, intercollegiate oratory, and debate flourished, but as extracurricular ac-

tivities under the supervision of boards of the faculty senate. Dramatic arts courses burgeoned after Edward C. Mabie joined the faculty in 1920. In the first year alone he personally offered courses in Dramatic Interpretation, Dramatic Production, and the Contemporary Stage. The production of plays in Macbride Hall, with its shallow stage and limited space offstage, was a nightmare for directors, but Mabie and his aides gave a professional touch to their productions. Mabie, moreover, began to obtain rights for the first production of plays outside of New York, a practice commended by such playwrights as Owen Davis, Eugene O'Neill, and Sydney Howard. When, with the help of a grant from the Rockefeller Foundation, a new theater was erected on the west bank of the Iowa River, the University had one of the most modern plants anywhere. Although the new theater did not open until 1936, it was with President Jessup's help that Mabie was able to assemble one of the finest college theater staffs in the country, notably Vance Morton in acting, Arnold Gillette in stage design, and Hunton Sellman in stage lighting. It was common talk in New York that for the best college training, aspiring actors should go to Yale, Carnegie, or Iowa. The establishment of a contest for high school drama students and of Professor Mabie's course on Practical Community Theatre Operation spread the influence of the University statewide.

The School of Letters

The School of Letters came into being in the spring of 1930, with Professor Norman Foerster as director. The school included English, classics, and foreign language departments. President Jessup was especially pleased with the appointment of Professor Foerster because he believed Foerster to be a strong man who would integrate the work in literature across the campus. Foerster did bring to the study of literature, especially that of England and America, a new emphasis on literature as a repository of human values. He was less concerned with historical scholarship than with critical interpretation. His influence was felt immediately in the two-year required undergraduate course in Literature and Writing, and in a greater emphasis in the Department of English on literary criticism and creative writing. While traditional scholars in English and the foreign languages resisted Professor Foerster's neohumanism, his ideas strongly appealed to such younger men as Joseph Baker, John McGalliard, and Seymour Pitcher. His appointments of the senior critics René Wellek and Austin Warren brought instant recognition to the School of Letters. It was while they were at Iowa that they wrote their *Theory of Literature*, a work that still remains a classic in the field of literary criticism.

Although Foerster was a brilliant man who created lively intellectual discussions on the campus, he was too doctrinaire and dictatorial to be a successful administrator. Once, for example, he tried to kill the *Philological Quarterly* (then edited by Baldwin Maxwell) in order to use the money for *American Prefaces*, a journal he had persuaded Wilbur Schramm to edit. Dean Seashore wisely found funds for both journals. In their different ways, both brought distinction to the University, *Philological Quarterly* by being the premier journal in Elizabethan and eighteenth-century scholarship and *American Prefaces* by being a journal devoted to literary criticism and creative writing, publishing works not only of Iowa faculty members such as Grant Wood, Paul Engle, John T. Frederick, Edwin Ford Piper, and Joseph E. Baker, but also by such writers as Stephen Vincent Benét, T. S. Eliot, James Hearst, Wallace Stevens, Jesse Stuart, and William Carlos Williams.

The school faded out for a time after Professor Foerster resigned in 1944, but its emphasis on the practice of imaginative writing as well as literary criticism continued in courses and theses in criticism and especially in the Writers' Workshop, which to this day is one of the University's top attractions.

The Experimental Schools

The experimental elementary and high schools and the Iowa Child Welfare Research Station got their start under Jessup's direction, first as dean of education, then as president of the University. As laboratories for the students in the College of Education, the University Elementary School opened in 1915 with Ernest Horn as director, and the University High School in 1916 with Ervin Lewis as director. These laboratories also served as desirable small schools for children whose parents wanted alternatives to public education. They probably could have been filled with "faculty kids" had there not been a policy of limiting children of faculty members to half of the total enrollment. U-High athletic teams were something less than powerhouses, but the academic training was clearly superior for those who were lucky enough to be taught by such department heads as G. Robert Carlsen, John Haefner, Vernon Price, Anne Pierce, and Camille LeVois or by such instructors as Shirley Harrison and H. H. Wubben. For financial reasons, President Boyd closed the school in 1972.

Established in 1917, the Iowa Child Welfare Research Station was the first center in the country to study by scientific methods the development of the normal child. Its first director was George D. Stoddard. In 1925 it was made the coordinating center for work being done on child study and parent education not only in Iowa City

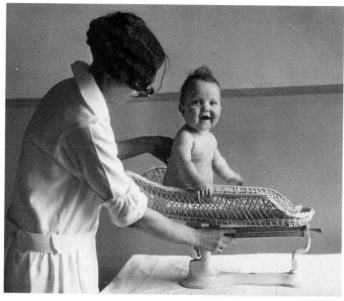

A nurse weighs a baby at the Iowa Child Welfare Research Station, 1928. The mission of the research station (later the Iowa Institute of Child Behavior and Development) was to study the normal child. Researchers at the facility, led first by Bird T. Baldwin (1917–28) and next by George D. Stoddard (1928–42), produced influential studies on children's IQ, speech, and physical development. They also contributed articles to such popular magazines as Better Homes and Gardens, *the* Ladies' Home Journal, McCall's, Parents' Magazine, *and* Wallaces' Farmer. *By 1967, when the institute celebrated its fiftieth anniversary, the bibliography of articles and books generated by researchers contained over two thousand entries.*

but also in Ames and Cedar Falls. Expenses were met by direct appropriations from the General Assembly and by grants and private donations. Its preschool became so highly esteemed that parents would register their children for it as soon as they were born. Some parents even tried—without success, it should be said—to register their children as soon as they were conceived.

The Campus Course

There has never been any course at the University quite capable of matching Benjamin F. Shambaugh's Approaches in Liberal and Cultural Education, better known as the Campus Course. Shambaugh, bothered by what he saw as overspecialization by undergraduates, began working on the Campus Course in the late 1920s and offered it for the first time in the summer of 1932. The goal of the course, said Shambaugh, was the "Realization of the Good Life." The approaches taken to get there included the scientific, humanistic, psychological, philosophical, religious, and contemporary, and the list of suggested readings for the course contained well over one hundred volumes. Students took no exams, but they did keep a diary, which they submitted to Shambaugh each week.

After 1934 the Campus Course met in a specially designed room on the third floor of Schaeffer Hall furnished with venetian blinds, tall Roman floor lamps, and 250 Windsor chairs. Students who arrived early listened to classical music and gazed at paintings (changed every week) prior to Shambaugh's dramatic lectures. The refinements of the Campus Course room, which also had a 2,000-volume library, only enhanced the course itself.

At stage center was the always impeccably attired Shambaugh, who started his students off with Genesis

A One-Man Operation, 1916–1934

Benjamin Franklin Shambaugh (1871–1940). Professor Shambaugh was born on a farm near Elvira, Iowa, earned his B.A. in 1892 and his M.A. in 1893, both at Iowa, and his Ph.D. in 1895 at the University of Pennsylvania. In 1895 he returned to Iowa City to join the faculty of the Political Science Department. Five years later he became head of the department, and he was appointed to the newly created office of superintendent of the State Historical Society of Iowa in 1907. On the campus he was an institution. He was tall, straight, and debonair, invariably sporting a red tie and pocket handkerchief and carrying a malacca cane. For many years he was chairman of the University Lecture Series. The legend continues that many went to hear his introductions rather than the addresses of the speakers. His wife, Bertha Horack Shambaugh, whom he married in 1897, was an amateur photographer and a historian of the Amana Colonies.

(though they later read Darwin as well), and then, according to *Time*, "went from there in all directions." The course transcended departments and colleges. In Shambaugh's view it was a synthesis of all modern knowledge, aimed at an audience of "men and women desiring a richer and fuller life—a life made vivid and exquisite with the maximum of intellectual and emotional experience."

Construction

"Westward Ho!" proclaimed the title of an article President Jessup wrote for the November 1918 *Iowa Alumnus*. In it he described recent construction and the plan to move the College of Medicine and all its hospitals to the west side of the Iowa River. The extension of the campus across the river was made possible by the construction of new bridges at Burlington Street in 1915 and Iowa Avenue in 1916, along with transportation provided by the interurban and the Iowa City streetcar system. In 1917 the University made its first westside land purchase and began construction of a children's hospital on the bluff above the river. The next year construction began on the SATC barracks south of the children's hospital, which after the war became the Quadrangle dormitory. The Armory, the Psychopathic Hospital, and Westlawn (a dormitory for nurses) followed in 1921. Then, on December 27, 1922, Jessup announced that the Rockefeller Foundation and the Rockefeller General Board of Education had awarded the University $2,250,000—at that time the largest gift ever granted in the United States to a tax-supported institution—to assist in building and equipping a new hospital and teaching laboratories. At the beginning of the new

year the General Assembly voted matching funds. Three years later, in 1926, the Medical Laboratories building was completed and construction of the General Hospital was underway one hundred feet to the west of it. In 1927 the Field House was dedicated, and a new stadium close by was ready for use two years later. After the dedication of the new hospital in 1928, the campus could no longer be thought of as facing the town. Rather, the dome of Old Capitol faced the hospital tower, which rose across the river above grounds between four and five times as extensive as those on the east side.

During the Jessup regime, the campus east of the river also began taking on its present-day appearance with the completion of Eastlawn in 1915, the Dental Building (now Trowbridge Hall) on North Capitol Street in 1917, the Chemistry-Botany-Pharmacy Building on North Capitol Street in 1924, University Hall (now Jessup Hall) on the Pentacrest in 1924, the Iowa Memorial Union in 1926, and the power plant on Burlington Street in 1928. Just across the river by the Burlington Street bridge was the Hydraulics Laboratory.

The Iowa Memorial Union

The need for a center for student social and cultural life became increasingly evident as the student body continued to grow. The University's first response, taken in 1911 during President Bowman's administration, was to renovate Unity Hall, the former Unitarian Church at the corner of Iowa Avenue and Clinton Street. But Unity Hall soon proved to be inadequate, and in December 1913 the Union moved to the rooms above the Brunswick Bowling Parlor, 121–123 Iowa Avenue. In March 1914 it again moved, this time to the St.

Digging the foundation of the Chemistry Building, 1921. Interest in chemistry mushroomed in the wake of World War I. The Chemistry Depart-ment's quarters, built in 1890, were found wanting. Chemical laboratories were scattered around the campus: in Close Hall, the Dental Building, an annex on Iowa Avenue, and an old mess hall.

Iowa Memorial Union, c. 1929. During the campaign for an Iowa student union, President Jessup said: "As Old Capitol is the center of our official life, this will be the focus of our social life." Fund-raising for the cultural and student center began in 1919, and in 1927 the first two units of the building were opened at a site near the river on Madison Street. The ballroom was the most impressive feature of the new facility, which also included a cafeteria, indoor and outdoor porches along the river, rooms for the Triangle and University clubs as well as the YMCA and YWCA, and a soda fountain serving chocolate sundaes for 15 cents. In the original plans, a theater and auditorium were to be included in future units to the south, but this changed when the arts campus developed across the river in the 1930s. A 1955 addition created more space for student organizations and recreational activities, and in 1965 a guest house called the Iowa House was built. Extensive renovations began in 1986 to expand the bookstore and rearrange much of the interior of the building.

James Hotel building across Iowa Avenue from Unity Hall. Unhappily, in April 1916 the St. James burned to the ground, and this time the Union had no place to go.

After the war, President Jessup, combining the need for a Union and the desire for a memorial to students who had been killed in action, proposed a Memorial Union, which would be the "hearthstone of the whole university." The Alumni Association immediately picked up the idea and created the Iowa Memorial Union Corporation headed by a board of trustees instructed to raise a million dollars for the construction of a suitable building. In July 1919 the Board of Education assured the alums of its "hearty and cordial cooperation"—but their cooperation stopped short of volunteering state funds. Then followed a series of fund drives, none of them notably successful. In October 1920 the trustees appointed Ralph G. Grassfield as the first permanent director of the Union. When he resigned less than three years later, the trustees selected Rufus H. Fitzgerald, the head of the campus YMCA. It was Fitzgerald's fearsome task to solicit further pledges, collect on the pledges already made, oversee the planning and construction of the building, and plan a program once the building was a reality. In 1923 the pledges totaled $537,409 but only $73,567 of this sum was in hand. Many of the students who had pledged said they had done so in the heat of a campaign when their judgment was skewed by University speakers. Some parents and local businessmen charged duress and threatened to take legal action when a collection agency tried to extract what they owed. Usually the Union trustees went lightly on the students, but they did press the case against recalcitrant business establishments.

Acting on the theory that much more money could not be raised until construction started, the trustees, after considerable discussion about sites, selected the plot

at the northwest corner of Jefferson and Madison Streets
and told the architects, Boyd and Moore, to draw up
plans for a building composed of interlocking units. On
September 29, 1924, contracts were signed for the construction of Unit I, the central part facing south plus the
large lounge and ballroom immediately to the north.
Somewhat later, when the contractor pointed out that the
trustees could save money by constructing Unit II while
he still had his equipment on the lot, the trustees signed
a contract for Unit II, roughly the northeast section of
the building fronting on Madison Avenue. Discouraged
by fund-raising campaigns, they turned to other ways of
obtaining revenue. For $50,000 they awarded the Trian-
gle Club, a 250-member male faculty club then meeting
in the Commercial Bank building, a lease for fifty years
and nine months on half of the second floor and all of the
third floor of Unit II. They also agreed to lease offices to
the YMCA and the YWCA on the first floor for a period
of fifty years for $19,000. In addition, the University
agreed to pay rent for the space it used for University
activities, and the Board of Education authorized one dollar from the tuition and fees of each student for the purchase of furniture and equipment. By the fall of 1927 the
two units were in use. The first big event held in the
Union was the Military Ball on February 4, 1928, which
sent local journalists to their thesauruses to find adjec-
tives adequate to describe such a gala. In September 1930
women were admitted as members of the Student Union
Board, an event considerably more significant than the
Military Ball, for from then on the Union was in truth
an enterprise for all the students. The activities it housed
ranged from University registration to professional conferences, from vespers to tea dances, from a browsing
library to a nonalcoholic nightclub called the Silver
Shadow. Under Ted Rehder the Union Dining Service

operated a catering service both inside and outside the
building so successfully that one segment of the downtown restaurateurs complained to the legislature. After
the Board of Education in 1929 added the directorship of
the new School of Fine Arts to Fitzgerald's duties, the
Union became even more closely tied to the cultural life
of the University and the community. When he retired
in 1934, President Jessup could look upon the Union as
one of the major achievements of his administration.

The Marshall Imbroglio

Jessup weathered many crises in his eighteen-year
administration. There was a conflict between the
military and athletic departments over the exemp-
tion of intercollegiate athletes from ROTC, some trouble
regarding faculty views on Prohibition, and Iowa's suspension from Big Ten play in 1930, to name but a few.
But these predicaments were minor indeed compared to
the investigation launched by Verne Marshall, the editor
of the *Cedar Rapids Gazette*. The majority of Marshall's
charges alleged financial impropriety or ineptitude on the
part of certain administration officials. But the last of his
twenty-one charges was a bit more personal. There Marshall characterized Jessup as having an "arbitrary, dog-
matic, stubborn and czar-like attitude as chief executive."

The opening salvo of this battle had been Marshall's
editorial of December 21, 1930, in which he blasted the
Jessup administration. A defense of the University by W.
Earl Hall, the editor of the *Mason City Globe-Gazette*,
failed to turn Marshall from his campaign. Eventually
Governor Dan Turner supported Marshall by asking for
an investigation of the University. The General Assembly complied, calling an investigation that began on Feb-

Night vigil at University Hall, 1931. The legislative investigation of the University took a dramatic turn on March 3, 1931, when agents of the State Bureau of Investigation were dispatched to Iowa City to impound University records. "Friendly hostility" ensued when University officials physically denied them access to the records. Shown here during the standoff are, from left to right: an unidentified reporter; Edward E. Bright, University accountant; J. V. Arney, a state agent; Ray Lapitz, a Chicago detective; William Wisdom, a special agent; and H. L. Finch, University engineer. Ultimately, the investigation exonerated the University.

ruary 23, 1931, and did not end until April 11. Seven members of the state senate and house heard eighty witnesses, and the official transcript ran to almost six thousand pages. After it was all over, Marshall claimed victory on eighteen of the twenty-one charges he had made, but the actual report, though it found laxity in many areas, disclosed no grounds for prosecution of any kind; nor did it request any resignations or dismissals. The minority report was even more favorable to the University. The State Board of Education thanked the Iowa faculty, students, and alumni for their loyalty to the University, and on April 27, 1931, the Iowa City Chamber of Commerce held a "vindication banquet" for several hundred friends and supporters of the University.

Student Life

The literary societies finally died out during this period. Six societies for women still existed in the mid-twenties—the Erodelphian, Hesperian, Octave Thanet, Whitby, Athena, and Hamlin Garland—and there were four for men—the Zetagathian, Irving Institute, Philomathean, and Rhoterian. The groups faced too much competition, however. The fraternities and sororities took over their social functions; men's and women's forensic councils and professional forensic fraternities such as Phi Delta Gamma, Delta Sigma Rho, and Sigma Delta Phi provided professional recognition far beyond what a local literary society could furnish; intercollegiate debates, including debates with Oxford University, attracted the best students away from intersociety debates; the *Iowa Literary Magazine* became semi-independent, with contributions no longer limited to members of the literary societies; and honorary organizations in music and journalism emerged, as did a variety of departmental

clubs. All this helped to bring about the demise of the
literary societies. By 1934 all were gone, though they
still retain a distinguished place in the history of the
University.

Since Jessup and many of the faculty and staff were
fraternity men, they encouraged the growth of both fraternities and sororities. They believed that such organizations contributed importantly to the process of student
maturation—and besides, the fraternity houses helped to
alleviate the tight housing situation. The number of such
organizations grew substantially. The *Hawkeye* for 1916
lists fifteen social fraternities, sixteen sororities, and
twelve professional and eleven honorary organizations.
This was the period of the elegant chapter house, with
fraternities and sororities trying to outdo one another
and, in some cases, piling up debts that took years to pay
off. One medical fraternity went bankrupt. In 1924 Alpha Chi Omega sorority purchased the magnificent Victorian house at Washington and Governor streets. Kappa
Kappa Gamma and Pi Beta Phi both built houses costing
$40,000. Sigma Alpha Epsilon built the first fraternity
house on the west side of the river at a cost of $65,000.
The *Daily Iowan* for April 11, 1926, reported that six
fraternities had plans for building chapter houses within
the year and that these would cost a total of $320,000.

This was the era of raccoon coats and the Charleston,
and Iowa fraternities and sororities were not going to be
left behind in Jazz Age display. Although the deans had
no direct control over how the student organizations
spent their money, the deans' offices did take over the job
of auditing the books of fraternities and sororities. Also,
they clamped down on Hell Week when the brothers
went so far as to injure their initiates, either emotionally
or physically.

Prohibition seems not to have agitated the students
particularly, partly because most of them apparently did

Union sun porch, c. 1934.

not drink and the others, according to old grads, had a high old time visiting blind pigs and making their own bathtub gin. The University simply continued its long-standing rules that there should be no liquor on University property and that drunkenness was cause for disciplinary action. Furthermore, while the board and the people of the state wanted the students to obey the law, sentiment against the Prohibition Amendment was strong enough to permit a bit of winking at minor infractions. The campus, therefore, never became a major Prohibition battleground.

Foremost among those monitoring the activities of the student body were Robert Rienow and Adelaide L. Burge. Rienow was one of the hardest workers during the Jessup years and was often called the conscience of the University. He had come to the University to assist Professor Forest Ensign, who was registrar, examiner, dean of men, and, as they said, director of everything else. When Professor Ensign left on a short leave in 1915, Rienow became dean of men, and he held that position until 1942. He and such deans of women as Nellie S. Aurner and Adelaide L. Burge were responsible for riding herd on all students, particularly the undergraduates, and keeping, insofar as possible, the antics of the mavericks out of the newspapers. Their areas of responsibility included student attendance, scholarship, student employment, student health, audits of the books of student organizations, supervision of the dormitories and discipline among fraternities and sororities, minor and major crimes, records of faculty and student committees on student affairs, visits to sick students in the hospitals, and conferences with individual students. To make the task still harder, the budgets for the deans did not go up as student enrollment increased. Given the complexity and tension of their work, Rienow and Burge well de-

served the honor of having dormitories named after them.

Even greater problems, however, were raised by student housing in the city, where many landlords charged whatever they thought they could get. Especially after it was discovered that the grade point average of students living in town was substantially below that of students living in dormitories and in fraternity and sorority houses, the administration required students to live only in housing approved by University inspectors.

Discrimination in the University's own housing was openly practiced. The administration did not intervene, for example, when residents of the Quadrangle dormitory insisted on the exclusion of nonwhites. Rienow took the position that it was unwise to create the dissension that would result when a small minority of students forced its presence upon the overwhelming majority. Instead, Dean Burge, President Jessup, and he encouraged blacks to take rooms in the Iowa Federation House for Colored Students. In the town Helen Lemme was especially active in finding housing for nonwhite students. By today's standards the policy was far from enlightened, but in the twenties and thirties it created little fuss because there were so few nonwhite students and because civil rights had not become a national issue.

Class attendance for undergraduates was mandatory; violators were hauled before the Committee of Admissions and Classifications, and their parents were notified. Students found guilty were placed on probation and, unless they mended their ways, had their registrations canceled. Students whose grades were seriously deficient were treated similarly. It was especially gratifying to Rienow that the academic standing of the men in the Quadrangle, where the University maintained a measure of control, was the highest for any housing unit. Fraternities could be—and were—put on probation for a year

Quadrangle dormitory, early 1930s. Quadrangle men thought of themselves as special. Although the dean of men took a special interest in the "Quad," the dormitory was largely self-governing, enough so that it was referred to as a "splendid example of American democracy at its best." The dorm had unusual spirit, and from 1927 to 1930 it produced and financed its own yearbook. Quad men invariably had the highest grade point average of all campus housing groups, and, in contrast to the women, male dorm residents had neither bed checks nor curfews.

when grades fell below the minimum. For a fraternity, probation was no light matter, because it meant the loss of social privileges and the right to pledge new members. As always, the grades of the athletes were a matter of concern. Some groups of athletes were above the average, some quite a bit below. In descending order of their grade averages were the gymnasts, swimmers, baseball players, track men, football players, basketball players, wrestlers, and—"Give me an A!"—cheerleaders.

Minor disciplinary matters were usually handled by faculty committees or college deans; more serious infractions were referred to the Senate Board of Discipline, which included the deans of men and women. The most common causes of disciplinary action were drinking, writing bad checks, dishonesty on examinations, and

mutilating library books. One student was disciplined for operating a still and another for insulting the dean of the College of Medicine. Occasionally the students stretched Rienow's famed patience too far, as they did in staging a rush on the Englert Theater in 1919 as a protest against the continuation of a war tax, and as they did again in vandalizing the railroad coaches on a "football special" to Minneapolis. The feud between the "laws" and the engineering students occasionally created havoc. In the winter of 1929, for example, a group of law students raided the Mecca Ball of the engineers and brought the dancing to a stop until they were thrown out. While a few of the students may have acted like the glamorous collegians pictured in the F. Scott Fitzgerald stories and the John Held, Jr., cartoons of the day, on the whole during the

Jessup years they seem to have been a reasonably well behaved outfit. The administration was pleased no end when big-band leader Paul Whiteman, after playing for a student dance in the Union, told its director that in all his experience he had never played for a finer group of young people. He even used the administration's favorite adjective when he called them "wholesome."

Athletics

By 1916, when Walter Jessup became Iowa's president, football was the undisputed king of sport, and rarely has it prospered as it did in the early 1920s, when Iowa fielded teams reminiscent of the great unbeaten teams of 1899 and 1900. From 1916 until 1919 Iowa's teams were good, though far from great, but midway through the 1920 season Howard Jones's Hawkeyes began to win. The team's star player was Fred "Duke" Slater, considered by many the finest tackle ever to play at Iowa and the recipient of innumerable all-American honors. In addition, it had quarterback Aubrey Devine, who in the 1921 defeat of Minnesota had a simply astonishing offensive game, passing for two touchdowns, running for four more, kicking five extra points, returning punts and kickoffs, and finishing the game with 464 total yards. On the same team were Lester Belding, who was voted to all-American squads in 1919, 1920, and 1921, and fullback Gordon Locke, whom John Heisman described as having "legs that gave the drive the momentum of a battle tank." Iowa won the last three games of the 1920 season, went undefeated and won conference titles in 1921 and 1922, and then won the first three games of the 1923 season before falling 9–6 to an Illinois team led by Red Grange. The twenty-game winning streak, by

far the longest in University of Iowa history, was enhanced by a 6–0 defeat of Yale, which had never lost to a western team, in October 1922.

Howard Jones, the head coach at Iowa during these glory years, left after the 1923 season for a job at Trinity College (now Duke University), and after that Iowa's football fortunes began to sag. The coach who followed Jones, Burton Ingwersen, was not popular with many alumni. Some thought it morally wrong that Ingwersen, though an Iowa native, had attended the University of Illinois. One unhappy alumnus said he wanted to keep "Iowa schools for Iowa boys." Others were less polite. Unfortunately, this opposition did not stop with talk. In fact, alumni interfered with the University's football program to such an extent that in May 1929—the year that Kinnick Stadium, then called Iowa Stadium, was built—the directors of the Western Intercollegiate Athletic Conference met and after long deliberation recommended that "the conference sever athletic relations with Iowa University" as of January 1, 1930.

On hearing news of the suspension, students demonstrated and marched on President Jessup's house, pelted the house of ousted athletic director Paul E. Belting with rocks, and demanded that Commissioner Griffith come to Iowa to explain the reason for Iowa's suspension. Griffith came, and the University launched an investigation to find out what, exactly, was going on. The officials discovered a slush fund for "loans" to athletes and the questionable practice of refunding tuition to athletes and using athletic scholarships improperly. But just as important was the conference's conviction that at Iowa the faculty was losing control of athletics. The upshot was that a number of football players were barred from competition, the University regained control of its football program, and the action suspending Iowa was rescinded on

The following newspaper front page is reproduced:

Chicago Sunday Tribune
THE WORLD'S GREATEST NEWSPAPER

10 CENTS PAY NO MORE

LAST MAIL

VOLUME LXXXI—NO. 42   OCTOBER 15, 1922.   ★ SEVEN CENTS IN CHICAGO AND NEAR RANGE | TEN CENTS ELSEWHERE.

IOWA ELEVEN SMASHES YALE

RAIL WAY MEN GET PAY BOOST OF $22,125,562

Rate Raised 2 Cents an Hour by Board.

THE FOUR ENEMIES OF GOOD GOVERNMENT

HAWKEYE LINE ATTACK BRINGS 6 TO 0 VICTORY

Parkin Star; Scores Only Touchdown.

Races in Coma to Set World Air Record

LLOYD GEORGE PUTS FATE IN PEOPLE'S HANDS

Contends He Kept Peace in Europe.

Parade on Washington Street after the Yale victory. Yale had never lost to a western team in the Yale Bowl, but on October 14, 1922, Iowa held Yale without a first down for the entire first half and went on to win, 6–0. In those days eastern football was considered far superior (all-star teams, for example, were divided into East and West squads), and Iowa's victory was headline news around the Midwest. The game also marked only the second time in football history that two brothers had opposed each other as coaches, in this case Howard Jones of Iowa and Tad Jones of Yale.

February 1, 1930. The reprieve did not help Iowa football much. It went through a series of ups and downs until the Ironmen arrived in 1939.

The second most popular sport at Iowa in those days was basketball, but it was relatively new and expectations were not high. A 9–10 record in the 1919–20 season, for example, was judged "highly successful" in the student yearbook. The primary problem was the game itself, which then emphasized defense and passing but not scoring and required a center-jump after each score. In the 1919–20 season, for example, the Iowa team scored an average of only twenty-four points per game. Slowly the crowds grew, especially in 1922–23, when Iowa tied for the conference championship. The Field House, built in 1927, had 7,500 seats, and 3,100 more were added in 1933. On January 15, 1934, a standing-room-only crowd of 12,000 fans watched Iowa beat Illinois, 36–14, and 3,000 other fans had to be turned away.

Track was on the decline just before the Jessup years. In fact, in 1916 the Athletic Board seriously considered discontinuing it as a University sport. Beginning in 1921 new coach George T. Bresnahan's aggressive promotion of track, at both the intercollegiate and intramural levels, and his creative coaching techniques—such as the use of motion pictures—renewed interest in track and field. Many still think of the Bresnahan years—1921 to 1949— as the golden age of the "thin clads" at Iowa. Among the many fine athletes who participated in track and field at Iowa were a number who became Olympians. George Saling won the 110-meter high hurdles at the 1932 Olympics, setting a new Olympic record and equaling the world record in the semifinals. Charles Brookins set the world record in the 220-yard low hurdles in 1923 and was a member of the 1924 Olympic team. Edward Gordon was the Olympic broad-jump champion in 1932, and

Frank Cuhel, Eric Wilson, George Baird, and Harold Phelps were all Olympic team members in the 1920s and 1930s.

As for other sports, some fared well during the Jessup era and others did not. Wrestling became an intercollegiate sport in 1911, and by 1916 Iowa had become a conference power. Swimming became an intercollegiate sport at Iowa in 1917, and the performances of the Seals and Eels clubs, and later the Dolphins, increased the sport's popularity. The squad of 1936 won the conference title, and Leslie Beers was a 1928 Olympic team member at 158 pounds. Tennis did not become an intercollegiate sport until 1922, though it had been quite popular on campus before that. Golf and gymnastics became recognized sports in 1923. In 1935 George Nissen from Cedar Rapids, the man who developed the trampoline, was a gymnast at Iowa and won the national intercollegiate tumbling title at Cambridge, Massachusetts.

Perhaps the most significant growth in athletics after 1920 was in intramural sports. Fraternities, dormitories, professional societies, and others had their own teams, and by 1927, when the Field House was built, some 2,500 men participated in sixteen different intramural sports, among them water polo, football, basketball, baseball, tennis, handball, fencing, golf, wrestling, boxing, and horseshoes.

At the turn of the century, women's athletics was headquartered in a basement room in Schaeffer Hall that the students lovingly referred to as "The Crypt." But by 1915, thanks to the new women's gymnasium, the women had a building that provided facilities equal to those enjoyed by the men. Women's physical education classes in the teens and twenties focused on dance and gymnastics, but there were also courses in hygiene, emergencies, playground activities, physiology, anthropometry, Girl Scout leadership, and a popular course in physiotherapy taught by Dr. Arthur Steindler of the Children's Hospital. Under Elizabeth Halsey, director of women's physical education from 1924 until 1956, the program grew strong. Intramurals for women began in 1924. Teams drawn from dormitories and sororities competed in volleyball, field hockey, tennis, basketball, swimming, golf, horseshoes, archery, and badminton. Intercollegiate athletics for women would not arrive until the 1970s, but Halsey's slogan, "Sports for every woman on the campus," was as close to fact as she could make it.

Induction parade, Iowa Avenue, October 1, 1924. A procession from Old Capitol to Iowa Field, led by the University band, and followed by students ranked by colleges and classes, and then by members of the faculty in academic costume, marked the beginning of the academic year during most of the 1920s. After an address by President Jessup at the opening of the 1926–27 academic year, the assembly pledged with upraised hands: "I pledge, here and now, lifelong loyalty to the ideals of scholarship and character of the founders of this institution to the end that I may loyally serve this University, this Commonwealth, and this Nation." Induction ceremonies were discontinued in 1968, but in 1984 President Freedman instituted a Fall Opening Ceremony.

Renovation of Old Capitol, 1921–24. Because Old Capitol had been the architectural centerpiece of Iowa City and the University for so long, and was thought to be so solidly built, many people could not understand the need for a nearly total renovation of the building in the 1920s. Yet the stone steps at the east entrance were so badly worn that they had been covered with planks, and the building had settled so far that an extra step had been added to the stairs in the center of the building. Renovation began in 1921, and when work was completed in 1924, little of the original interior of Old Capitol remained. Structural steel beams replaced the rotting old oak floor joists; new copper gutters hung in place of hewn-out walnut logs; new woodwork and replastered walls and ceilings brightened the rooms; a completely redone freestanding spiral staircase dominated the building's interior; and the west portico, planned in 1840, was finally built.

Rebuilding the staircase in Old Capitol, 1921–24.

The Pentacrest, from Newton Road, 1925. For travelers coming from the west in the 1920s, this was the first view of the Iowa campus. The approach over the river on Iowa Avenue had recently been widened and landscaped, and new walkways and plantings led up the slope to the west portico of Old Capitol. In the early 1920s the center of the campus was still called the "Five-Spot," but that name had come to sound less and less suitable. On December 11, 1924, the Daily Iowan's headline read: "Five-Spot Called Weak Name for Iowa's Campus; Seek Another." In that article, Professor Edwin Starbuck said, "I should call the designation 'five-spot' rather low-brow and commonplace," while Benjamin F. Shambaugh thought the "only appropriate title is 'Old Capitol Campus.' " After the Daily Iowan held a naming contest, the term "Pentacrest" became the official designation.

Herbert Hoover visiting Old Capitol, 1928. From left to right in the center of the picture are Mrs. Hoover, President Jessup, Hoover, and George T. Baker, chairman of the Board of Education. Not long after he received the Republican presidential nomination in 1928, Herbert Hoover *returned to his native Iowa for a campaign visit. He stopped first in West Branch, his birthplace, where he was greeted by a crowd of 18,000. He then visited Iowa City and Old Capitol and moved on to Cedar Rapids. The major issue in his Midwest campaign? Farm relief.*

Chemistry lecture, c. 1925. Enrollment in chemistry classes doubled between 1917 and 1921, and the department moved into its new building in 1923. In the mid-1920s the chemistry department had the largest staff and offered more courses than any other department at Iowa.

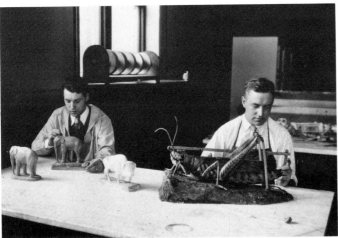

Museum Methods, 1928. "The courses in museum methods given by the University are unique," said Homer Dill, director of what was at the time the only museum training program in the country. The curriculum combined study in the natural sciences with special training in clay modeling, specimen mounting, and exhibition.

Wilbur J. Teeters (1870–1959) and his pharmacognosy class, 1926. Teeters planned to be a practicing pharmacist when he graduated from the University of Michigan in 1895, but Iowa wanted him so much that he came to teach for a year. By 1903 he was a professor of pharmacy, and in the following year he was named dean of the college, a post he held for the next thirty-three years. Teeters was involved in all aspects of University life, his door was always open, and even after his retirement in 1937 he taught a course in toxicological analysis. He was the mayor of Iowa City from 1943 to 1946.

Stephen Hayes Bush (1878–1960), wearing the uniform of the French Foreign Legion. "No matter what Bush was scheduled to teach, he always taught Bush," said one of the many students of the man who ran the Department of Romance Languages at the University of Iowa from 1906 to 1946. Bush arrived at Iowa in 1901, and in his early years taught French twenty hours a week. In his first year, 193 students were enrolled in French, but by 1919, in the aftermath of World War I, the department taught over five times as many. Bush did not sit idly by during the Great War. He was rejected by the American army but served in the French Foreign Legion with such distinction as to earn the croix de guerre and medaille commemorative from the French government. Bush also volunteered to serve in North Africa in World War II but was turned down because of his age (sixty-four), even though he had taken up mountain climbing in the Rockies in the late 1930s and was immensely fit. He was famous (or infamous) on campus for scheduling student conferences at six o'clock in the morning.

Carl Emil Seashore (1866–1949) and George D. Stoddard (1897–1981), who between them headed the Graduate College from 1908 to 1946. With a Ph.D. from Yale, Seashore came to the University in 1897 as an assistant professor of psychology. In 1908 President MacLean appointed him dean of the relatively new Graduate College, a post he held until he retired in 1936. He was succeeded by George Stoddard, but when Stoddard left Iowa in 1942 Seashore was persuaded to reassume the position. He retired for the second and last time in 1946. More than any other single person, Seashore built Iowa's reputation for experimentalism in both the sciences and the arts. As a psychologist, for example, he developed a laboratory training program for undergraduates, and among graduate students he encouraged the design and manufacture of psychological instruments. As a dean he stressed the usefulness of experimental techniques in such disparate areas as music (his second enthusiasm), speech, religion, aesthetics, audiometry, child welfare, and literature and plastic arts. He emphasized the development of individual capabilities and encouraged new methodologies, interdisciplinary research, and creative efforts as acceptable alternatives to scholarly work. Nationally, he is probably best remembered for his Seashore Measures of Musical Talent. Rigorous in his scholarly demands but dapper and affable as a human being, he was for decades at Iowa "Mr. Dean."

After earning his doctorate at Iowa, George D. Stoddard was from 1925 to 1942 a member of the psychology department. He was also the director of the Iowa Child Welfare Research Station (1928–42), head of the Psychology Department (1938–39), and graduate dean (1936–42). In 1942 he left Iowa for the presidency of the University of the State of New York and after that the presidency of the University of Illinois and a host of other prominent positions nationally and internationally. While at Iowa he ably carried on the tradition of experimentalism stressed by Seashore. In 1940 he was a leading candidate for the presidency at Iowa.

Frederick M. Pownall (1887–1979). Pownall had been the editor of the Des Moines Daily Capital *before he was appointed assistant professor of journalism in 1927. Before he finished his long career at Iowa he was also named manager of printing services, manager of mailing services, director of student publications, and publisher of the* Daily Iowan. *Chances were if the University published something, Pownall was involved. Pownall had the well-deserved reputation of being the best yarnspinner on campus, and he was just as good with one-liners. After he had passed his ninetieth birthday he declared that he was so old he didn't even know the people in the obituaries.*

Frank Luther Mott (1886–1964). Mott taught American literature and short-story writing in Iowa's English department from 1921 until 1927, when he was named director of the School of Journalism. Mott won the Pulitzer Prize for volumes two and three of his four-volume History of American Magazines *in 1938 and the Bancroft Prize for volume four in 1958. Mott left Iowa in 1942 to head the University of Missouri's School of Journalism.*

John T. Frederick (1893–1975). Teacher, poet, critic, novelist, editor, and scholar, Frederick was for six decades a professor of English at four major universities. After receiving his B.A. from Iowa in 1915, he joined the University's English Department and taught a course in short-story writing

that routinely enrolled over one hundred students. As a teacher, Frederick was extraordinarily effective. Carefully organized and informative, his lectures were delivered slowly and in a surprisingly deep voice. What won the students particularly, however, was that he seemed "all there" for each of them, that he cared personally and warmly about their small pleasures and large bewilderments. He left Iowa in 1930 to teach at Pittsburgh, Northwestern, and Notre Dame, and to host "Of Men and Books," a CBS radio program quite popular in the 1930s and 1940s. He returned to his alma mater in 1970 to serve as a visiting professor and in 1973 was honored as a UI Distinguished Alumnus.

Ernest Horn (1882–1967). Horn was literally and figuratively a man of many words. In 1920 he coauthored (with E. J. Ashbaugh) the Horn-Ashbaugh Speller, *and in subsequent years wrote roughly a dozen spelling books for students at the elementary, junior high, and high school levels. A professor of education from 1915 to 1952, Horn was also the director of the University elementary school. In addition*

to his nationally known spellers, Horn wrote Methods of Instruction in Social Studies *(1937) and* A Basic Writing Vocabulary: 10,000 Words Most Commonly Used in Writing *(1926), which for decades was a standard text. An excellent golfer, a topflight gardener, and an indefatigable storyteller, Horn was also a collector of dictionaries and Elizabethan jest books.*

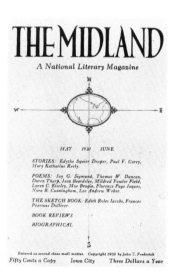

Midland *magazine. The flyer claimed that "the general interests of the Middle West will receive proper attention only in the pages of a Middle Western magazine." That magazine was the* Midland, *a monthly begun in 1915 by John Towner Frederick. Ruth Suckow,*

MacKinlay Kantor, James T. Farrell, Loren Eiseley, and Paul Engle were among those who published work in the Midland *between 1915 and 1933. H. L. Mencken in 1923 called it "probably the most influential literary periodical ever set up in America."*

Laurence C. Jones (1884–1975), back row, center, and students at the Piney Woods School, Piney Woods, Mississippi, c. 1921. Jones, the first black graduate of Marshall-town High School, worked his way through the University of Iowa tending furnaces and waiting on tables, graduating in 1907. Though he had thoughts of going into business, he decided instead—according to his autobiography, Piney Woods and Its Story *(1925)—"that my duty was down in the black belt among the less fortunate of my people." Jones went to Mississippi and worked to save money to start a school. Inspired by the Hampton and Tuskegee institutes, Jones in 1909 opened Piney Woods Country Life School in an abandoned log cabin on a few acres of land in Rankin County in rural Mississippi. The students cooked all their own meals, made the bricks with which they constructed the school's buildings, learned carpentry, ran a producing dairy farm, and canned vegetables, all this in addition to attending classes. In 1954 Jones appeared on the popular television show "This is Your Life," and host Ralph Edwards suggested that viewers send a dollar to support Piney Woods. Within three days $245,000 had rolled in, and the total eventually reached $776,000. By 1967 the school Jones had started on a wish and a prayer had an endowment of four million dollars and owned 1,600 acres of land.*

Philip Greeley Clapp (1888–1954), 1930. Pianist, composer, critic, and teacher, Clapp ran the University's School of Music from 1919 until shortly before his death. In his early years, when some doubted the worth of university-level instruction in music, Clapp told them, "No state will permit a dog to receive treatment from any but a qualified veterinary, but any quack can ruin voices and pervert the musical taste of the rising generation." Clapp, as egotistical as he was gifted, brought Iowa's music program to national prominence. His radio course in music appreciation, broadcast statewide for nearly three decades on WSUI, entertained and educated countless Iowans. Clapp also had a rather unusual special interest—trains. He subscribed to the 1500-page Official Guide of the Railways and read numerous technical railroad publications. "My most absorbing hobby is railroad operation," he said, "probably because of a certain symphonic quality which I find in 'choo-choo.' "

Moot court, Gilmore Hall, 1924. Moot court has been a feature of legal education at Iowa for over a century, and around the turn of the century the court was staged in an interesting fashion, with cases based on well-known topics in history and fiction. In March 1903, for example, Iowa law students put Hamlet on trial for murder, with Hamlet pleading not guilty by reason of insanity. Other law schools copied the idea. In the 1930s and 1940s the results of mock trials were reported regularly in local newspapers. In 1939 townspeople and students were invited for the first time to serve as jurors for mocktrial cases ranging from simple traffic offenses to murder.

E. C. Mabie (1892–1956), far right, and students, in front of Macbride Hall. Edward Mabie was one of the strong men President Jessup brought to Iowa. He took a small, rather ordinary speech department and turned it into one of the largest and most distinguished in the country. Not content with simply offering courses in public speaking, he developed programs in public address and debate under Craig Baird; phonetics and a speech laboratory under James Curtis; television, radio, and film under Clay Harshbarger; and speech pathology and audiology under James Curtis. In this last program, the Stuttering Clinic, directed by Wendell Johnson, became world famous. In the mid-1940s Mabie even directed the new freshman program in communication skills. His main interest, however, was in dramatic art and the theater. As soon as he arrived in Iowa in 1920 he began offering courses in acting, play production, and community theater.

Soon, with the help of such faculty as Arnold Gillette and Hunton Sellman, he began expanding the course offerings and producing plays in both a community series and an experimental series. Especially in the summer, he added nationally and internationally known experts to his staff. As early as 1933 he imported a Los Angeles cameraman to conduct a course in cinematography. Many of the students who studied in his playwriting course later wrote for Broad-way and for film and television. Though always demanding—many thought excessively demanding—and always in strict control of his department, Mabie had his soft side and would often, for example, lend or give money to hard-up students. At home his hobby was raising prize chickens. The main auditorium in the enlarged theater building was named the Mabie Theatre in 1973.

Carl Menzer (1900–1986), WSUI studio, 1924. Menzer was a pioneer in educational radio and television. He began his career in broadcasting in 1917 while a freshman at the University and earned his B.S., M.S., and E.E. degrees at Iowa. He was director of the University radio stations, WSUI and KSUI, from 1921 to 1968. The station, which became WSUI, was granted its first broadcasting license in 1922, and the radio facilities were housed on the third floor of the Engineering Building. Operator, repairman, program director, production manager, and announcer of home football and basketball games—in the early years Menzer did it all. He worked with Edwin Kurtz to create television station W9XK in 1932 and also planned an educational FM network for the state of Iowa. In 1938 he was awarded a Rockefeller Fellowship and spent 1938–39 working for the relatively new National Broadcasting Company in New York. Later Menzer worked at Los Alamos and was present for the atomic bomb tests at Bikini Atoll in 1946.

Physics library in MacLean Hall, c. 1920.

Speech broadcast studio, 1931. The "Little Theater of the Air" performed plays that were broadcast over WSUI in the 1930s. Many of them were works written by faculty or students of E. C. Mabie's class in playwriting. The performers made up for their lack of visual presence with elaborate sound effects.

First W9XK broadcast, showing President Jessup, 1932. On January 25, 1932, President Jessup and the University's deans went to the Electrical Engineering Building to watch a broadcast that began: "Gentlemen, you are watching the first sight and sound program from the television station

W9XK at Iowa. You will see and hear a scene from the play 'The First Mrs. Fraser.'" W9XK, the first educational television station in the country to broadcast sight and sound programs (the sound was provided by WSUI), intrigued the public. More than one thousand Iowa Citians

turned out for a public demonstration of television in March 1933. Engineering professor Edwin Kurtz, who installed station W9XK, was feeling the pulse of the future when he said that "the surprising thing is how easy it is to become absorbed in the program." W9XK ceased broadcasting in 1939.

Hydraulics Laboratory, 1934. The first wing of the University's Hydraulics Laboratory was built in 1929, and in 1933 the five-story central and south wings were added. The building was constructed over two river-channel study models, one ten feet wide and three hundred feet long, and the other sixteen feet wide and one hundred feet long. In 1934 the Iowa Institute of Hydraulic Research was already internationally known for its research in such areas as flood protec-tion, water storage, naviga-tion, irrigation, water power, and the construction of bridges. Many projects relating to the Upper Mississippi River Basin were undertaken in co-operation with the U.S. Army Corps of Engineers, which rented space in the Hydraulics Building. During World War II the Hydraulics Laboratory was the site of military research on such subjects as the draft of stationary ships in flowing wa-ter and fog dispersal on mili-tary airfields.

B. P. Fleming (engineering, class of 1915), designer of the tunnel running under the Iowa River along the Burlington Street dam. Beneath the cam-pus run several miles of tun-nels that pipe steam and water and furnish electricity to Uni-versity buildings. The oldest tunnel, probably dating back to 1870, carried steam pipes to Old Capitol. A network of tun-nels built before World War I ran in various branches under about sixteen blocks between several heating plants, extend-ing as far north as Currier Hall. After more tunnels were added in 1924 and 1928, the system was extended under the river to supply the medical laboratories and the hospital.

During the Depression and World War II, many itinerant workers and tramps slept in the tunnels on straw or news-papers and devised methods of cooking underground, too. Some even made coffee from condensed steam leaking from a valve. (The smell of smoke in Currier Hall repeatedly brought the Iowa City fire de-partment to the scene, and af-ter a number of false alarms, a search revealed that hoboes cooking their meals in the tun-nels were the culprits.) There were apparently even a few students who, lacking the money to rent rooms, carried mattresses labeled with their names down into the tunnels as well.

A student tent in Tent City, 1932. Though the administration called the area the "University Summer Camp," its residents (and most other people) called it "Tent City." It was home for many of the graduate students who attended Iowa's summer session, which had grown from one hundred students in 1900 to 4,363 students in 1932. The University brochure described the facilities: "The popular summer camp developed by the University has all the conveniences of the modern tourist home. With thirty-five families maintaining residence at the site this summer, there is activity on the streets all times of day." No doubt this was especially true in 1935, when nearly half of the camp's slightly more than one hundred residents were children between the ages of two and six. Tent City, located near the present site of the Veterans' Administration Hospital, was self-governing and elected its own officials. Each twelve-by-fourteen-foot platform tent was provided with electricity and city water, at a rent of five dollars per week. The Daily Iowan reported that "everyone becomes acquainted in this little town, which probably has the highest IQ per capita of any city in the world."

Postal substation, Quadrangle, 1929. The Quadrangle was a small city unto itself. Among the conveniences provided for its three hundred residents were a barber shop, a pressing room, many lounges, a cafeteria, tennis courts adjoining the dormitory, and a postal substation where letters from home were delivered twice daily.

Dental infirmary, Trowbridge Hall, 1919. An intimidating sight for patients, the new infirmary contained 160 dental chairs, each with running water, electricity, and compressed air. Construction of the new facilities was prompted by the merger of Drake University's dental school with Iowa's in 1914.

Nurses in Eastlawn, on the southwest corner of Iowa Avenue and Gilbert Street, 1919. Before Eastlawn was opened in 1915, nurses were assigned to private houses rented by the state. By the 1920s the University's medical facilities were widely dispersed. Besides the University Hospital (now Seashore Hall) on Iowa Avenue, there was an isolation hospital for patients with contagious diseases on the corner of Jefferson and Gilbert streets, a maternity home on Jefferson Street, a venereal disease clinic in a formerly private home next to the hospital, an annex for diabetics, a urology clinic, and a convalescent home. The main hospital was so overcrowded, despite periodic additions of new wings, that proposals to enlarge existing facilities gave way to a plan to move the entire medical complex across the river.

Children's Hospital waiting room, 1919. As a result of the passage of the Perkins Act in 1915, orthopedic and pediatric patients came to Iowa City from across the state. The act provided that any child suffering from a curable ailment whose parents could not afford to pay for proper treatment could be taken to University Hospital at state expense. Up to this time, one of the main weaknesses in medical training at the University had been its limited supply of patients. It was argued that Iowa City simply did not have the population to support a teaching hospital. Therefore the upsurge in clinical cases brought by the Perkins Act was an incalculable benefit to the medical school. Even with a new addition, the hospital on Iowa Avenue quickly became inadequate. In 1917, without a single dissenting vote, the General Assembly appropriated $150,000 for construction of the Children's Hospital on the west side. In 1919 the Haskell-Klaus Act extended state-supported medical care to indigent adults as well. Many other states were to pattern legislation after Iowa's indigent patient laws.

Hospital "tank," c. 1920. After the construction of the Children's Hospital, which began to accept patients in 1919, the University's medical facilities were located on both sides of the Iowa River. Doctors, nurses, and dieticians were issued free tickets to ride a battery-operated bus between the old hospital and the Children's Hospital, and then the new hospital after its completion in 1928. It was always a question whether the hospital-gray bus could make it up the hill by the Engineering Building at the end of the day when the batteries were worn down.

New ambulance, 1925. In 1932 a statewide ambulance service was set up for patients unable to pay for their own transportation.

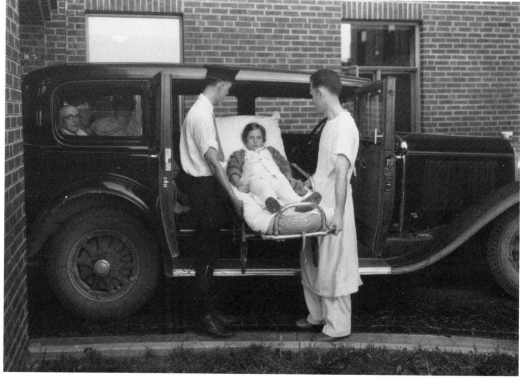

University Hospital's tower under construction, 1928. Two men, Abraham Flexner and William R. Boyd, were in large part responsible for the University's securing a gift of $2,250,000—half from the Rockefeller Foundation and half from the General Education Board (also a Rockefeller offshoot) for the construction of a new medical complex. Flexner's report to the Carnegie Foundation had exposed the shortcomings of the University's medical training program. After a decade of self-scrutiny and rehabilitation, the medical school began to receive recognition for its improvement. Flexner saw Iowa as an ideal place for the Rockefeller Foundation to initiate its new policy of aiding tax-supported schools. He served actively as a liaison between the University and the foundation boards, and he argued that improving medical education at one midwestern school would inspire other states to follow suit with funding for their own institutions.

W. R. Boyd, chairman of the finance committee of the Board of Education from its formation in 1909, sustained a vision of the medical school's potential during a time when others despaired of the school's future. He sought to enlarge the Uni-versity's hospital and to attract both an eminent resident faculty and patients in numbers sufficient for clinical training. After his active role in obtaining the Rockefeller grant, Boyd worked to balance the demands of the various departments in the medical school and oversaw the planning of the new medical facilities.

The grant for construction of the hospital and the adjacent Medical Laboratories was announced on December 27, 1922, conditional upon the state legislature's matching it dollar for dollar. There was little opposition to making the appropriation, and the Iowa house and senate passed bills that committed the state to spending $450,000 annually for five years, beginning in 1923, for construction of a new medical unit. The cornerstone for the hospital was laid in 1926, and the Medical Laboratories building was occupied in 1927. Dedication ceremonies for the hospital were held in November 1928.

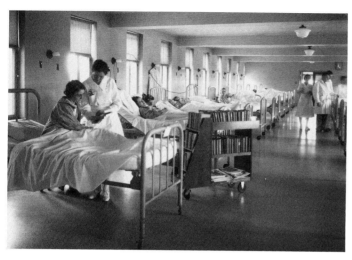

University Hospital ward, c. 1929. The new hospital opened with a 750-bed capacity. In its dedication issue the Daily Iowan *reported that there were over 2,000 windows and about 1,600 doors in the new building, along with the 1,350 feet of tunnels linking the General Hospital to the other units in the medical complex: the Children's Hospital, Westlawn (the new "Nurses' Home," completed in 1921), the Psychopathic Hospital (also ready for use in 1921), and the Medical Laboratories. The hospital's silent paging system, with physicians' call numbers lighting up on boards, was seen as a noteworthy innovation. Gowns for use in the hospital were—according to the* Daily Iowan—*sewn in a linen room on the premises. And "Helioglass" sun porches were advertised as permitting "the passage of vital ultra-violet rays, so necessary as a healing property." When the hospital was ready, 350 patients were moved across the river by ambulance and bus. With kitchens operating on both sides of the river, the transition period was a nightmare for nutritionists. Special meals, in particular, seemed to go astray.*

Arthur Steindler (1878–1959). An early advocate of state-supported health care for needy children and adults, Steindler was active in obtaining financial support for the Children's Hospital and played a major role in designing the building. He received his M.D. from the University of Vienna in 1902. Five years later he left Vienna, his native city, because, he said, "It was plain what was going to happen in Europe. There was nothing but privilege and preference. The working man had no chance. And nothing but aggression could come out of the policies of the government." In the United States he first worked as an orthopedic surgeon at the Home for Crippled Children in Chicago and then at the Iowa Methodist and Lutheran hospitals in Des Moines. In 1910 he became a professor of orthopedic surgery at the Drake medical school, and then commuted between Des Moines and Iowa City to teach until the Drake medical school closed in 1913. Internationally renowned, Steindler was head of the University of Iowa's Orthopedic Department from 1915 until he left the University in 1949 to establish a private practice at Mercy Hospital in Iowa City. He was awarded honorary fellowships by many institutions, including England's Royal College of Surgeons and Royal Society of Medicine, the College of International Surgeons in Geneva, the German Orthopedic Association, the National Academy of Medicine of Mexico, and societies of orthopedics and traumatology in France, Spain, and Brazil. He continued to practice into his eighties while sustaining a strong interest in classical and modern languages, music, mathematics, and history. In his honor the Children's Hospital was renamed the Steindler Building in 1983.

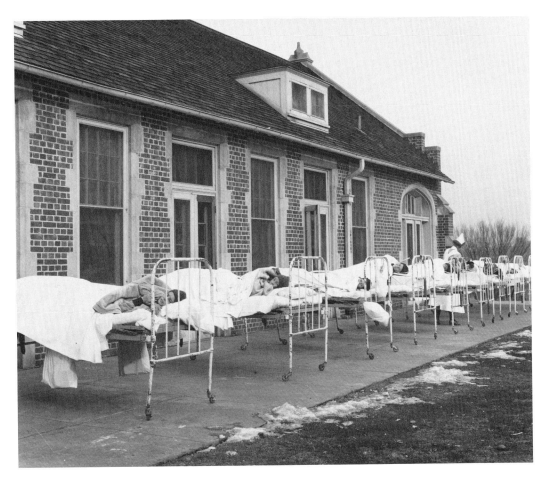

Children's Hospital, children sunning, 1923. As the first University building begun on the west side of the Iowa River, the Children's Hospital was ready in 1919 to accommodate increasing numbers of patients and staff. Broken only by the two-story central administrative section, the pavilion design of the east orthopedic wings and the west pediatric wings eliminated stairways and elevators, both safety hazards, and provided easy access to the outdoors. All of the patients' beds could be rolled out through French doors that opened onto a concrete patio from each room. Sunshine and fresh air were regarded as an important part of the therapy year-round. The Children's Hospital included a gymnasium with corrective exercise equipment and a school for patients under long-term care.

P. G. Mott with a patient in the Children's Hospital brace shop, 1920. The orthopedic shop was equipped with lathes, forges, and machines for cutting, shaping, and punching steel in order to manufacture appliances for use by orthopedic patients. P. G. Mott came to the Children's Hospital at the same time as its first director, Dr. Steindler, and headed the brace shop for seventeen years. With only a single course in experimental anatomy to his credit, his extraordinary skill in constructing braces and casts was largely self-taught. Handicapped by a bad leg himself, Mott managed to humanize the brace shop through a special feeling for his patients' plight.

Corner of Washington and Dubuque streets looking south-west, 1925. In this transition period, streetcars lingered on, though buses began to displace them. Traffic lights had not made traffic policemen obsolete, and the Jefferson Hotel was in its heyday.

Iowana float, 1921. The girls from Alpha Chi Omega won first prize among the many sorority float entries in the May Carnival parade for 1921. The girl on the right, Edna "Jerry" Gingles of Onawa, Iowa, was chosen Queen of the May.

Corn monument on the corner of Clinton Street and Iowa Avenue, 1935. At the Homecoming celebration in 1925, the Daily Iowan *reported that "Old grads cheered themselves hoarse, and some of them were a bit wheezy before they started cheering." No wonder—Homecoming then was an endless round of breakfasts, conferences, tours, games, dinners, and parades designed so that alumni would become completely reacquainted with their alma mater. When Iowa's first Homecoming was staged in 1912, three hundred alumni attended. The following year a more widely publicized Homecoming brought well over one thousand alumni to campus, many of them returning for the first time in fifteen or twenty years. The first corn monument, constructed by hydraulic engineering students from 3,000 ears of red, yellow, and white corn, appeared in 1914. In 1919 the engineering students as a whole decided to collaborate on the corn monument, but three groups continued to build separate monuments as well. The civil engineers fashioned bridges and arches, the electrical engineers produced lighted signs, and the chemical engineers concocted lighted water fountains. After 1934 the engineers limited themselves to one impressive display. Homecoming grew so quickly in popularity that in 1915 extra bleachers had to be added on Iowa Field to accommodate the football crowds, and in 1916 hundreds of students were unable to squeeze into Macbride auditorium for the pep rally prior to the Homecoming game. Leading the cheers was Charles Sumner "Doc" Chase, professor of materia medica and pharmacology, whom the* Daily Iowan *described as "a very dynamo of pep."*

Waiting for football tickets at Whetstone's, c. 1920.

"Yell leaders" at Iowa Field, 1920.

Aubrey Devine vs. Minnesota, 1921. In the 1921 game with Minnesota, Iowa's Aubrey Devine ran for four touchdowns, passed to Lester Belding for two more, kicked five of six extra points, and even returned kickoffs and punts in Iowa's 41–7 victory. The game was played in Minneapolis, but when Devine went to the bench he received a standing ovation for his outstanding play.

Iowa vs. Wisconsin, Iowa Field, November 7, 1925. Photographer Fred Kent somehow kept a camera working on the sidelines as unbeaten Iowa dueled Wisconsin in a driving snowstorm. Two weeks earlier on the same field Iowa had defeated Red Grange's Illinois team, 12–10, and appeared to be on its way to a Big Ten title. On this day, however, the elements won. Fans huddled under blankets or gathered around bonfires at the edge of the field while the players exchanged fumbles and frozen punts. Between them the two teams fumbled thirty-two times. The sole attempted forward pass (by Iowa) fell incomplete onto the snow-covered turf, where it stuck. Finally, late in the game, Wisconsin blocked a kick deep in Iowa territory and pushed across the only score to win, 6–0.

Wrestling match in Old Armory, 1921. The first wrestling meet held on the Iowa campus took place in 1909, and the first intercollegiate match in 1911. Official recognition as a University sport came in 1913.

Exercise class, Halsey Gymnasium, 1924. During the first week of physical education classes, all students were screened for "orthopedic defects." The women thought to have such deficiencies were assigned to Corrective Exercise and Posture Training (later simply Posture Training). The men's equivalent, required of those with "cyphosis, lordosis, scoliosis, flat feet, fallen arches, round shoulders and flat chest," was called Corrective Gymnastics.

Tobogganing on the Pentacrest, 1926.

Baseball at the old Iowa Field, 1925.

Women's physical education dance class, 1923. Women from the Physical Education Department performed this routine during commencement week ceremonies at the President's House.

"Iowater Regatta," women's canoe race, Memorial Day, 1925. Five thousand spectators crowded the riverbank at City Park to watch a program of water sports sponsored by the Eels and Seals clubs. The schedule of events included a men's river swim, a women's canoe race, a fancy diving contest, a blindfolded boxing match on a raft, a human fish stunt, and a procession of decorated floats.

The Field House, 1927. Called "a gargantuan cathedral of sport" by English novelist Hugh Walpole at its dedication in 1927, the Field House originally seated 7,500. Basketball became so popular, however, that 3,100 seats were added in 1933. In addition to serving as the home for intercollegiate teams, the Field House was the site of countless intramural activities. In its first year the facilities were used by 2,500 students.

Football game, the Armory, 1927. None of Iowa's home intercollegiate football games has ever been played inside. Shown here is the varsity team giving a demonstration at the dedication of the adjacent Field House in January 1927.

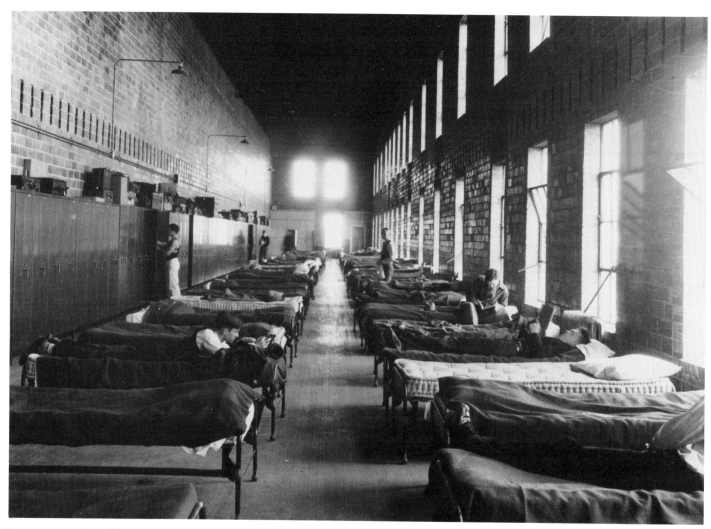

Dormitory in the Field House, c. 1930. In the 1930s nearly one hundred men paid a dollar a week for a cot on the third floor of the Field House. Each student had a steel locker near his bed, and a room for studying was set up at the end of the corridor. Showers were three flights down, in the basement locker room. Homer Calkin (B.A. 1935, M.A. 1936, Ph.D. 1939) remembers that although the University provided sheets and blankets, the high ceilings and drafty windows made it "pretty cold during the night in the winter. I was lucky. A radiator was at the end of my bed to keep my feet warm." This was during the Depression, and according to Calkin, "Most of the students worked at some job to help meet their expenses. This could be board jobs at the hospital—one hour for each meal; erecting bleachers for basketball games at 34 cents an hour; or as student janitors in University buildings at 26 cents an hour." By working full-time at the hospital, Calkin said, "I was thus able to build up a supply of meals for later when I wouldn't be working."

FIVE

Cautious Change,
1934–1964

Registration in the Field House, 1950.

In these decades the University once more had to gear itself up for participation in a world war and then to accommodate itself to the changes the war would leave behind. Thousands of students enrolling under the GI Bill had to be housed and new courses and programs developed to meet their interests. Moreover, the postwar faculty demanded a greater role in the governance of the University, and the worldwide explosion of knowledge required more highly specialized research by the faculty and their graduate students. Profound changes, in short, were taking place despite cautious leadership at the top.

Eugene A. Gilmore

Eugene A. Gilmore was appointed president only six years before he reached retirement age. Fortunately, his background prepared him well for assuming the position without a period of apprenticeship. Not only had he been a member of the law faculty at the University of Wisconsin for twenty years but he had also been vice-governor of the Philippines for six years. For fifteen months of this time he was the acting governor-general of the islands. In 1928 he succeeded Henry Craig Jones as Dean of Iowa's College of Law and served until 1934, when he was tapped for the presidency of the University. His work as dean was so astute that even during the Depression the number of both the law students and the full-time faculty in the College of Law increased. From personal experience, therefore, he knew the challenges and pitfalls of public higher education. In his six years as president of the University of Iowa he encountered plenty of both.

Although President Jessup may have left the University far stronger than he found it, he did not—could

not—leave it without serious economic problems. The collapse of farm prices and the decline in land values brought on by the Depression had been followed and aggravated by a two-year drought. Salaries of the faculty and administrative officers of the University had been lowered by 15 to 25 percent. Positions had been left unfilled or filled at reduced salaries, and all educational services had been cut to a minimum. Spending on laboratory equipment, for example, had been reduced by 50 percent and library expenditures for books by 70 percent. Still worse, faculty members, especially bright young scholars, were leaving Iowa for institutions that had begun to recover from the Depression more quickly than Iowa.

When he took office in 1934 President Gilmore had lost no time in appealing to members of the legislature and the Board of Education to reverse the downward slide. As dean of the College of Law he had come to know many of them personally, and as a high officer in the Philippine colonial government he had learned how to work with governing bodies. A university cannot suffer a continuing loss of support, he argued, and remain the same university. He requested $3,188,500 for each year of the 1935–37 biennium but got only $1,950,000. Nevertheless, he could claim that the slide had been stopped, for the new appropriation provided an annual increase of $150,000 over the preceding one. He believed the University was on the road back, and he was right. By the 1939–41 biennium, thanks to more generous appropriations, the institution was able to operate at almost a pre-Depression level.

Ironically, the construction that went on during Gilmore's presidency gave the impression of boom times. The capital value of the University plant increased by over $3.25 million, of which $1.25 million went for new

*Eugene Gilmore (1871–1953),
twelfth president, 1934–40.*

structures and improvements on old ones—a remarkable figure against the backdrop of the Depression. Only one-seventh of the amount available for buildings, however, came from the state, either through appropriation or through transfers of funds from the general account. The remainder came principally from the Rockefeller and Carnegie foundations and the federal Public Works Administration and from bonds for dormitory construction. Construction for academic purposes included the Theatre and the Art Building (made possible so close to the river by the construction of a stone retaining wall by the Civilian Conservation Corps), the Botanical and Pharmaceutical Laboratories, and two buildings for radio education and transmission. New dormitories included the Law Commons, Hillcrest, and a Currier Hall addition. With the possible exception of the theater, none of these was architecturally arresting, but they were reasonably functional and hence most welcome additions to the life of the University. Unfortunately, a fire in Close Hall, which was occupied by the School of Journalism, destroyed the two upper floors. As restored without these floors, the building was easily the ugliest on the campus.

In his six years Gilmore managed to increase salaries for the full-time staff by over 9 percent, which was no mean achievement, given Iowa's economic condition. Furthermore, he persuaded the board to adopt the tenure plan recommended by the American Association of University Professors. It called for one-year appointments for instructors, three-year renewable terms for assistant professors, and indefinite tenure for full and associate professors. The plan became effective July 1, 1939, and still persists, though assistant professors, unless promoted, are rarely retained after two terms. In approving promotion and salary raises for associate professors and salary raises for full professors, Gilmore followed the pattern already common in major universities of giving priority to research and only secondary, but not necessarily negligible, consideration to teaching. In 1938 in a report to the North Central Association (the regional accrediting agency), Dean of Liberal Arts George F. Kay wrote that "we have a few full professors who have attained this rank on the basis of fine teaching alone, though such a case is relatively scarce."

Curriculum innovations designed to broaden the students' perspective by interdisciplinary study received strong support from the administration. They included a marriage course taught by members of the liberal arts and medicine faculties, a seminar in social and collective behavior sponsored by the various social sciences, and a program in American civilization promoted by Norman Foerster of the English Department and Professor Harrison J. Thornton of the History Department. This last combined the approaches and subject matter of literature, history, and the social sciences to illuminate American life and letters. The Iowa program was one of the first of its kind in the country. Alexander Kern was its first and longtime director, from 1947 to 1975. Two new programs in the Gilmore period—the Iowa Writers' Workshop and the program in nuclear physics—would later add uncommon lustre to the University. One compromise brought relief from the continuing hassle over a duplication of effort with Iowa State in engineering and home economics: on the recommendation of Samuel P. Capen, chancellor of the University of Buffalo, who was called in as a consultant, the Board of Education agreed that enrollment in engineering at Iowa should not exceed five hundred students and that graduate work in home economics should be confined to nutrition and child welfare.

Other developments during Gilmore's six years in-

Cockroft-Walton atom smasher, MacLean Hall, 1938. Installed in 1936 and completely rebuilt in 1942, the Cockroft-Walton atom smasher assisted University physicists in their research into nuclear structure and dynamics. The "huge metal monster," looking like something out of a low-budget science-fiction film, operated on the third floor of the Physics Building (now Mac-Lean Hall). In 1948 a more sophisticated and powerful Van de Graaff atom smasher was put in service in an underground room connected to the Physics Building.

Chester A. Phillips (1882–1976), acting president, 1940.

Frank Lloyd Wright (second from left) touring Old Capitol, 1939. Just to his left in the white shoes is his host, Earl E. Harper, who was the director of fine arts from 1938 to 1963. Wright arrived in Iowa City on July 21, 1939, "driving a sleek, streamlined automobile painted bright red," and as always full of opinions on the dreary state of American culture. His lecture drew a crowd of over 1,500, which, according to the Daily Iowan's *report,* "enjoyed [Wright's] chastisement of American culture and architecture." Of the Iowa campus, Wright said: "All your buildings are very bad . . . and they are destructive of me and my work." Which University building did Wright think the absolute worst? Old Capitol. Wright said the houses in Iowa City were "only big boxes with holes cut in them and some junk dragged in for furniture."*

cluded the installation of an underground atom smasher just east of the Physics Building, an increase in WSUI's power to five thousand watts, the establishment of a blood bank and a training center for the study of cancer, and progress in the control of dental caries, or tooth decay. Help for students included a new cooperative housing program, additional housing for minority students, an International House for foreign students provided by Professor and Mrs. George W. Stewart, and an expansion of student centers supported by religious denominations. The most widely publicized happenings were the annual festivals in the arts sponsored by the School of Fine Arts. The first one, in 1939, featured a new play, Ellsworth P. Conkle's *Paul and the Blue Ox*, concerts by the University symphony, and an art exhibition focusing on paintings by Grant Wood and Marvin Cone. Special guests included Lawrence Tibbett and Frank Lloyd Wright, who did not exactly enter into the spirit of the occasion when he warned Iowans to "forget your sentimentality for Old Capitol else you are doomed to destruction."

In short, Eugene Gilmore, though by no means a daring reformer, had a full and productive presidency. Even he, however, would probably have admitted that all of the other accomplishments that marked his term were eclipsed in the popular mind by those of a young Phi Beta Kappa from Adel named Nile Kinnick, who ran, passed, blocked, and kicked his way to the Heisman trophy and, besides, was so splendid a human being that his death on a Navy practice flight in the Caribbean was mourned as a national tragedy.

Chester A. Phillips

When the Board of Education could not decide between George D. Stoddard, the graduate dean, and Paul C. Packer, the dean of education, as a successor to Gilmore, they appointed as acting president Chester A. Phillips, who had demonstrated his administrative ability in building up the College of Commerce during his twenty years as dean. Phillips served as acting president from July 13 to November 2, 1940. He was careful to maintain the operation of the University without approving anything that might embarrass the next president. When relieved of his duties as acting president, Phillips returned to being the dean of the College of Commerce and a professor of banking. From then until almost the day he died at the age of ninety-four he continued to walk to his office almost every day and turn out carefully researched books and articles on banking. One anecdote connects Phillips with novelist Sinclair Lewis. In the summer of 1940, when Phillips was acting president, he refused to join Norman Foerster and George Stoddard in requesting that the Board of Education appoint Lewis as a lecturer in fiction writing. Phillips had heard that Lewis was a drunkard (actually, Lewis had been on the wagon for three years). Lewis was outraged, and so were many people in Iowa City. A few weeks later Phillips was partly vindicated when Lewis, while teaching at the University of Wisconsin, walked out of his class after the fifth meeting, never to return.

Virgil M. Hancher (1896–1965), thirteenth president, 1940–64. Hancher is shown here speaking at the Navy Pre-Flight School inauguration ceremonies in April 1942. Iowa became the "Annapolis of the Midwest" when the Navy Pre-Flight School was commissioned on April 15, 1942. Governor George A. Wilson, University President Virgil M. Hancher, and Rear Admiral John Downes presided over the ceremony. Soon two thousand aviation cadets would be on campus preparing to fight in World War II. In all, 21,000 cadets completed the program before it was disbanded in December 1945.

Virgil M. Hancher

Conservative, even cautious, in the guidance he gave the University, Virgil M. Hancher nevertheless successfully presided during its period of greatest growth. While he was president, the University more than doubled the size of its student body and staff and more than tripled the size of its campus. The value of research grants when he retired was twenty-four times what it had been when he took office. A handsome man and an eloquent one, Hancher's public performances were always impressive.

Hancher received his B.A. from Iowa in 1918. As an undergraduate he was elected to the Zetagathian literary society, the All for Iowa men's honor society, Phi Beta Kappa, and the presidency of his senior class. After he had spent two years as a Rhodes scholar, Oxford awarded him an A.B. in jurisprudence. Then he returned to the University of Iowa to add the degree of doctor of jurisprudence. From 1924 to 1940 he worked for a law firm in Chicago as a specialist in corporation law, after which he once more returned to the University of Iowa, this time as its president. Though not always comfortable in dealing with the politicians in Des Moines or the faculty on campus, Hancher remained committed to the liberal and humane tradition and what he liked to call "humanology." The focus of a university, he told *Time* in 1952, should be upon those things that "concern *men* and *women* as *men* and *women*." During his presidency he was appointed to many national boards and commissions, including in 1958 the United States delegation to the United Nations. After his retirement in 1964 he went to India as a specialist for the Ford Foundation's South and Southeast Asia Program. He died in New Delhi on January 30, 1965.

World War II

Like President Jessup, Hancher hardly had time to adjust to his new position before war broke out. The Japanese attack on Pearl Harbor on December 7, 1941, interrupted life on the campus just as it interrupted activities throughout the nation. When he spoke to the students the next month, Hancher asserted that the University must be an "Arsenal of Education," and that "we must be in this thing not only for the duration of the war, but for the duration of the peace that follows the war. This time we must achieve, and keep, the Victory. . . . We must prepare for Peace." The war years were perhaps Hancher's finest as president, for he almost magically kept the regular program of the institution alive while handing over a great part of the campus to the military.

In the spring of 1942, with the approval of the Board of Education, Hancher ordered a speedup in the academic program that put it on a twelve-month schedule. The spring break and examination weeks were eliminated, and the summer session started the day after spring commencement. Freshmen could enter at the beginning of the summer session and during it could complete a year's requirement in social science, speech, and either science or mathematics. Thus a full undergraduate program could be completed in three calendar years. The earliest summer session ever began on April 24, 1944. Many courses were modified to include material relevant to the war, and in the fall of 1942 a yearlong course, "The World Today," was initiated. It dealt with the impact of the war on the contemporary world and was taught by faculty from subject areas ranging from history to biology, economics to public health, and psychology to international law.

What chiefly distinguished the war years on campus, however, was the presence of a variety of military programs. The largest of these was the Navy Pre-Flight School, which operated at Iowa from April 1942 to December 1945. The pre-flight school took over Hillcrest and Quadrangle dormitories, four-fifths of the Armory and Field House, and the adjacent campus areas. The University maintained the buildings and the campus areas and furnished food service at the rate of $1.20 per cadet per day, a figure that was revised upward as costs climbed during the war. Although the navy exerted considerable pressure on him, President Hancher refused to allow the cadets to take over the entire Field House or to make use of Currier Hall, which throughout the war continued to house 550 women students. Given all the possibilities for conflict, there was surprisingly little friction between the military and the University, or between the military and the town. Except for their off-duty hours on Saturday and Sunday, the cadets kept strictly to the west side, so much so that many in town were hardly aware of their existence. John Glenn, the future astronaut and U.S. senator, was one of the pre-flight ensigns.

In late 1942 the University agreed to serve as one of the bases for an Army Air Corps pre-meteorology program. This program opened in March 1943, when the first group of two hundred men arrived. More closely integrated with the University's regular curriculum than were the pre-flight school cadets, the Army Air Corps men were housed in the Law Commons and went to class in Schaeffer Hall and what are now Jessup and MacLean halls. They were taught in their academic program by regular members of the University faculty. Before it was discontinued, 443 men took part in the program, the last to complete it being transferred, to their great disappointment, to the infantry and the Signal Corps because the Army Air Corps meteorology units were full.

In May 1943 classes opened for the Army Specialized Training Program (ASTP). Those in the ASTP lived in fraternity houses and ate in the Union. Sections were activated or abandoned as the need for specialists in one area or another rose or declined. They, too, were taught largely by regular faculty in such areas as language, psychology, engineering, medicine, dentistry, optics, and examinations and testing.

Altogether, 32,879 individuals received wartime training at the University:

Navy Pre-Flight School	21,014
Army Specialized Training Programs	2,562
Civilian Pilot Training and War Training Service	1,028
Cadet Nurse Corps	448
Army Air Corps Pre-Meteorology Program	443
Reserve Officers Training Corps	51
Civilian Program in Engineering, Science and Management War Training	7,333

Of the roughly 12,000 University alumni engaged in military and government service during the war, three hundred were counted among the known dead.

Thirty-three members of the liberal arts faculty with the rank of assistant professor or above put on uniforms, and 184 other staff members added their expertise as civilians to the war effort. A few examples demonstrate the variety of the faculty's contributions. Curt Zimansky (English) was a senior advisor on the famous Ultra staff at Bletchley Park in England. It was his responsibility to help interpret and analyze German air and ground commands sent out in code. He was later recalled for similar duty during the Korean War. C. H. McCloy (physical education) was a consultant to the surgeon general and the War Department, and wrote the navy's *Physical Fit-*

Pre-flight training near the Art Building, 1942. "Our cadet's day will begin at 6 o'clock every morning and for 16 hours thereafter he will have few idle moments," said Rear Admiral John Downes at the dedication of the navy pre-flight program at Iowa. "He will chop wood, dig ditches, go on 40-mile hikes, wrestle, box and in all sorts of sports build up a strong, tough body."

Aviation simulator, Shelter House, 1941.

All-woman Daily Iowan *staff, 1944–45, from left: Ruth Wilson, Roberta Wheelan, Dorothy Klein, Gloria Weiser, Terry Tester, and Rose Ericson. Since 1901 the* Daily Iowan *has had fourteen women editors. In 1917–18 Mildred Whitcomb became the DI's first woman editor and the first woman editor of an American college daily. It was unusual, though, for the DI editorial staff to consist entirely of women, as was the case in 1944–45. One of the staff members, Phyllis Chesney, reported in the* Iowa Journalist *in 1984 that it "could never have happened without the war. The war provided a tremendous breakthrough for women."*

ness Manual. George W. Martin (botany), working at the mycological laboratory of the quartermaster's depot at Jefferson, Indiana, directed research on fungi that impaired the utility of military equipment. Lothrop Smith (chemistry) worked on the Manhattan Project at Oak Ridge, Tennessee, and Alexander Ellett (physics) headed work on the "VT" or radio proximity fuse, which was called "second in importance to the Atom Bomb" in bringing about an Allied victory.

From the faculties in the professional schools, to take only a few examples, members of the College of Engineering worked on torpedo design for the navy and on methods of fog dispersion over English and Alaskan airports. In addition they produced films to show gas dispersion on the ground in different conditions for the Chemical Warfare Service. In the School of Nursing, a training program begun before the war to prepare women as ward helpers during emergencies became the model for nationwide training. The School of Nursing also prepared women for the Red Cross and reserve nurses' corps of both the army and the navy. The College of Medicine was the most severely affected by wartime demands. By the fall of 1943, 270 of 312 medical students were in uniform, and few new students applied, because the services preempted the selection of students for military needs. Departments, moreover, were forced to teach with reduced staffs. In Internal Medicine, half of the faculty entered military service in July 1942, leaving the remaining half to carry the teaching load through July 1945. Nevertheless the college accelerated its program and went on a twelve-month calendar. It added special war courses in treatments for exposure to gas, shell and shrapnel wounds, shock, and medical problems stemming from high altitudes, dive bombing, and compression and decompression. Dr. Robert Hardin was in charge of the Blood Transfusion Service for the European

theater of operations at the time of the Normandy invasion, and Dr. Elmer L. DeGowin served on the committee on blood and blood substitutes of the National Research Council. The Department of Hygiene and Preventive Medicine added a course in tropical diseases taught by staff who had been in the tropics. And the Hygienic Laboratory examined blood tests of draftees mailed in by draft boards across the state. By the end of 1944, 340,000 specimens had been examined for the Selective Service, the Navy pre-flight program, the WACS, the WAVES, and other military groups.

During the 1942–43 academic year the School of Fine Arts started a War Art Workshop. Students created posters for the Office of War Information and for local use (that is, in high schools), murals and sculpture for army camps, signal code flags, relief maps, and other instructional material for the pre-flight school. In the spring of 1944 the Office of War Information used the Iowa campus to film a motion picture to be shown in allied and neutral countries on the role of education in a democracy. And at the request of the Federal Security Agency, the University set up a Key Center for the promotion of civilian morale. Involved were the Extension Division, the Department of Speech, and the War Information Committee.

The women—students, faculty, and faculty wives— were hardly less busy than the men. The Women's Association, the Women's Recreation Association, and the YWCA mounted the "Double V" war service program ("Victory in War for Victory in Peace"). Concerned with health, education, and service, they did everything from feeding and bathing patients in the Children's Hospital to clerking in the Civilian Defense office, soliciting for bonds and war-chest drives, making surgical bandages, and serving as hostesses in the USO center. Women students took over the Highlanders, joined the Marching Band,

and assumed top positions on the staffs of the *Hawkeye, Frivol,* and the *Daily Iowan.* One woman even became the sports editor of the *DI.* After the war, women continued to hold many of these positions. Several times the women Highlanders journeyed to Scotland and astonished the Scots, who had been quite sure that women did not have enough wind to blow a proper tune on the pipes.

Aftermath of the War

In the aftermath of the war, housing for both students and the younger staff became a crucial issue. In the fall semester of 1945–46 academic year, there were 4,853 students, by spring there were 6,787, and by September 1946 there were 9,783, an increase in one year of over 100 percent. Roughly 6,000 of these were veterans returning on the GI Bill or the rehabilitation program. Over 30 percent were married, and many had children. With the help of federal funds for veterans, the University erected "villages" of temporaries (trailers, quonset huts, and barracks). They were located on Old Iowa Field (the Hawkeye Trailer Village), along or near the river (Templin, Riverside, Quonset, and South parks), near the nurses' dormitory (Westlawn Park), and west of the athletic complex (Finkbine and Stadium parks). At the peak there were 680 barrack apartments. All told, more than five thousand families were housed in temporary buildings, with the University spending $683,825 on their erection, and the federal government $1,529,072. Although they were clearly not enchanted with their living quarters, veterans and their wives made do and often developed close and lasting friendships. It was a case of closing ranks in the face of adversity.

In addition, many of the faculty and staff had to make use not only of "temporaries" but also of such obsolete firetraps as Old Dental, Electrical Engineering, and Close Hall. There were thirteen clusters of temporaries used primarily for classrooms, laboratories, offices and work space, and storage. Communication Skills and Social Work occupied Old Armory Temporary, and the Writers' Workshop was housed in a temporary north of the Union. Some law school activities took place in temporaries, and the Student Infirmary filled two temporaries south of the General Hospital. Many University services held forth under metal roofs, too, even the Campus Police. Much of this housing lasted so long that the term "temporary" became a campus joke. But how could it have been otherwise? State appropriations for permanent buildings did not begin to keep pace with the need for space created by the students, on the one hand, and the faculty and staff on the other. For two bienniums in the postwar years the legislature voted no funds at all for building construction. During the twenty-four years of the Hancher administration, the only new permanent buildings constructed for student housing were the South Quadrangle, the Parklawn Apartments, the Hawkeye Drive Apartments, and the Kate Daum dormitory. New permanent structures contributing to the educational program were the Communication Center (journalism) and the first section of the Main Library in 1951, the Medical Research Center in 1957, a new law library and classrooms adjoining the remodeled Law Commons in 1962, and the Pharmacy Building in 1963. Danforth Chapel opened in 1953.

To cope with the influx of students and the consequent growth of the faculty, the president had to increase the size of his administrative staff substantially. Although the administration did not become as overpowering as it did in many other universities, to some of the Iowa faculty it looked like the beginning of a bureaucracy in which relations between faculty and administration might

Margaret Bourke-White, the Life photographer, at work on the west steps of Old Capitol, April 15, 1947. Thanks to the GI Bill, 1.8 million veterans nationwide were attending college in April 1947. At the University of Iowa, six thousand men and women—60 percent of the total enrollment—were veterans, which changed profoundly the nature of the campus. Life magazine saw Iowa as "typical of American institutions of higher learning in 1946" and dispatched its most flamboyant photojournalist, Margaret Bourke-White, to do the photography for an article on "Veterans at College." The piece appeared in Life on April 21, 1947, and included photographs of temporary housing, overcrowded classrooms, and veterans' families.

Hawkeye Trailer Village, Old Iowa Field, 1947. This was the first of eight temporary villages constructed in the wake of World War II to house the huge numbers of married veterans (and their families) going back to school on the GI Bill. The tenants of the 128 trailers in the Hawkeye Trailer Village shared communal showers and wash houses. By the early 1950s the trailers were not holding up well, and the administration declared its policy to be: "If a major repair costing $50 or more is necessary, the trailer is abandoned and removed from the area." The last of the temporary housing was razed in 1975.

become so depersonalized that faculty members could no longer communicate with the president directly but would have to "go through channels." Between the president and the faculty there came to be a provost, three vice-presidents, and an administrative dean, and they in turn were served by the necessary lower-level administrators. Hancher's top appointment was that of Harvey H. Davis, who as provost brought both an understanding and an accessibility that eased many tensions, even those between the doctors and the hospital administrator. Allin Dakin, the administrative dean and an old friend of the president's, rode herd on the budget. Vice-presidents, at least in the last years of the Hancher administration, included Ray L. Heffner for instruction, John C. Weaver for research and graduate study, and Elwin T. Jolliffe for business and finance. In addition, Hancher appointed Robert F. Ray as head of the extension division.

Medical Service Plan

In the clinical areas of the College of Medicine it had long been the case that department heads served only as part-time faculty members, maintaining private practices and charging their patients fees while using the University's hospitals free of charge. All other medical faculty were on straight salary, and any fees earned in private practice either accrued to the department head or went into a departmental fund. A plan to remedy this inequity was developed by Dr. Henry S. Houghton (dean of the College of Medicine from 1928 to 1933), was pushed forward by Dr. Stuart Cullen, and was supported by President Hancher. Under this plan, all medical faculty were to receive a base salary, established by rank, which could be supplemented by pooled earnings from private practice in the clinical departments (by up to 100 percent

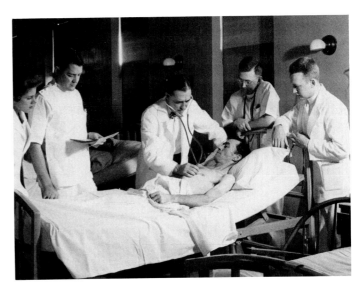

Dr. Willis Fowler making rounds, 1947. During World War II Dr. Fowler was one of only four doctors on the Internal Medicine staff. He headed the Department of Medicine from 1946 to 1948, following Dr. Fred Smith and preceding Dr. William Bean.

of the base salary for department heads and other full professors, 75 percent for associate professors, and 50 percent for assistant professors).

The Medical Service Plan, as it was called, began a two-year trial period in July 1946 but not without dissension. Dr. Frank R. Peterson (the head of Surgery) and Dr. John W. Dulin (second man in Surgery) both resigned, and a committee of the State Medical Society decried the plan, calling it "a compulsory leveling of income . . . clearly a form of socialized or communistic medicine." But President Hancher pointed out that the plan, because it was not part of a "larger scheme where production, distribution and exchange were in the hands of government," was not socialistic. Further, he argued, without the plan the disparity in income between medical department heads and younger staff had been much greater than any difference in medical skill, and the old system had fostered unwarranted insecurity and low morale among the junior faculty. The Medical Service Plan, a model for similar plans instituted by medical schools across the country, was eventually adopted on a permanent basis and, with some changes, has been reapproved by the Board of Regents at regular intervals.

Faculty Salaries

Faculty salaries in general continued to be a major headache for the administration. At a time when expenses were ballooning in an extraordinary fashion, the University had the bad luck of having to deal with excessively conservative governors—Robert F. Blue (1945–49) and William S. Beardsley (1949–54)—who placed no great priority on higher education. Instead of getting the University faculty and staff solidly behind him, President Hancher, with his customary caution,

tried to go it alone but got nowhere. Iowa's salaries were at the bottom of the Big Ten, in fact substantially below those of the university that was in ninth place. As a ploy to avoid utter catastrophe in some later year, the president began putting badly needed money aside for an even rainier day—some say over a million dollars—only to have Governor Beardsley send an auditor to discover what was going on. No illegality was found, but the governor felt less inclined than ever to increase the appropriation when he discovered that the University was already getting more than it was spending. The immediate result of the investigation was that the legislature passed a bill requiring the University to return all unspent funds to the state at the end of each biennium. No one knows what would have happened had not Dewey B. Stuit, the dean of liberal arts, in the early fifties proposed at a meeting of the deans that legislators be invited to visit Iowa City to observe the needs of the University firsthand. When the legislators proved to be lukewarm to this idea, Dean Stuit suggested that members of the University faculty and administrators visit them in their hometowns. Although the president was out of town, Stuit was warmly supported in his proposal by Provost Davis, James Jordan, director of the University Information Service, and Max Hawkins, then in the Alumni Office and later for many years the able lobbyist for the University in Des Moines. So that the effort would be in support of the regents, not just the University, the Iowa City group enlisted the willing cooperation of the faculty and administrative officers at Ames and Cedar Falls. Singly or in twos they visited all candidates for the legislature, Republican and Democratic. The payoff came when the 1957 legislature appropriated funds sufficient to raise Iowa's faculty salaries to third in the Big Ten. Hershel C. Loveless, a more liberal governor, promptly approved the appropriation. Before too long, faculties in other universities began to receive sizable increases also (without having to make time-consuming visitations), and ultimately Iowa's salaries began sliding back until they were once more in ninth or tenth position. Nevertheless, the campaign gave the University a boost just when it needed it most. The higher salaries in the 1950s, following the adoption of a funded retirement program (TIAA) in 1944, made Iowa a distinctly more attractive place for the faculty.

Fragmentation of Interests

The huge increase in student enrollment during the Hancher years—from 6,667 to 14,700—and the consequent quadrupling of the size of the faculty resulted in the University's becoming a federation not just of colleges but of schools and departments. By 1964 the chemistry faculty alone was larger than the whole University faculty had been at the beginning of the Schaeffer administration. Scattered across campus, often in their own buildings, departments seldom turned out in great numbers for major University events except, possibly, football games. This geographical separation was less serious, however, than the separation caused by the increasingly diverse interests of the faculty. The source of this fragmentation lay in the contemporary explosion in knowledge that made intense specialization necessary if a faculty member were to make a significant contribution to learning and thus to earn a reputation as a scholar or a scientist. While preaching the necessity for liberal education (called "general education" in the 1940s and 1950s), deans and department heads in all universities competed for the productive specialists and thus aggravated the fragmentation of their own faculties. Iowa was no exception. By the end of Hancher's presidency,

Dewey B. Stuit, Dean of Liberal Arts, 1949–77. Stuit joined the University in 1938 as associate professor of psychology and supervisor of the Entrance Testing Program. He was briefly the assistant graduate dean before taking a position during World War II in the Test and Research Section of the Bureau of Naval Personnel. Returning to Iowa in 1946, he became the first director of the newly constituted Student Personnel Service. In 1948 he became the acting dean of liberal arts and the next year the dean, a post he held for twenty-seven years. As dean he provided both stability and order. Although too conservative for the more liberal members of the faculty, he nevertheless unwaveringly supported his departmental executive officers even when they wanted to experiment with innovative programs or to add faculty members with exciting but not necessarily conventional talents. His one demand was that both faculty and programs be of the highest possible quality. Through the years he earned two of the highest accolades that can be awarded any administrator: "One always knew where he stood" and "He never went back on his word."

the Iowa faculty had spread their specialties so widely that undergraduate degrees were being awarded in thirty-eight fields, and graduate degrees in eighty-six. Among the new divisions were the Departments of Chinese and Oriental Languages (later Asian Languages and Literature), Speech Pathology and Audiology, and Russian; the School of Social Work; the Bureau of Dental Hygiene; the Bureau of Labor and Management; the Institute of Public Affairs; the Radiation Research Laboratory; and the Graduate Program in Health and Hospital Administration. The Sociology and Anthropology Department alone had six subdivisions. As at all universities, for most of the top scholars at Iowa, research became more of a preoccupation than was teaching, and priorities shifted so that loyalty to one's discipline came first, then loyalty to the department, and finally loyalty to the university.

Faculty Participation in Governance

Both in the University as a whole and in the College of Liberal Arts the faculty succeeded in organizing itself, something that had happened in other Big Ten schools considerably earlier. President Jessup had wanted no part of an active faculty organization. He tolerated a University senate because it was a powerless group of 130 with himself as head. As a body it was rarely called together, and then mainly for ceremonial purposes. Its chief service was to give authority to faculty committees that oversaw activities in such fields as athletics, discipline, and campus lectures. Jessup did call his deans together rather regularly but usually just to announce what was happening. When he sought advice it was usually from such individuals as Dean Seashore, Dean Packer, and William H. Cobb, the business man-

ager and secretary. President Gilmore was more receptive to faculty wishes but did not change the overall structure. Given the choice, President Hancher would probably have liked to continue Jessup's one-man operation, though in a more low-key and gentlemanly fashion. But the faculty he inherited after the war was not about to be ignored. Many of them veterans, they had had their fill of being ordered about, and many of those recruited from other universities had experienced faculty participation as a way of life. Whatever the reasons, the faculty in the mid and late 1940s crowded into the Iowa chapter of the American Association of University Professors (AAUP) as a way of making their collective voice known in high administrative circles. At one time Iowa had the second largest AAUP chapter in the country. Most of the medical faculty belonged and all of the members of several liberal arts departments. Spearheading this movement was Ralph E. Ellsworth, the director of libraries, whose imaginative help on a new library building the president greatly valued but whose liberal political views he found upsetting. Out of such activity, two documents emerged almost concurrently: a constitution for a University council and a manual of procedure for the College of Liberal Arts.

After conferences with Ellsworth and others, and with some reluctance, the president in May 1947 authorized a committee headed by Professor Lloyd Knowler of the mathematics department to draw up and present to him a proposal calling for the organization of a University council (later the president insisted that for legal reasons it be called the University Faculty Council). In the spring of 1948—after the proposal was drawn up and approved by the faculty, the president, and the Board of Regents— the fifteen-member council became a fact of University life. To allay the president's apprehensions, the document emphasized strongly that the purpose of the council was advisory, not legislative or administrative. More specifically, the council was to be a means of communication between the faculty and the administration, and to that end it was to meet regularly with the president. Once the members had been elected by their designated constituencies and had selected Professor Knowler as chairman of the group, the council got down to work on the main concern of the faculty: parking! Other topics that soon surfaced, however, were faculty housing, sabbatical and research leaves, the synchronizing of college schedules, and, of course, salaries. The council continued until 1968, when it became in effect the executive committee of the University Senate. During its short life it served the faculty—and the president—well. By the time Hancher retired, the University had established not only a Faculty Council but also an Administrative Council, a Graduate Council, a Research Council, and a Council on Teaching.

Meanwhile, members of the College of Liberal Arts began meeting with Dean Earl J. McGrath to draw up a manual of procedure for the college. Two plans were necessary before a faculty committee produced one that the president believed safeguarded his authority. As finally approved by the regents, the manual went into effect early in 1950. Fortunately, Dewey B. Stuit of the Department of Psychology had been part of the drafting committee and was consequently heartily behind the manual when he became dean of liberal arts in 1949. During his long tenure as dean, Stuit followed the manual meticulously, as did his successors, Howard J. Laster and Gerhard Loewenberg.

Revision of the Liberal Arts Curriculum

In no other period, perhaps, were so many changes made in the University to help orient the students and to individualize the training, insofar as that could be done in a large institution. Student services were expanded to such a point that they became a miniature bureaucracy in themselves.

No development had more far-reaching effects upon undergraduate study, however, than the revision of the liberal arts curriculum in the mid 1940s. This took place in the broad context of a nationwide discussion of the means and ends of liberal education. At one extreme was Robert Hutchins, president of the University of Chicago, who, believing in the immutability of human nature, argued for education based on the Great Books. At the other extreme were the followers of John Dewey, who believed that a liberal education must reorganize and reconstruct contemporary experience.

At Iowa, the extremes were asserted, on the one hand, by Norman Foerster and his followers in the New Humanism movement, and on the other by the "educationists." With somewhat different terminology, the battle came close to being the old fight between the classicists and the pragmatists that had erupted in the faculty in the first years of the University and that had reached its height in the controversy between President George Thacher and the physicist Gustavus Hinrichs. Probably the argument would not have come to a head during the war years if the liberal arts dean, George F. Kay, had not reached retirement age in 1941. In the ensuing discussion of the characteristics desired in a new dean, the ends and means of undergraduate education received a thorough examination. When on September 1, 1941, the Board of Education appointed Harry K. Newburn the new dean of liberal arts, Norman Foerster and his follow-

Grant Wood and Thomas Hart Benton (seated), SPCS club, 1935. In 1935 the Times Club, an organization of faculty and townspeople which brought important cultural figures to Iowa City to lecture, gave birth to the "Society for the Prevention of Cruelty to Speakers" (SPCS), a group of sixteen faculty, students, and townspeople. The main function of the SPCS—created largely through the efforts of Grant Wood (art), Clyde Hart (sociology), and Frank Luther Mott (journalism)—was to host after-lecture parties for prominent speakers and performers who came to the University. Among those entertained by the SPCS were Thomas Hart Benton, Stephen Vincent Benét, James Weldon Johnson, W. C. Handy, Langston Hughes, MacKinlay Kantor, and Gilbert Seldes. The SPCS rooms were located above Smitty's Cafe and were decorated in lavish Victorian fashion by SPCS members. One of the group's favorite pastimes was to pose for photographer Fred Kent wearing false beards and mustaches and old-fashioned clothing. The portraits went into the SPCS's red plush photo album.

ers were outraged. To their thinking he was not a learned man. He had a Ph.D. in education from Iowa and was an associate professor of education and principal of the University High School. Furthermore, he was a protégé of Dean Packer of the College of Education, a fact that by itself was enough to damn him in the eyes of the Foersterites. But Newburn was not a person to underestimate. He had an alert mind, a considerable understanding of what was going on in American higher education, and, though affable, was not easily pushed around. A few months after he became dean he appointed a steering committee with himself as chairman to review the current curriculum and make recommendations for improvements. During the meetings of the steering committee, and of the subcommittees it appointed, the chief disruptions came from Foerster (when he discovered that his four-semester required course in literature and writing was being whittled down to two semesters plus an individualized program in communication skills) and from Edward B. Reuter, a professor of sociology, who believed, in contrast, that the proposed program largely ignored areas of vital importance to the modern world. Both men and their followers eventually teamed up to vote against the document.

Although hampered by war activities, the committee was able to finish its work by the spring of 1944 and to present the "New Program in Liberal Arts" for a vote of the faculty on April 5, 1944. It passed 108 to 50. Basically it was a plan designed for the education of the whole heterogeneous student body of a state university rather than an elitist plan for the most intelligent students. It called for general education to liberalize the mind as well as for specialized training to prepare the student for a vocation. In addition, it allowed for both required and elective courses. More specifically, it established re-

quirements in communication skills, and, later, in mathematics skills, in four "core" or general education courses, and in an area of concentration. Also, it set up physical education requirements and an impressive guidance program. A distinctive feature was that students had to stay in the skills programs until they could test out of them. (One athlete distinguished himself by staying in communication skills for seven semesters.)

In little more than a year, three of the main figures in the development of the new curriculum were gone from Iowa City: Foerster and Reuter, who both left in protest, and Dean Newburn, who left to become president of the University of Oregon. But President Hancher continued to support the new curriculum, saying that it was one of the greatest achievements of his administration. Paul Russell Anderson, special consultant to the American Council on Education, called it "an exceedingly forward-looking and yet practical program." Also, scores of college administrators wrote for information about it.

A Library Building at Last

For both students and faculty, the greatest event of the Hancher years was, perhaps, the opening of a library building. For a hundred years or more the University's collection of books and journals had been shunted from one building to another and never adequately housed. Prospects brightened in 1939 when the Board of Education accepted President Gilmore's request for $300,000 to begin construction of a main library. But hopes were dashed when the women's gymnasium at Iowa State burned down and the regents, to replace it, withdrew the funding for a library in Iowa City. President Hancher renewed the request, however, arguing that

Main Library, 1950s. While the current generation of students and faculty may take the Main Library for granted, behind its modern facade is a saga worth telling. The University's library began with the arrival in Iowa City in November 1855 of two boxes containing about fifty books purchased by President Dean. Originally a four-by-four-foot cubicle in the Mechanics' Academy, the library moved to Old Capitol in 1859, to North Hall in 1882, and to Schaeffer Hall in 1902. In 1908 books were moved from various rooms and corridors in Schaeffer to the main floor and part of the basement of Macbride.

No matter where it was located, the general collection was always bursting its bounds, and as it grew it was dispersed among many departmental libraries. (The Law Library has been a separate entity from the earliest days.) Until the opening of the Main Library building in 1951, none of the spaces provided was originally designed for library use. During the construction of Macbride Hall, for example, the regents decided to modify the building by removing interior walls and replacing them with columns so that the University's general library could be "temporarily housed therein." It was a temporary arrangement that was to last well over forty years, during which time the basement floor was lowered and divided into two separate floors to increase shelf space.

no other university of Iowa's size was without a central library building. The collection—under the direction of the long-suffering Grace Wormer—was scattered in seventeen locations, and almost 80 percent of the volumes were housed in buildings in which fire was a serious threat.

Yet progress was still tortuously slow. It looked as though funds would once more be shifted to Ames when the Agricultural Engineering Building there burned down in 1941, but at last $300,000 was allocated for construction of a library at the University of Iowa. When World War II broke out, however, plans were again suspended, and after the war, when bids overran the architect's estimates, the original plan was pared down to construction of only the first unit. At long last the builder broke ground in 1949, only to have construction stalled for most of the year, first because of a steel shortage and then because of a strike. When the first unit finally opened in 1951 it lacked sufficient space from the start, so 60,000 books were shipped that spring to the Midwest Inter-Library Center in Chicago. Happily, the building was expanded by two more small units in 1961 and 1965, and a major addition in 1972 doubled its capacity by adding fourth and fifth floors along with a new entrance facing south and *away* from the campus.

Ralph E. Ellsworth, who had come to Iowa from the University of Colorado, was not only a librarian but also an authority on library buildings and their uses. To make the library a center for faculty discussion as well as research, he installed a faculty lounge on the second floor just above the north entrance, where coffee was made available in midmorning and midafternoon. When Ellsworth returned to Colorado, his successor, Leslie W. Dunlap, was eager to run a tighter ship. He immediately closed the faculty lounge, though retaining one for the staff. Dunlap was followed by his hardworking assistant,

Reserve library, Old Armory, 1938. A "Library Annex" was opened in the Old Armory in 1927, housing under a perennially leaky roof the Reserve Reading Room, the Serials Department, and Government Documents. Students shared the reading room with occasional bats, and librarians dispensed fly swatters, set out flypaper, and sprayed with Flit.

Dale M. Bentz in 1982, and he in turn by Sheila D. Creth in 1987. Served by an extraordinarily knowledgeable and helpful staff, students have crowded even the expanded library, so that on many an evening every seat—and every possibility for parking—is occupied.

Nationally Recognized Programs

Of all the research and creative activity that took place during the Hancher presidency, five programs in particular won widespread national attention. These were in quite diverse areas: speech pathology, educational testing, the fine arts, creative writing, and physics. James F. Curtis and Wendell Johnson attracted scores of patients to Iowa City for their work on cleft palates and stuttering. As part of their therapy, stutterers walked along the sidewalks of Iowa City startling passersby by asking them, "D-Do you have the t-time?" and "D-Does my st-stuttering b-bother you?" In the field of testing, Everet F. Lindquist's high-speed scoring machine revolutionized the scoring and storage of objective test results. His fear that the consequent popularity of objective testing would lead to education simply for isolated facts led to his encouragement of test questions requiring comparison, inference, and judgment as well as recall. In the fine arts, the Big Three—Mabie, Clapp, and Longman—were at the zenith of their powers. Mabie's new theater made even more imaginative productions possible; Clapp developed singers and instrumentalists of professional caliber; and Lester D. Longman, head of the Art Department, after making the campus intolerable for Grant Wood, more than made amends by importing an extraordinary faculty, which included such painters as Byron Burford, Stuart Edie, Philip Gus-

ton, James Lechay, and Eugene Ludins; printmaker Mauricio Lasansky, and sculptor Humbert Albrizio. In creative writing, Paul Engle took over the Iowa Writers' Workshop, first directed by Wilbur Schramm, and with entrepreneurial skills as well as poetic talent brought it to nationwide attention. Engle raised private funds in order to bring to the campus many of the finest poets and writers of the time. He unearthed funds, too, to bring scores of talented students to Iowa. Although the Iowa workshop was widely imitated, under Engle—and later under Eugene Garber, George Starbuck, Jack Leggett, and Frank Conroy—it has remained the one with the greatest appeal to aspiring writers.

James Van Allen's stunning discoveries in space during this period brought the greatest attention to the University. In the first months of 1958, the Explorer I and III satellites revealed high densities of radiation in the Earth's upper atmosphere. When the information was released on May 1, 1958, the attention of the world scientific community focused on Iowa City, and a year later space physicist James Van Allen appeared on the cover of the May 4 issue of *Time* magazine. What he discovered in the magnetosphere became known as the Van Allen belts.

James A. Van Allen

James Van Allen was born in Mount Pleasant, Iowa, graduated from Iowa Wesleyan, and earned his Ph.D. in physics at the University of Iowa in 1939. After working on the radio proximity fuse during World War II and spending four years at Johns Hopkins, he returned in 1951 to his alma mater to succeed Louis A. Turner as a professor and head of the Department of

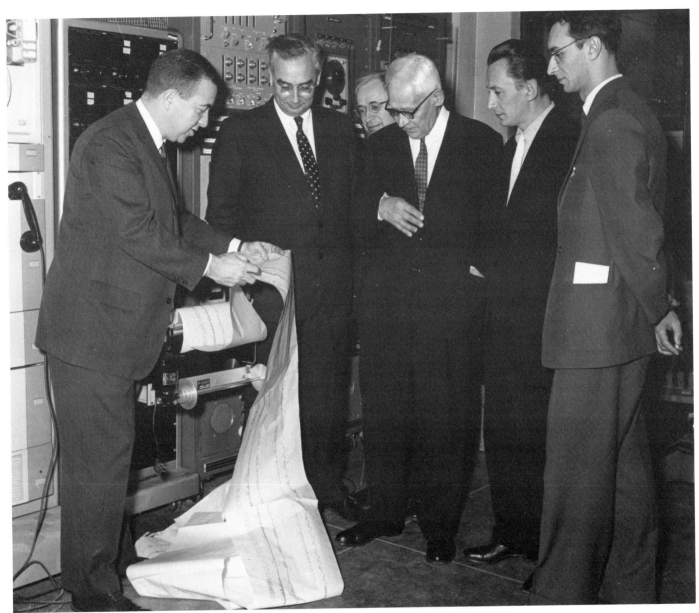

Explorer IV program 1959, from left to right: James Van Allen, L. I. Sedov, V. I. Krassovskii, A. A. Blagonravov, and two interpreters, one American, and one Soviet. When a group of Soviet scientists visited the campus, Van Allen described to them the analysis of data transmitted from University of Iowa equipment on an early satellite, Explorer IV.

Physics. Van Allen soon began to experiment with balloon-rocket ("rockoon") launchings. Working from a government ship sailing off Greenland, Van Allen managed in October 1952 to send one rockoon 250,000 feet into the Arctic atmosphere. The goal, as Van Allen said, was always to go higher: "The satellite is a natural extension of rockets, which are natural extensions of airplanes and balloons, which are natural extensions of man's climbing trees and mountains to get up higher and thus have a better view."

From what they learned on the rockoon experiments, Van Allen and his staff were able to provide instruments for the country's first lunar probe (Pioneer I) and for the first satellite to escape the Earth's gravity (Pioneer IV). In the 1980s, plasma wave detection instruments designed by a former student of Van Allen's, Professor Donald Gurnett, have gathered data from Jupiter, Saturn, and Uranus on board Voyagers I and II.

During his long career Van Allen has won many honors, among them the medal for Exceptional Scientific Achievement from NASA (1974) and the Gold Medal of the Royal Astronomical Society in London (1978). A year after his retirement in 1986 he was awarded the National Medal of Science, the United States' highest honor for scientific achievement.

Athletics

With the hope of defusing the rising tension in a longstanding rivalry, Minnesota governor Floyd B. Olson and Iowa governor Clyde Herring in 1935 decided to make a friendly bet on the annual football game between the states' two major universities. When Minnesota won, Floyd of Rosedale (brother of Blue Boy, the hog featured in Will Rogers's movie *State Fair*) was dispatched to Minneapolis. Floyd was then sent to a St. Paul artist, Charles Brioschi, whose bronze sculpture became the trophy awarded annually to the winner of the Iowa-Minnesota game. Floyd aside, Iowa football fans did not have much to cheer about until Coach Eddie Anderson's Ironmen—so named because many members of the undermanned team played both offense and defense—arrived in 1939. Star of the 1939 team was Nile Kinnick, who was named to every major all-American team and won the Heisman, Maxwell, and Walter Camp trophies. Kinnick was also named the Associated Press Athlete of the Year in 1939.

Although after 1939 the fortunes of varsity football would decline until the early 1950s, some first-rate football was played at Iowa during World War II by a team drawn from the hundreds of officers and cadets attending the Navy Pre-Flight School. Called the Seahawks, the squad included many former collegiate and professional football stars. In 1942 the Seahawks beat Kansas, Northwestern, Minnesota, Michigan, Indiana, Nebraska, and a team representing the military garrison at Ft. Knox on their way to a 7–3 season. The leading scorer was quarterback Forest Evashevski.

Iowa's football fortunes were reversed in 1952 with the hiring of the same Forest Evashevski (quarterback of the Michigan team that gave Iowa its only loss in 1939) as head coach. He led Iowa to Rose Bowl wins in January 1957 and January 1959 before resigning after the 1960 season to become athletic director. In his nine seasons as head coach, Evashevski compiled a record of 52-27-4. Among the Iowa football players who went on from the teams of the 1940s and 1950s to play professionally were Wally Hilgenberg, Emlen Tunnell, Alex Karras, Paul Krause, and Calvin Jones.

Meanwhile, basketball was becoming the University's second most popular sport. Iowa had several fine teams between 1934 and 1964, among them the 1943–44 team, which had fourteen freshmen and still went 14–4; and the 1945 team, which went 17–1 and was ranked third nationally; and, of course, the 1954–55 and 1955–56 teams, both of which went to the NCAA Final Four. Coached by Frank "Bucky" O'Connor, who died tragically in an automobile accident in 1958, these teams were the Big Ten champions both years, and after the second Final Four appearance Iowa was ranked second in the nation. Among the best of the players who played for coaches Rollie Williams (1930–43), "Pops" Harrison (1944–50), Frank O'Connor (1950–58), and "Sharm" Scheuerman (1958–64) were Dick Ives, Murray Weir (NCAA scoring champion, 1947–48), and Don Nelson, for many years an NBA player and coach of the Milwaukee Bucks.

Iowa also had its share of standouts in other sports in these years. Otto Vogel came to Iowa to coach baseball in 1925 after two years with the Chicago Cubs and stayed on for nearly four decades, producing Big Ten champions or cochampions in 1927, 1938, 1942, and 1949. In wrestling, Iowa grew stronger and had frequent top ten finishes at NCAA meets in the 1940s and 1950s, but its total dominance of the sport would come later. Swimmer Wally Ris was the national AAU 100-yard freestyle champion from 1945 to 1949 and received gold medals in the 1948 Olympics in the 100-meter freestyle and as part of the 800-meter relay team that set world and Olympic records. Bowen Stassforth, breaststroker, won a silver medal in the 1952 Olympics at Helsinki.

In 1948 Iowa's current mascot was created by journalism instructor and 1942 graduate Dick Spencer III, and a statewide contest was run to give the hawk a name. The

An early Herky on the sidelines at Kinnick Stadium, c. 1948.

winning entry, Herky, was provided by John D. Franklin of Belle Plaine. But there had been other mascots before Herky. During the 1909–10 season there was a black bear named "Burch" that somehow drowned in the Iowa River. In the 1920s came a Great Dane named Rex, and then Rex II, who also drowned in the river. A St. Bernard then served as an informal mascot until Herky's arrival.

Nile Kinnick and Coach Eddie Anderson before the Northwestern game, 1939. Hired to replace Irl Tubbs, Eddie Anderson arrived at Iowa in 1939 after coaching Holy Cross to a 47-7-4 record in six seasons. A native of Oskaloosa, Anderson learned his football at Notre Dame from Knute Rockne and later played professionally for the Chicago Cardinals while earning his M.D. at Rush Medical Center in Chicago. At Iowa he divided his time between the gridiron and the urology clinic at the University Hospitals. Anderson coached the Hawkeyes for eight seasons from 1939 to 1942 and from 1946 to 1949 (during World War II he was a major in the Army Medical Corps). It is his first team, however, the 1939 "Ironmen" led by Nile Kinnick, that Iowans remember best. Kinnick scored or passed for 107 of Iowa's 130 points during that season. He led the nation in kickoff returns and in interceptions, and he ranked among the top ten in total offense. After this remarkable year, Kinnick topped the voting on both the Associated Press and United Press all-American teams, won the Chicago Tribune's Silver Football award, the Heisman Trophy, the Maxwell Trophy, and

the Walter Camp award, and he was named the Associated Press's Athlete of the Year ahead of Joe DiMaggio. The consummate student athlete, he graduated Phi Beta Kappa. During World War II, Kinnick joined the Navy. On June 2,

1943, he took off on a practice flight from the U.S.S. Lexington, but his plane developed an oil leak and went down in the Caribbean. Kinnick's body was never found. In 1972 the University's football stadium was renamed in his honor.

Nile Kinnick scoring the winning touchdown against Notre Dame, November 11, 1939. Midway through the 1939 football season, undefeated Notre Dame came to Iowa City. The Ironmen were ready for them, and led by the legendary Nile Kinnick, they beat the Fighting Irish, 7–6. Kinnick punted for an average of forty-six yards, scored Iowa's only touchdown, and then drop-kicked the extra point. He was one of eight Hawkeyes to play all sixty minutes that day.

"Crack-the-whip" on Clinton Street, Homecoming, 1941. Celebrations following the big Iowa football victories often lasted into the following school week. Following Iowa's big victory over Notre Dame, according to Mason Ladd, students "stampeded the buildings, broke into classes, occupied seats in somewhat of a sitdown strike fashion and made it impossible to conduct classes." In the fall of 1941 President Hancher asked the deans to issue a statement prohibiting absences after football games.

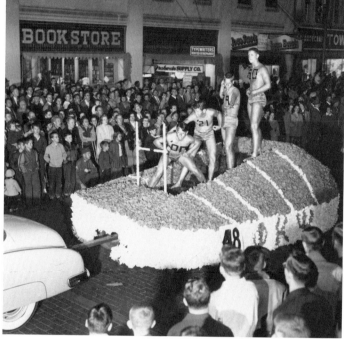

All-male Scottish Highlanders at Kinnick Stadium, 1939. The Scottish Highlanders bagpipe band was founded in 1936 by Colonel F. N. Dailey (head of the University's ROTC program), and in 1937 Dailey brought William Adamson to Iowa as director. Adamson, whose father ran a bagpipe importing firm in Boston, began playing the bagpipes at age nine as therapy to strengthen a left arm and hand weakened by polio. It was Adamson who gave the Scottish Highlanders their name, turned them into a performing group, and directed them until his death in 1965.

The band was all-male until 1942, when World War II called seventy-two of its seventy-eight members to active duty. The world's largest bagpipe band then became all-female until 1972, when men were once again allowed to join—and women were allowed to join the Hawkeye Marching Band. The Highlanders traveled to Europe every four years between 1952 and 1976, and have performed at countless parades and festivals around the country. In July 1956 they appeared on the "Ed Sullivan Show."

Phi Kappa Psi float passing the reviewing stand on Clinton Street, Homecoming, 1950. The first time that a Homecoming program listed a parade was in 1921. The event was called a pageant, and it was directed by none other than E. C. Mabie.

Leaving for the Rose Bowl, December 1958. Approximately 18,000 Iowans traveled to Pasadena to watch the Hawkeyes beat the University of California on January 1, 1959. Eleven hundred students and alumni rode on a special train sponsored by the Santa Fe Railroad. The forty-two-hour trip featured conga lines, cheers, and countless card games. Because students were allowed to take only one suitcase, the Daily Iowan's *special Rose Bowl Edition devoted an entire article to the subject of how to pack for the trip west. Those who drove to California may have enjoyed the trip less, especially the hundreds of Iowa fans trapped in a New Mexico blizzard two days before the game.*

Coach Forest Evashevski along the sidelines at the 1959 Rose Bowl. All-American quarterback Randy Duncan got a kiss from Jayne Mansfield, the Hawkeye Marching Band got new uniforms and was directed by Meredith Willson, and Forest Evashevski rose from his sickbed against his doctor's advice to lead Iowa to a 38–12 victory over California in the 1959 Rose Bowl. The game's most valuable player was Bob Jeter, who gained 194 yards on only nine carries, and the team as a whole rushed 429 yards, then a Rose Bowl record. The bowl win followed an 8-1-1 season, which earned the University of Iowa the Grantland Rice trophy as the nation's top-ranked team.

University Marching Band performing in downtown Los Angeles, 1957. The first official University band was founded in 1881, and it served as the main concert band until the 1930s, when it underwent division. The concert band continued to play concerts on the Pentacrest lawn and around the state, while the varsity, or sports band, played at football and basketball games and pep rallies. Until the 1930s the band was in the Military Department, but in 1936 it became part of the School of Fine Arts. Under the direction of Frederick C. Ebbs, who became band director in 1954, the Hawkeye Marching Band began to do the colorful maneuvers and "flash" routines for which it is known today. In 1957 the principal bands grew to three in number. The Symphony Band toured the state and gave formal concerts, the Hawkeye Marching Band performed at football games, and the Varsity Band, a training unit for the other bands, handled basketball games. In 1966 the Symphony Band toured Europe and gave a twelve-encore concert at the Soviet Opera House in Kiev.

The best known of the many songs the Hawkeye Marching Band plays is "The Iowa Fight

Song," composed in 1950 by Meredith Willson. A native Iowan and creator of the musical The Music Man, *Willson premiered the song on NBC's "The Big Show" on December 31, 1950, with a forty-seven piece orchestra and sixteen singers.*

It was introduced to the Iowa campus on February 12, 1951, at an Iowa-Indiana basketball game. Willson led the Hawkeye Marching Band in a performance of his popular composition at both the 1957 and 1982 Rose Bowl games.

The "Fabulous Five," left to right, Sharm Scheurman, Bill Logan, Carl Cain, coach Bucky O'Connor, Bill Schoof, and Bill Seaberg. In the 1955–56 basketball season, Iowa's "Fabulous Five" went all the way to the championship game of the NCAA tournament before losing 83–71 to a University of San Francisco team led by Bill Russell and K. C. Jones. Each man in the all-senior starting lineup averaged in double figures. The only Iowa team ever to go to the NCAA final game, the 1955–56 Hawkeyes won the Big Ten title and finished at 20–6.

Old Gold Days, 1958. Sponsored by the Dolphin Club, Old Gold Days were held during the time when high school students from around the state came to see life at the University. Activities included water skiing on the Iowa River, diving from the Union footbridge, and canoe jousting. But a pall hung over the events in 1958, for earlier in the week highly popular Iowa basketball coach Bucky O'Connor had been killed in an automobile accident.

Dolphin Follies, October 31– November 2, 1941. Each year from 1921 until 1977 members of the Dolphin Club swimming fraternity put on popular water shows, first at the Old Armory pool and later at the Field House pool. The shows featured fire diving, synchronized swimming, trampoline acts, and a trapeze act performed fifty feet above the water. The *shows adopted a different theme each year ("Rhythm in Aqua," "Aquatropolis," "Soggy Sawdust," "Davey Jones' Locker") and always included aquatic comedy routines, as in this 1941 show, "Tropical Tradewinds," where six swimmers purport to demonstrate the "Six Lessons from Madame LaZonga."*

Teeing off at Finkbine, 1932. The University's first golf course opened in 1923. Built on land given by William O. Finkbine of Des Moines, one of the University's most generous alumni, the old course was pared to nine holes when a new eighteen-hole championship course was constructed in 1954.

Entrance to the Silver Shadow on the east side of the Iowa Memorial Union, 1937. In 1936 University of Iowa students created their own nightclub, the Silver Shadow. Located in the basement of the Iowa Memorial Union, it served no alcoholic beverages and was acclaimed by all as wholesome entertainment. So appealing was the notion of this sort of club, in fact, that an article about the Silver Shadow appeared in Good Housekeeping in 1946. It read in part: "On Saturday nights the place has an air about it, with its chic decor of silver jewel cloth and everybody in formal dress. It provides a happy ending that ends on a pleasant note instead of in the ditch or with nerves wrecked by visions of expulsion."

Under the Whetstone's clock, 1950. The Whetstone's soda fountain, featuring Persian sherbet, was a favorite gathering place for students from 1927 to 1962.

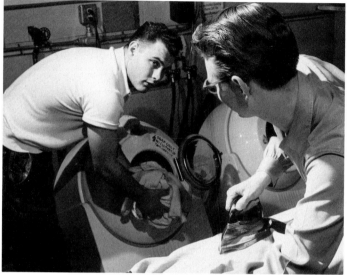

Hillcrest at night. Built in 1938, Hillcrest originally housed 250 men on four floors. It expanded to make room for 400 the following year, and additions in 1949 and 1956 made it the largest residence hall on campus until Burge Hall was completed in 1959. In the 1950s and subsequent decades, Hillcrest was the preferred dorm for men, especially Iowa's intercollegiate athletes.

Doing laundry at Hillcrest, c. 1956. "Remember those wonderful old canvas bags we used to send home to mother regularly—always bulging with laundry?" asked the S.U.I. News Bulletin in 1954. "And recall the way they came back with clean clothes and always a box of home made cookies, a cake, or some other prize winning goody from the home kitchen?" For most students, those days were gone by the early 1950s. Postage rates had risen and coin-operated washers and dryers were installed in the dorms and in laundromats in town. Doing laundry became a social occasion for many undergraduates.

Soda fountain, Currier Hall, 1953. The Currier Hall soda fountain, added to the dormitory in 1939, served sandwiches, milk shakes, ice cream, and Cokes daily from midmorning until 11 P.M. In the 1970s it was replaced by a bank of vending machines.

Dance, 1950s. In the 1940s and 1950s students at the University of Iowa held major dances every other week. In 1947–48, for example, students could attend the following dances: the Inter-Fraternity Pledge Prom, Commerce Mart, Harvest Holiday, Spinster's Spree, Homecoming, Newman Nocturne, Barristers' Ball, Miami Triad, Dad's Day, Gadabout, Carnival of Bands, Tinsel Twilight, Mecca Ball, Spring Frolic, Caps Caprice, Military Ball, Hillcrest Hobo Party, Pastel Prelude, Woodchopper's Ball, Diane's Delight, Prize Prom, University Prom, Aesculapian Frolic, and Sophocles' Serenade.

Burge Hall lobby, 1963. Occupied in 1958, though not ready to house its full complement of nearly 1,300 women until 1959, Burge Hall was named to honor Adelaide Lasheck Burge, Iowa's dean of women from 1920 until 1946.

Senior Nurses' Hayride, 1942.

"Dents" in front of Trowbridge Hall, 1944. During the war, many of the University's "medics" and "dents" were members of Company C in the Army Specialized Training Program (ASTP).

Iowa Memorial Union during a flood, June 1947. Before the completion of the Coralville Reservoir in 1958, flooding was a frequent and occasionally severe problem on campus. On June 17, 1947, the Iowa River crested at 18.6 feet, causing one of the worst floods in Iowa City history. A dike large enough for trucks to drive on was erected to protect the Union, and an all-night vigil was maintained by University maintenance crews. University High's basement was half-filled with water, and the power plant was threatened as water poured into the tunnels. Pumps operated around the clock until the swollen river returned to its banks.

Law Commons. The Law Commons was the first unit in what was to be a self-contained College of Law. Built in 1934 with Public Works Administration money, the Law Commons housed 150 students, who each paid five dollars a week for board and less than half that for their room. University officials apparently did not want anyone to think of the building as a dormitory, however. "Properly understood," a 1934 SUI News Bulletin sniffed, "it is a junior lawyer's club."

Pharmacy Building, 1963. After seventy-eight years of sharing quarters with other departments, the College of Pharmacy finally had its own building in 1961. The five-story structure located just west of Quadrangle dormitory was shepherded into existence by College of Pharmacy dean Louis Zopf. Zopf, dean from 1952 until 1972, established a continuing education program now mandatory for Iowa pharmacists, lengthened the curriculum from four to five years, and faced down experts who would have painted the building's interior "battleship gray, penitentiary green," and "depraved brown." The Pharmacy Building contains the Pharmaceutical Laboratory, which performs research and development on new drugs and which manufactures drugs for trial use, and the Iowa Drug Information System, a computer-based, medication information retrieval system offered by no other college of pharmacy in the country.

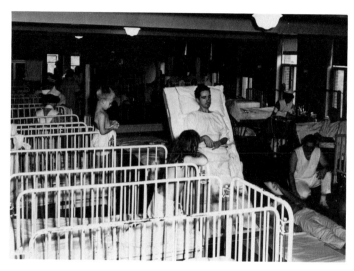

Polio Clinic in Children's Hospital, 1950. In 1950 the University Hospitals admitted 560 patients to its polio ward, and within two years that number was exceeded by more than a hundred. Although all patients seeking admission found beds, there was severe overcrowding in the clinic, and rooms that normally had two beds housed four adults or six children. One room housed eleven cribs, leaving scarcely enough room for doctors and nurses to move around. Those suffering from poliomyelitis spent most of their time in a horizontal position, and, as shown here, had slowly to become accustomed to an upright position. Jonas Salk's discovery of a polio vaccine in 1955 made the polio clinic happily obsolete.

Clyde Berry (facing) and Thomas McCorkle, of the Institute of Agricultural Medicine (seated), discuss farm safety with a local farmer, 1957. The technology of agriculture advanced rapidly in the 1940s and 1950s, but the understanding of how this affected the health of farmers did not keep pace. In response, the Institute of Agricultural Medicine was established within the College of Medicine in September 1955 with the assistance of a grant from the Kellogg Foundation. The institute delved into such problems as the relationship of machine noise to deafness, the connection between chemical sprays and skin and lung disorders, machine safety, and farm-related diseases. The Institute of Agricultural Medicine was the first of its kind in the Americas (a similar program had already been established in Poland), but not the only institute at Iowa coming to the aid of farmers. In 1954 the College of Law established its Agricultural Law Center in cooperation with Iowa State College and the U.S. Department of Agriculture for the purpose of bringing together legal scholars and experts in agricultural economics and farm management.

Wendell Johnson (1906–65). Johnson is best known for his pathbreaking research into stuttering, and the fact that Iowa's speech and hearing clinic bears his name is testimony to his achievements. That he was himself a stutterer, said Johnson in 1961, "led to my becoming a specialist in my own distress." To aid others similarly afflicted, Johnson founded the Demosthenes Club and set enough experimental and therapeutic programs in motion that Iowa City came to be known as "the stuttering capital of the world." But Johnson was more than a speech pathologist. A genial and gentle man, he was closely involved with research in clinical psychology and in a new field called general semantics. First taught in 1939, his course in general semantics became wildly popular, the sort of course that attracted students to the University. Because there was no text, Johnson wrote People in Quandaries *(1946), which is still in print. Johnson wrote constantly, and between 1928 and his death in 1965 published over two hundred articles and books, including some potboilers he wrote during the Depression under the pseudonyms of Dr. Robert Clark and Dr. George Hall. When a student asked him why he worked so hard, Johnson replied, "I enjoy what I do, so I do a lot of it."*

E. F. Lindquist (1901–78) and his test-scoring machine. In the field of educational testing, no man is more prominent than Everet F. Lindquist, the man who developed the Iowa Tests of Basic Skills, taken by millions of school children across the country. Lindquist was also responsible for the Iowa Tests of Educational Development, was founder in 1953 of the Measurement Research Center, and was cofounder in 1959 of the American College Testing Program. In the 1950s he invented the electronic scoring machine, which revolutionized the entire business of educational testing. A native Iowan, Lindquist joined the Iowa faculty in 1927, and from 1930 until his retirement in 1969 he was the director of the Iowa Testing Programs. He arranged for the profits from the Iowa tests to go into a University fund for educational research and capital expenditure. Some of the money earned from Lindquist's pioneering work went to build an educational research building, fittingly called the Lindquist Center, which houses the Weeg Computing Center, the Iowa Testing Programs, the Iowa Information Center, and the division of Educational Psychology, Measurement, and Statistics of the College of Education. The Lindquists donated the main curtain in Hancher Auditorium.

Computer installation, 1961; standing, left to right: E. F. Lindquist, Provost Harvey Davis, James Van Allen, and James Dolch, the director of the computer center; seated, an IBM representative. The University's first computer center was established in September 1958 with the installation of an IBM 650 in East Hall (now Seashore). This computer quickly became ob-
solete and was replaced with an IBM 1401 and the IBM 7070 seen here. James Dolch was the first director, and he was followed in 1964 by Gerard P. Weeg, after whom the present computing center was named. In its early years, and with a succession of different mainframe computers, the computer center dealt largely with two major customers. One was James Van Allen,
who needed to have the information gathered by the many satellites under his supervision processed. The other was E. F. Lindquist's creation, the Measurement Research Center, which scored thousands of tests from across the country. For years the computer center's operations were a mystery to most of the campus. As late as 1974 there were only seventy terminals on campus capable
of hooking into the main computer, and only ten of those were available to students. All that has changed. There are now well over two thousand computer work stations on campus, constantly busy computer clusters for students at sixteen locations around campus, and a new computer facility, the Weeg Computing Center, located in the Lindquist Center.

Construction of the arts campus, 1934. One of the University's most significant achievements came in the middle of the Depression when the arts campus was developed on the west side of the river. Funded in part by grants from the Carnegie and Rockefeller foundations, an arts "colony" was es- *tablished with the construction of the Art Building in 1934 and the Theatre Building in 1936. Plans also called for a music building and a performance hall, but that had to wait until the 1970s, when the Music Building, Clapp Recital Hall, and Hancher Auditorium were completed. In the meantime,* *concerts were held in the Union ballroom and in the Old Music Building on Gilbert Street. It was not the collection of buildings, however, that made the arts campus so important. In the 1930s, Iowa's School of Fine Arts was the only program in the nation in which students could earn ad-* *vanced degrees by producing a creative thesis, whether in art, theater, music, or writing. Between 1948 and 1962 the University of Iowa was first in the nation in the number of graduate arts degrees conferred.*

Painting studio, 1940. In the late 1930s, Lester D. Longman, head of the new Department of Art (a combination of the old department of Graphic and Plastic Arts and the History and Appreciation of Art), introduced a new graduate program in art that combined studio training with classroom learning in the history and theory of art. The Art Building was the testing ground for this *philosophy. Built on land that was originally a swamp and city dump but which had been reclaimed by three years of landfill dumping, the building contained a large gallery, numerous studios (all with north light), and an auditorium seating three hundred. Funds for the new building came from the Carnegie Corporation, the Works Progress Administration, and Iowa alumni.*

Grant Wood (1892–1942) and painting student, c. 1940. When he was hired by the University in 1934, Grant Wood was a nationally known painter (he had completed American Gothic *in 1930) and the Iowa director of the Public Works of Art Project (PWAP), a New Deal program. A series of murals he designed for the library at Iowa State was carried out in part by students in his mural-painting class, who received stipends from the federal government as well as academic credit for their work.* *It was hoped that Wood would create a similar set of murals for buildings on Iowa's campus, but the PWAP ended in June 1934 before they could be started. In the fall of that year, Grant Wood opened a Saturday "Art Clinic" for artists from Iowa and surrounding states who sought professional advice on their work. Students worked at home and traveled to Iowa City every three weeks for critique sessions in what had been the operating amphitheater of the old University Hospital (now Seashore Hall).*

Four painters, left to right: Stuart Edie, James Lechay, Eugene Ludins, Byron Burford. By 1945 Iowa had 154 graduate students in art, whereas its closest competitor—New York University—had only a hundred. To staff his program, Longman hired art historians with doctoral degrees, on the one hand, and professional artists on the other, particularly artists experienced in the various forms of modern art (four of whom are pictured here). As a result of the new program, Grant Wood's regionalism went into eclipse and virtually disappeared after he died in 1942.

Humbert Albrizio, with a sculpture student, c. 1960. One of the country's leading sculptors, Albrizio studied in several schools in New York and privately with José de Creeft, Gutzon Borglum, and U. A. Ricci. Among the many galleries at which he exhibited were the Metropolitan, the Whitney, the Brooklyn Museum, the Chicago Art Institute, and the National Academy of Design. Viewers marked not only the form of his sculptures but also the qualities he brought out in his materials: their texture, color, and high polish. Yet as Lester Longman once said about Albrizio's works, one does not get one's literal and prosaic answers from them: "If you do not see the poetry, you see nothing."

Mauricio Lasansky (second from right) and students in the printmaking studio, c. 1960. A master craftsman in the intaglio printmaking process, Mauricio Lasansky came to the United States from Argentina in 1943 on the first of five Guggenheim fellowships. Two years later he joined the art faculty at Iowa. In his years at the University, Lasansky brought the print department into national prominence and taught hundreds of students, many of whom are now established artists and teachers in their own right. Lasansky is best known for his portraits and for the stark Nazi Drawings series. In 1976 a room in the Carver Wing of the Museum of Art was dedicated to a permanent display of his work.

Beaux Arts Ball, Art Building, March 4, 1940. The Art Department at Iowa was pioneering in many respects, but one incident demonstrates that its progress was not always smooth. In the fall of 1939, prominent art historian H. W. Janson, then teaching for the first time, took a group of students to see a major Picasso exhibit at the Art Institute of Chicago. Such "modern" art was so controversial in those days, at least at Iowa, that Dean of Fine Arts Earl Harper fired Janson for making the trip. He was later reinstated after some of his colleagues objected. The whole affair was lampooned by the students at their Beaux Arts Ball the next semester when they staged an all-Picasso costume party.

Arnold S. Gillette with a model of the new Theatre Building. Gillette, who taught set design and construction at Iowa for forty years, had an important role in the planning of the University Theatre. Author of the classic Stage Scenery: Its Construction and Rigging *(1959), Gillette designed a thirty-six-foot revolving stage within the larger stage, which allowed a new set to be brought into view every thirty seconds. Among the 500-seat theater's other important features was a "flexible remote control" lighting system located in a glass-paneled room in the rear of the theater. The system greatly facilitated the work of Hunton D. Sellman, who taught lighting in the Theatre Department.*

Two Hundred Were Chosen, *Theatre Building, November 1936. Ellsworth P. Conkle's* Two Hundred Were Chosen, *based on a true story about midwestern farmers sent by the United States government to colonize Alaska, was the first play staged in the University's new Theatre Building. It was an appropriate choice, for a number of reasons. Conkle that year earned the first Ph.D. ever awarded by the Department of Speech and Dramatic Art for a creative thesis. Conkle's thesis consisted of three plays, one of them* Two Hundred Were Chosen. *The play was representative of the regional theater movement so dear to E. C. Mabie, and it took advantage of the new theater's special features.*

"Sciopticon-effect machines will give the illusion of rain, fog, and mist," Hunton D. Sellman told the Daily Iowan. *"Mountains will jut upward on the cyclorama by means of lens-projections. The shimmering colors of Alaska's aurora borealis will come from a Linnebach lighting instrument." The play received national attention as well. Two weeks after Conkle's play was performed in Iowa City, it opened on Broadway.*

Backstage in the new Theatre Building, 1936.

Death of a Salesman, *1952. In April 1952 the University's Theatre Department put on eight performances of Arthur Miller's* Death of a Salesman. *Robert Paulus (center) played Willy Loman, Gerald Tippit (right) was Happy, and Jerry Silberman (left) had the role of Biff. Silberman (B.A., 1955), known now to moviegoers as Gene Wilder, went on to star in such films as* Young Frankenstein, Blazing Saddles, Stir Crazy, *and* Silver Streak.

The Marriage of Figaro, *Macbride Auditorium, July 1955. Herald Stark and Harold Shiffler directed, and Arnold S. Gillette built the sets for, this 1955 production of Mozart's* The Marriage of Figaro. *Produced jointly by faculty in speech, drama, and music, and performed July 26–28 in over ninety-degree heat in Macbride Auditorium, the opera was the climax of the University's seventeenth annual Fine Arts Festival. The tradition of staging a major opera began in 1939 as a collaboration between the Theatre and Music departments and continues to this day. Then, however, opera lovers paid only $1.50 or $2.00 for their tickets.*

James Dixon (left) and Dimitri Mitropoulos, 1952. While still a student at Iowa, James Dixon (B.A. 1952, M.A. 1956) twice conducted the University Symphony when Dimitri Mitropoulos was guest pianist. Mitropoulos, for years internationally famous as the conductor of the New York Philharmonic Orchestra, became Dixon's mentor. Dixon's first job as a resident conductor was with the Seventh Army in Germany (1953–54). From there he returned to Iowa to fill the void left by the death of P. G. Clapp, and he stayed for five years. In 1959 he became the conductor of the New England Conservatory Symphony Orchestra, in 1961 the associate conductor of the Minneapolis Symphony Orchestra, and in 1962 returned once more to Iowa. Dixon has been awarded the Gustav Mahler Medal (1963) and the Ditson Conductor's Award (1980) and has recorded with the Royal Philharmonic of London and the American Composer's Orchestra.

Iowa Writers' Workshop class, c. 1962, left to right: Edmund Keeley, R. V. Cassill, Paul Engle, Vance Bourjaily. In his introduction to Midland: An Anthology of Poetry and Prose (1961), Paul Engle said of the Writers' Workshop that it could offer young writers "hard criticism and decent sympathy." The workshop's method of teaching, which more or less embodies Engle's words, demands that each week one to three students "put up their work" by turning in a short story or a selection of poems. Each class member gives the work a close reading prior to class, and in class the stories or poems are critically assessed. Over the last half century, the Writers' Workshop faculty and alumni have won virtually every prize, fellowship, and grant the literary world has to offer, and their work dominates recent poetry and short-fiction anthologies. A short list of those who have taught or studied at Iowa would include John Cheever, Gail Godwin, John Irving, Tracy Kidder, Galway Kinnell, Robert Lowell, James Alan McPherson, Flannery O'Connor, Philip Roth, W. D. Snodgrass, Kurt Vonnegut, and Robert Penn Warren.

Winter 1958, showing the offices of the Writers' Workshop (in the nearest temporary) and the Art Building across the river. The temporary had the distinction of having fiercely hot water in its only toilet.

SIX

A Major Teaching and Research Institution,
1964–1987

Preparation of a freeze-dried
anticancer drug, College of
Pharmacy, c. 1980.

Despite lean budgets and disturbing student demonstrations, the University during the Bowen, Boyd, and Freedman years experienced probably its most exciting times. Enrollment climbed to near the thirty thousand level, over a dozen major new buildings provided additional space for teaching, research, and entertainment, and in 1986–87 gifts and grants for the first time totaled over $100 million in one year. Even the athletic teams prospered as never before. Every college developed programs that carried the work of the University throughout the state. Iowa was being richly repaid for the support it had given its university.

Howard R. Bowen

Selected by the Board of Regents from among several distinguished candidates, Howard R. Bowen brought a new type of leadership to the University. A noted economist and an educational philosopher, he possessed a willingness to break with tradition in order to create the kind of university he thought Iowa should be.

Partly a homegrown product—he earned his Ph.D. in economics at Iowa after receiving his earlier degrees at Washington State University—Bowen taught economics at Iowa from 1935 to 1942. During World War II he worked for the Department of Commerce, and later he was chief economist for the House Ways and Means and Senate Finance committees. From 1945 to 1947 he served as chief economist for the Irving Trust Company in New York City, and he was then successively the dean of the College of Commerce at the University of Illinois, a professor of economics at Williams College, and the president of Grinnell College before returning to the University of Iowa in 1964 as its fourteenth president.

President Bowen spelled out much of his thinking about higher education in his inaugural address and, at greater length, in a 108-page Green Book, which he distributed in September 1965 as a working paper for the regents, faculty, and staff. In both he made it clear that though there were practical advantages in bigness, he was not enamored of bigness for its own sake. Indeed, he opposed most of the trends of the current "multiversity": its impersonality, the unrestricted proliferation of programs and courses, and the emphasis on research at the expense of teaching, especially the teaching of undergraduates. He wanted the University of Iowa to be a community in which the atmosphere was intellectually stimulating and in which the individual was valued. Even in the professional schools, he hoped for education that would result in graduates who were broadly trained as well as specially prepared for a vocation. In many ways he was hoping to transfer the goals of a good liberal arts college, such as Grinnell, to the larger scene of a major university. Nevertheless, he inherited bigness. In the five years of his presidency, enrollment climbed from 14,480 to 21,221.

Unhappily, because of the student protests that broke out in the last two years of his administration, President Bowen never had a chance to put into effect all of the plans he had developed. As the protests grew more strident, long-range goals became obscured by crises of the moment. On January 26, 1969, he announced that he would resign to take a position in the Department of Economics at Claremont College in California. He expressed a desire to return to teaching and a concern for Mrs. Bowen's health, but many suspected that being essentially a quiet scholar, he found the hassle with the students too unnerving.

Governance of the University

President Bowen's method of administration was in marked contrast to that of President Hancher. Hancher had been an old-style administrator: somewhat paternal and even dictatorial in a genteel way. He had not been enthusiastic about widespread faculty and student participation in University affairs. Bowen, on the other hand, encouraged as much participation as possible. He made it a rule, he said, that every part of the administration should be under the responsibility of someone besides himself. The person he leaned upon most heavily was Willard L. Boyd, whom he appointed vice-president for academic affairs and dean of the faculties shortly after he took office. Bowen and Boyd quickly developed a symbiotic relationship, with Bowen being principally the idea man and Boyd the one who converted the ideas into action. Besides Boyd, President Bowen appointed other officers who shared his liberal view of administration: David H. Vernon, for example, as dean of the College of Law, Hunter Rouse as dean of the College of Engineering, Donald J. Galagan as dean of the College of Dentistry, and Duane C. Spriestersbach as dean of the Graduate College. Holdovers such as Dr. Robert Hardin in medicine and Laura Dustan in nursing also worked with him closely and cordially. Bowen and Dean Dewey B. Stuit of the College of Liberal Arts, however, had their differences, the chief being over departmental autonomy. Stuit believed that departments should have a high degree of independence, whereas Bowen believed that deans should provide departments with direction and guidance. Furthermore, Bowen held that the College of Liberal Arts, with over forty departments and major programs, was too large an organization for any dean to oversee adequately. He proposed

Howard R. Bowen, fourteenth president, 1964–69, addressing Governor Hughes's staff, November 1964.

that the college be broken into three or four smaller colleges, each with its own dean. In opposing the idea, Stuit received considerable support from his departmental executive officers, especially from those heading strong departments that prospered from being left alone. The situation was still a standoff in 1969 when Bowen resigned, and the issue was dropped.

The desirability of a faculty senate had been discussed frequently in the Faculty Council before Bowen arrived on campus, and the council had even appointed a committee to investigate the possibility of creating one. But the work of this committee stalled when President Hancher insisted that it meet with a committee of his choosing headed by Sidney Winter, dean of the College of Business Administration. The purpose of the joint meetings, Hancher explained, was to discuss the disadvantages of a faculty senate as well as the advantages. Thus the progress toward a senate was back almost at square one when Howard Bowen became president. Hancher advised Bowen to kill the senate idea, but Bowen had had experience with such a body at Grinnell and strongly believed that its advantages far outweighed its disadvantages. So he gave the council the go-ahead. In the next eleven months a council committee on faculty participation, headed by sociology professor J. Richard Wilmeth, drew up a constitution for a senate. In a long process it was approved by the council, the faculty, the president, and the regents, and it finally went into effect on July 1, 1967. As the "representative and deliberative organization" of the faculty, the approximately 75-member senate's chief functions were to formulate and recommend policies to the president, to appoint faculty representatives to all-University committees, and to consult in the selection of central administrative officers, including, on invitation of the regents, the selection of the

president. The council continued as the senate's administrative agency. At the first meeting of the new organization, Jerry Kollros of the Zoology Department was elected chairman and thereby became chairman of the council as well. The senate was created none too soon, in view of the fact that the student unrest just ahead often called for a group that could speak authoritatively for the faculty.

Willard L. Boyd

Willard L. Boyd was one of the brilliant young law professors whom Dean Mason Ladd recruited for Iowa's College of Law. He came to Iowa in 1954 after earning two degrees at the University of Minnesota and two at the University of Michigan. He had also practiced law for two years in Minneapolis. Hired initially as an instructor, he quickly rose to the rank of full professor and had just been made associate dean in the College of Law in 1964 when President Bowen appointed him vice-president for academic affairs and dean of the faculties. He had, therefore, a running start for the presidency when Bowen resigned in 1969. He accepted the position knowing full well, to use his own words, that he was not slipping into "a snug harbor."

In fact, it was not a harbor at all, but the open seas, and rough seas at that. Many, like State Representative Charles Grassley, had opposed his appointment on the grounds that he was too lenient with student activists. Others thought him too young and inexperienced for the presidency. State appropriations were not meeting the needs of the institution, and a $250 hike in in-state tuition put into effect just before Boyd took office fueled the student protests that had been flaring intermittently for two years. Furthermore, student demonstrations on other campuses, notably Berkeley and Wisconsin, made it clear that the worst was yet to come.

Boyd surrounded himself with a balanced staff. For his provost he selected Ray L. Heffner, who had been provost under President Hancher and more recently had been president of Brown University and provost at Indiana University. Later, when Heffner requested permission to return to the teaching of Elizabethan drama, Boyd named May Brodbeck, who was dean of graduate studies at the University of Minnesota, to be vice-president for academic affairs and dean of the faculties. Brodbeck had taken her Ph.D. at Iowa, working in philosophy under Gustav Bergmann, and was a shrewd, tireless, and compassionate administrator. Among other vice-presidents were Duane C. Spriestersbach (educational development and research), Dr. Robert C. Hardin (health affairs), and Philip G. Hubbard (student services). As did other presidents, Boyd made frequent use of the executive talents of Samuel L. Becker (communication studies) and David H. Vernon (law)—and of the abilities of the intrepid Mary Parden, who was secretary to five presidents.

Boyd was a man of strong convictions. Among these was the belief that a quality university is impossible without a quality staff and therefore that faculty salaries must have first priority in the disposition of university funds. Another was that a university can attain greatness only through democratic processes. For him that meant participation by students as well as faculty and staff. He strongly supported the liberal arts, holding that a liberal arts education gives the students the flexibility they will need to shape and enjoy their careers. He also championed the cause of human rights, putting the prestige of his office behind an affirmative action program as well

as programs designed to strengthen the position of minority groups.

As proud as he was of the new buildings that went up during his presidency, Boyd always maintained that his real interest was in people, not structures. He was never able to do as much for the faculty as he wished because state appropriations during his years were so limited. One year in the early 1970s there was no increase at all, and salaries had to be frozen. But with the help of Vice-President Brodbeck, Boyd persuaded the regents to create one of the most generous developmental leave programs in the country. It permitted a faculty member with a research project that had been peer reviewed and approved to take a semester off at full pay for research and writing every fifth year. In addition, the administration encouraged the departments to develop their own named professorships. To set an example, Boyd encouraged Roy Carver to include enough money for five distinguished professorships in one of his multimillion-dollar gifts to the University. In the Boyd years the faculty won more than a half billion dollars in federal and private grants for research, training, equipment, and student financial aid. Every college began to establish research centers, institutes, or laboratories—the College of Medicine alone created at least five distinguished research centers as subdivisions of the college.

When Willard Boyd resigned in 1981 to become president of the Field Museum of Natural History in Chicago, he left a university with a reputation for flexibility and tolerance. He had proved himself to be a capable administrator and a superior fund-raiser—and an appealing human being whom even the freshmen dared to call "Sandy."

Willard L. Boyd, fifteenth
president, 1969–81.

First Carver professors; in back, from left to right: Gustav Bergmann (philosophy), James Van Allen (physics and astronomy), Allan D. Vestal (law); in front: Donald C. Bryant (speech) and Hunter Rouse (hydraulics). Muscatine industrialist Roy Carver, in the back row at right, gave the University $3.5 million in 1971, a substantial portion of which was used to establish professorships for a select few of the University's faculty. Carver professorships have since been given to William Aydelotte (history), James Clifton (internal medicine), George Forell (religion), John F. Kennedy (hydraulics), John Paul Long (pharmacology), Sherman Paul (English), Stow Persons (history), and Vernon Van Dyke (political science).

Student Demonstrations

A change in attitudes became evident on campus in the mid-1960s, when in ever-increasing numbers the students began to register in the humanities and social science courses that they believed would help them deal directly with human values. Relevance, they maintained, was what they were seeking. In response, some of the faculty changed the approaches in their courses in order to highlight current human concerns, and in the spring of 1968 an Action Studies Program began to offer sessions taught by unpaid faculty volunteers on such topics as the Vietnam War, urban ghettos, business ethics, underground newspapers, peace, and sex. In the meantime, hundreds of students began to protest whatever they deeply believed was unjustifiable and immoral. They attended rallies on the Pentacrest, gathered to hear the speakers at the Soapbox Soundoff in the Union, crowded the Union ballroom to applaud off-campus antiwar speakers, and engaged in sit-ins in the president's office. Their targets at the rallies and sit-ins were various: beauty salons and barbershops, for example, where blacks could not have their hair cut, tuition hikes, the cost of textbooks, and, of course, the war in Vietnam. Occasionally they carried placards saying "Make Love, Not War" and handed out flowers and jelly beans. The protests that caught the headlines, however, were the more violent ones, such as the burning of draft cards, the smashing of windows in downtown stores, and the blocking of streets and highways. Both Presidents Bowen and Boyd, often agreeing with the students' objectives and admiring their commitment, defended their right to assemble peaceably, but they strongly opposed the students' use of violence and any attempt to interrupt University operations.

The first major attempt to interrupt University operations occurred on November 1, 1967, when a crowd of antiwar students blocked the entrance to the Union, where Marine Corps recruiters were attempting to sign up prospects. A similar confrontation occurred on December 5, when the representatives of the Dow Chemical Company, makers of the napalm used in Vietnam, tried to recruit employees. This time the demonstrators not only blocked the Union entrance but also marched through the library and some of the classroom buildings chanting "Stop Dow now!" Eighteen were arrested, including David Sundance (David S. Grant), who had been living in a tent outside the Union dressed as "Death," and Jerry Sies, who had made a citizen's arrest of State Senator Thomas Riley of Cedar Rapids, who was on campus to observe the goings-on. Bowen warned that the next students who disrupted University operations would be suspended or expelled.

When he became president in 1969, Willard Boyd inherited an uneasy campus. Student demonstrations in Old Capitol were so common that to preserve the furnishings, especially the portraits of former presidents, he moved the president's office to Jessup Hall and locked the doors of Old Capitol. The worst demonstrations came in the spring of 1970 after the military intervention in Cambodia and especially after the killing on May 4 of four Kent State students by Ohio National Guardsmen. On May 7 the ROTC Governor's Day activities had to be postponed, and University buildings were patrolled at night by faculty volunteers. Boyd created a "command post" on the Oakdale campus, thereby giving the confrontations the appearance of real warfare. With him in this bunker, as some of the faculty called it, were Deans Spriestersbach, Hardin, and Vernon, and Arthur Bonfield from the College of Law. At 2 A.M. on May 8 well over

Demonstrator being dragged away from the Union protest, November 1, 1967. A total of 108 demonstrators were arrested for blocking the entrance to the Iowa Memorial Union during a protest against Marine recruitment on campus. Police were called in by President Bowen after a confrontation between demonstrators and taunting counterdemonstrators (including several football players) escalated into violence. Those arrested were released on twenty-five dollars bail and later fined fifty dollars each. None of the counterdemonstrators was arrested.

Dean of Students M. L. Huit lights the cigarette of a demonstrator during a sit-in against Marine recruiting, Iowa Memorial Union, October 28, 1968. Huit also passed around a statement asking the protestors to disperse, saying that they were "disrupting the orderly process of the University." Along with President Bowen and other members of the administration, Huit felt strongly that the individual rights of all students must be protected and therefore that such recruitment should be allowed.

May 1970. Campuses nationwide were shattered by the death of four student demonstrators at Kent State University on May 4. A crowd of over two thousand gathered on the Pentacrest and blocked intersections in mostly peaceful protests. In the days that followed, however, confrontations between students and members of various law-enforcement agencies grew increasingly violent. Governor Robert D. Ray stationed the National Guard outside of town but ultimately found that state troopers were sufficient to keep the campus under control. Attempts were made to block Highway 6 and Interstate 80, windows downtown and in the National Guard Armory were smashed, and the Rhetoric Building adjacent to Old Armory was burned.

two hundred students were arrested for disorderly conduct, and at 3 A.M. the following morning Old Armory Temporary was mysteriously set afire and burned down. Even though they had been warned that the building was a target, many of the rhetoric instructors who had offices in it lost typewriters and unfinished theses. All ninety of them had to find space in the already crowded English-Philosophy Building. (Later the fire marshal decided that the fire was due to faulty wiring!)

On Sunday, May 10, Boyd gave all students who felt personally endangered the option of going home (the semester was almost over), with the choice of completing their semester's work at a later date, accepting a pass or withdrawal grade, or taking a grade on the work completed through May 3. So many students stayed in their dorms after opting to go home that Philip Hubbard, the dean of academic affairs, had to warn them to be off campus in forty-eight hours. By May 11 a total of 11,796 students had elected to go home, and undergraduate classes were little more than formalities. Although protesters believed that they had succeeded in shutting down the University, President Boyd could rightly claim that they never forced him to close its doors or cease its operation. On May 12 the faculty senate approved by one vote a resolution to terminate the ROTC program on campus, but neither the administration nor the regents supported the action, and it never took effect. On May 13 Governor Robert D. Ray withdrew the National Guardsmen he had stationed just outside Iowa City but, to his great credit, had never ordered to move onto the campus. State troopers were also withdrawn. They had patrolled the campus unarmed and with instructions to be as friendly as possible with the students. (They had even been issued pipes to make them seem chummy.)

The faculty reacted in various ways to all this. A few of them joined with the students in some of the alterca-

tions with police and state troopers, and many took part in peaceful demonstrations. But most served as monitors and as building guards or simply continued to teach their classes and work in their studies and laboratories. For several years in the late 1960s and early 1970s an antiwar group kept a silent vigil every Friday noon on Clinton Street across from Whetstone's Drug Store. George W. Forell of the School of Religion, Dean Philip Hubbard, and Robert E. Engel, assistant to the president, deserved at least minor decorations for dampening down rallies before they became violent—as did the mayor of Iowa City, Loren Hickerson, and the city manager, Frank Smiley.

Sporadic outbursts occurred during the academic year of 1970–71 but began to fall off in the autumn of 1972, and by 1973 they were only a memory. During the height of the disturbances, the regents, under the chairmanship of Stanley F. Redeker, adopted rules for campus behavior that were probably designed more to protect the University from vindictive legislators than to clamp down on faculty and students. In the early 1970s the faculty senate adopted policies on faculty ethics, and a senate committee headed by Professors Dee Norton (psychology), William Hines (law), and James F. Curtis (speech pathology and audiology) worked for months on a statement on grievance procedures that was finally adopted and is still in force.

Today the small display windows of the bookstore across the street from the Pentacrest, installed when it became too costly to replace the large plate-glass windows shattered by rocks, are the only visible evidence of the most hectic period in the University's history. At the time the disruptions seemed alarming, but in retrospect they appear mild compared with those at such institutions as Berkeley, Columbia, Wisconsin, and, of course, Kent State. Only a small minority of students at Iowa engaged in acts of violence, and the reactions of the regents and city officials were remarkably restrained. There were no deaths or serious injuries, and the only major property loss was Old Armory Temporary.

Human Rights

President Boyd may well be remembered best for his contribution to the cause of human rights, for it was he more than any one other person who brought to the campus the national concern over human rights during the Kennedy and Johnson administrations. While still a professor in the College of Law, Boyd made his distress over discriminatory practices so evident that President Hancher in late January 1963 made him chairman of a University committee on human rights. The committee was charged with the responsibility of "marshalling the resources of the University to provide leadership in the field of human relations." It was composed of three University staff members (Boyd, Philip G. Hubbard, then of mechanics and hydraulics, and Donald B. Johnson of political science), two alumni living in Iowa City (William Nusser and Samuel Saltzman), and two students (Edward J. Bennett from Newton and Sara Elizabeth Brogan from Thornton). Conceiving of its task as considerably broader than simply responding to complaints, the committee appointed eight advisory subcommittees on consumer services, employment, housing, education, public affairs, adjudicatory procedures, research, and counseling. All but the last two of these advisory committees contained townspeople as well as faculty members. Spurred on by Boyd, the committee and the advisory groups soon tackled such sore points as University employment procedures, private information demanded by University records, discrimination against

members of minority groups by contractors working for the University and for fraternities and sororities, and, especially, discrimination in off-campus student housing. Needless to say, the activities of the committee were not universally welcomed, either on or off the campus. Even President Hancher and the registrar, Ted McCarrell, opposed recommendations that would put pressure on local landlords for more equitable treatment of minorities. Once he became provost and then president, however, Boyd increased the pressure for fairer practices with respect to women and minority groups. He strongly supported the American Civilization program, for example, when in 1969 it introduced Afro-American studies, first headed by Philip G. Hubbard and Robert Corrigan, and later by Charles Davis from Pennsylvania State and still later by Darwin T. Turner from Michigan. In 1972 American Civilization (later American Studies) also offered itself as an initial haven for women's studies, headed by Margaret McDowell, an assistant professor in rhetoric.

The organization that made the biggest impact on campus was affirmative action, the federally mandated program designed to enhance the roles of women and members of minority groups. Early on, Boyd had made the position of women and members of minority groups an important part of his committee's overall concern, but the primarily white male faculty had taken little action until forced to by the federal legislation of 1972, which required that women be treated equitably in hiring, salaries, and promotion—and sent out inspectors to see that they were. Boyd strongly supported the goals of affirmative action because, as he contended, they were morally and legally right. He delegated the administration of the program to Provost Heffner and later to Vice-President May Brodbeck and to Celia H. Foxley, its first director.

Affirmative action brought to Iowa, as well as to al-

Representatives of the Iowa NAACP address the Board of Regents, November 14, 1968. In an attempt to stop the discriminatory hiring practices of many construction firms doing business with the state's educational institutions, officials from the National Association for the Advancement of Colored People (NAACP) and the Iowa Civil Rights Commission met with the Board of Regents in November 1968.

most every other university, not only modifications of academic practices but also minor revolutions in manners (men no longer rose when a woman colleague entered the room), in language (the term *chairman* gave way to *chair*), and in salaries and promotions (at least some departments began to make fewer decisions on the basis of sex). It was fortunate for affirmative action that it had such vigorous backing from the central administration, because at Iowa, as elsewhere, it was not universally welcomed by the deans and the faculty. Many thought it scandalous that largely untrained inspectors from the federal Department of Health, Education and Welfare should have the right to tell them how to carry on their own business. What HEW called "goals," they argued, were really quotas, and "equal opportunity," was simply reverse discrimination. Celia Foxley and her successors as director of the affirmative action program tried to make the goals and procedures as palatable as possible, but they did not meet with total success. The system prevailed, however, because it had the backing of the central administration and of the federal government—and, it should be added, of many of the faculty. Over the years the percentage of women on the faculty rose perceptibly, though the percentage of members of minority groups did not keep pace, except possibly in the College of Law.

Later consequences of the human rights movement may be seen in the Afro-American Cultural Center, the Chicano/Indian American Cultural Center, the Women's Resource and Action Center, and the International and Comparative Studies Center. But the ultimate result appears in the statement on human rights carried in current University catalogs: "The University is guided by the precept that in no aspect of its program shall there be differences in the treatment of persons because of race, creed, color, national origin, age, sex, and any other classifications that deprive the person of consideration as an individual, and that equal opportunity and access to facilities shall be available to all." Although many of the faculty and staff, notably Michael J. Brody in pharmacology, George Kalnitsky in biochemistry, and Dee W. Norton in psychology contributed to the establishment of such a policy and the practices it requires, the major share of the credit for it must go to President Boyd, who demonstrated that one person can make a difference.

Construction

Bowen's presidency may be best remembered for the planning and construction that took place at the time. Twenty buildings were completed while he was in office, seven were under construction, and ten were scheduled for ground breaking. The architect's office under George L. Horner and Richard Jordison may well have been the busiest on campus, even though most of the major structures were designed by off-campus firms. The cost of the structures has been estimated at $125 million, with by far the greatest part of the money coming from the federal government, foundations, private gifts, and bonds. The program was striking not just for its size but also for its stress on architectural beauty. Bowen brought in consultants with national reputations to help him plan the campus and, ignoring the old shibboleth that the University had to use Iowa architects, sought the best architects he could find. In doing this, he relied heavily on the advice of Frank Seiberling, head of the Art Department. Bowen, it has been said, "discovered" the river, for he insisted that whenever possible new buildings be related to it. For instance, in the case of the English-Philosophy Building, Bowen had the blueprints turned around when he discovered that the archi-

tect had the stairwell end of the building facing the river and the office wing overlooking the dubious grandeur of the CRANDIC tracks.

Major buildings that were begun in the Hancher period but that were finished during Bowen's presidency were Phillips Hall (business administration), Van Allen Hall (physics), the English-Philosophy Building, and an addition to the Zoology Building. Structures begun and completed in Bowen's five years included the Agricultural Medicine Facility, the Spence Laboratories, and Carrie Stanley Hall. The ones that especially redound to his credit, however, were designed during his presidency but were finished in President Boyd's. In the arts area these included the Museum of Art and an addition to the Art Building, the Music Building, Clapp Recital Hall, and Hancher Auditorium, all designed by Harrison and Abramovitz of New York. In the science area were the Basic Sciences Building (now the Bowen Science Building) and the Health Sciences Library, both designed by Walter Netsch of Skidmore, Owings, and Merrill of Chicago; the Nursing Building, designed by George Herbert and Associates of Des Moines; and the Dental Science Building, designed by Smith, Hinchman, and Grylls of Detroit.

Dormitories were a special problem during the Bowen years. At first they were in such short supply that students had to be turned away because there were literally no beds for them in Iowa City or Coralville. Carrie Stanley Hall was rushed to completion for single women, Rienow I for single men, and Hawkeye Court Apartments for couples, and other residence halls were contemplated. Unanticipated by the administration, however, enrollment did not continue to increase at the same rate, and developers crowded Iowa City, Coralville, and the environs with private apartments, the largest being the Mayflower on North Dubuque Street, now owned by the University. Attracted by the more independent

Interior court, Bowen Science Building, 1972. Howard R. Bowen was a strong supporter of the sciences, and among the many buildings constructed during his presidency were the Spence Laboratories of Psychology, Van Allen Hall, and a six-story building for the basic sciences. Known now as the Bowen Science Building, it houses the Departments of Anatomy, Biochemistry, Microbiology, Pharmacology, *Physiology, and Biophysics, and the Animal Care Unit. Much of the funding for the Bowen Science Building came from a 1967 National Science Foundation (NSF) grant of $5.1 million, which was part of the NSF's program to develop Centers of Excellence around the country. The grant money also helped to fund forty new faculty and support staff positions, thirty graduate assistantships, and new equipment.*

living available in private housing, students left the dormitories in such numbers that the administration was faced with the possibility that there might not be enough income to pay the interest on the bonds. Plans for additional housing were shelved and Rienow II (now Slater) was built only because the regents overruled Bowen's recommendation that it, too, be put aside. The dormitories refilled only after the regents required freshmen, and briefly some sophomores, to live in them. Also, to make them more attractive the regents permitted men and women students to live in the same building. Formerly there had been so much concern over the proper behavior of the students that not only were there separate dormitories for men and women but they were kept on opposite sides of the river, the women on the east side and the men on the west.

Major structures that were designed and constructed during the Boyd presidency were the Lindquist Center (education and the computer center), and the Carver-Hawkeye Arena. The construction work nearest the heart of President Boyd, however, was the renovation of Old Capitol under the direction of Professor Margaret N. Keyes, with Mrs. Virgil M. Hancher as head of the Restoration Committee. The work began in 1970 and ended in 1976 in time for the renovated building to be the University's contribution to the United States Bicentennial. The U.S. Department of the Interior has since designated it a Historic Landmark. The restoration was unique in that it returned the building to three periods of its life, one part as it was in territorial times, one as it was in early state government times, and one as it was about 1920, when the University used it as an office and classroom building.

Construction during the Freedman presidency included the Communication Studies Building, containing state-of-the-art broadcasting equipment; the Willard L. Boyd

Law Building, which finally gave the College of Law the library space that it had always needed; and the Colloton Pavilion, Phase B, another handsome addition to the bewilderment of wings and towers that make up the main hospital. Near the stadium rose the Indoor Practice Facility, designed to keep football coach Hayden Fry and his talented athletes out of the cold and wet, and in the center of the campus the Iowa Memorial Union was once more being renovated. Construction of the Human Biology Research Facility, a major addition to the medical complex, got well under way. In brief, the campus between 1964 and 1987 acquired a physical complexity and yet an architectural interest that was undreamed of in previous years.

Planning the restoration of Old Capitol, 1972; left to right: Margaret Keyes (home economics), Mrs. Virgil M. Hancher, and President Boyd.

Duane C. Spriestersbach

When Willard Boyd left Iowa on September 1, 1980, the regents appointed Duane C. Spriestersbach, the vice-president for educational development and research and graduate dean, to be acting president. Spriestersbach needed no learning period. He had come up the University ladder, first as a graduate student and a faculty member in speech pathology and audiology, and then as graduate dean and finally also as vice-president, in which job he presided over seventeen University offices and more than thirty committees. As expected, then, he turned out to be no casual interim appointee. In his first meeting with the faculty he delivered a long speech in which he identified the major issues facing the University and suggested the actions necessary if the institution were to "keep humming." To the delight of the faculty and students, he kept it humming. To help him he appointed James Johnson, director of the Weeg Computing Center, as special assistant to the president

Duane C. Spriestersbach (center), acting president, 1981–82, chairs a meeting in Gilmore Hall, March 1982. Left to right: John Simmons (University of Iowa Press), Don McQuillen (publications),

Dwight Jensen (Office of Public Information), Spriestersbach, Mary Jane McLaughlin (Division of Sponsored Programs), Peter Husak (Business Office), Charles Mason (Graduate College).

James O. Freedman, sixteenth president, 1982–87.

for information and communication policy. In addition, he worked especially hard for a supplementary appropriation to make faculty salaries more competitive, to give fiscal stability to the College of Medicine, and to strengthen student aid and library acquisitions. Not normally given to attending football games, he took a ribbing from his friends when as acting president he and his wife had to put in an appearance at the Rose Bowl on New Year's Day, 1982. As his friends tell it, he became one of the most rabid Hawkeye fans. After Freedman was appointed president, Spriestersbach returned to his multiple duties as vice-president. He was due to retire at the end of June 1987, and was even about to go through the rigors of a farewell banquet, when the regents asked him to continue another year as vice-president because both President Freedman and Dorsey Ellis, vice-president for finance and university services, had unexpectedly resigned, and the central administration seemed to be melting away. Spriestersbach attended his farewell banquet—even sang at it—and started immediately to take charge of his offices and committees once more.

James O. Freedman

James O. Freedman brought a fresh point of view to the University. Ivy League all the way, he was a native of New Hampshire and had earned a bachelor's degree cum laude at Harvard in 1957 and an LL.B. from Yale Law School in 1962. Then, after serving briefly as a clerk for Supreme Court associate justice Thurgood Marshall, he taught in the law school at the University of Pennsylvania for eighteen years. For three of those years he was also the law school dean. He came to Iowa as president on April 1, 1982, and immediately showed himself to be a man of great energy and resourcefulness, one who impressed people both on and off campus as totally committed to building the quality and influence of the University. But though he maintained that he was sinking his roots in Iowa, it became clear that he had deeper roots in New Hampshire when he left Iowa for the presidency of Dartmouth College on July 1, 1987.

Freedman had some rough days as president. He arrived when Iowa was in the second year of its worst economic slump since the early 1930s. Farm prices were down, farms were being foreclosed, and the legislators had once more grown especially cautious about doling out funds for higher education. During his first years, Freedman, despite a supportive Board of Regents, saw faculty salaries remain at or near the bottom of the Big Ten schools. Then in May 1985 students held a sit-in, demanding divestment of Iowa's stock in companies doing business in South Africa. Tuition increases angered the students still more. And although enrollment climbed to over 29,000, there was little increase in the size of the permanent faculty.

Undeterred, Freedman turned to private funding for the "margin of distinction" that he believed Iowa needed to make it one of the twenty-five most distinguished universities in the country, public or private. In May 1983 he made a proposal to the members of the board of the University of Iowa Foundation that left them gasping. What he requested was $100 million or more by the year 2000 for senior and junior professorships, graduate student fellowships, and an interdisciplinary center for advanced study. Later he added to his plans for what became known as Iowa Endowment 2000 an international emphasis as well as an emphasis on what the University could do to enhance the state's economy. Always the key words were *quality* and *excellence.*

The emphasis on academic excellence became apparent in tighter admissions standards, a president's list for straight-A students, and at least seven new categories of scholarships and fellowships designed to encourage students to work up to their capacities. Top awards won by students were widely publicized: two Rhodes scholarships, three Truman scholarships, a Marshall scholarship, and awards from *Time*, the National Research Council, the National Science Foundation, and the Mellon Humanities Foundation.

During the Freedman presidency the University became more internationally oriented. It strengthened its international course offerings, added to its centers for international study, and increased the number of exchange agreements with foreign universities. A two-million-dollar gift from the Stanley family in Muscatine made possible a Center for Asian and Pacific Studies, and a half-million-dollar grant from the Ford Foundation resulted in an innovative Critical Language Program to train high school teachers of Chinese, Japanese, and Russian. Along with Dean Gerhard Loewenberg of the College of Liberal Arts and Robert Leutner, an associate professor of Asian languages and literature, Freedman traveled to the People's Republic of China in the spring of 1987 to sign agreements for student and faculty exchanges. Between 1982 and 1987 the registration of foreign students had risen from 1,357 to 1,874.

Freedman also took a leading role in relating the work of the University more closely to the social and economic needs of the state. With his support, the University strengthened its Small Business Development Center, established a Technology Innovation Center, and developed plans to use the University's share of the state's lottery proceeds to support areas of emerging knowledge. And the approval by the legislature and governor of a $25.1 million bond issue for a Center for Laser Science and Engineering promised many new possibilities for research and for practical applications of that research.

Internal changes included enhanced support for the University of Iowa Press, directed by Paul Zimmer, and the establishment of the Center for the Book, a program in bookmaking and book restoration directed by K. K. Merker. Introduced also were a Presidential Lecture Series for distinguished members of the faculty to report on significant aspects of their work, an annual faculty convocation to recognize faculty awards, and a spring buffet to honor members of the University staff for meritorious service. New key appointments by Freedman were Richard D. Remington (vice-president for academic affairs and dean of faculties), Dorsey D. Ellis (vice-president for finance and university services), George Daly (dean of the College of Business Administration), Gerhard Loewenberg (dean of the College of Liberal Arts), Robert S. Wiley (dean of the College of Pharmacy), and Emmett K. Vaughn (dean of the Division of Continuing Education). In addition, he appointed Sheila Creth as University librarian. Vice-President Remington became interim president after the resignation of President Freedman, while Samuel Becker and his search committee sought a new chief executive.

Athletics

Iowa's football fortunes once again declined in the 1960s and 1970s, and football fans were forced to live off memories of the Evashevski years until the early 1980s. Jerry Burns, later head coach of the NFL's Minnesota Vikings, took over from Evashevski in 1961; in Burns's first season the team went 5–4, the last winning season the Hawkeyes would see until 1981. Burns was followed by Ray Nagel (1966–70) and Frank X. Lauterbur (1971–73), under whom the football team hit bottom in 1973 with a record of 0–11. The next head coach was Bob Commings (1974–78), an ex-Hawkeye who had been the team's most valuable player in 1957. While the brand of football played at Iowa in the 1960s and 1970s was not what fans had become accustomed to under Evashevski, a number of future professionals played for the Hawkeyes, among them John Niland, Craig Clemons, Wally Hilgenberg, Ed Podolak, John Harty, and Joe Devlin.

Hayden Fry came to Iowa in 1979, and in his third year coached Iowa to an 8–4 record. It was the first winning season in twenty years, and it concluded with a trip to the Rose Bowl on January 1, 1982. Since then, Iowa has gone to a bowl game every year: the Peach Bowl (1982), the Gator Bowl (1983), the Freedom Bowl (1984), the Rose Bowl (1986), and the Holiday Bowl (1986). Among the notable players from this era were Andre Tippett, Mark Bortz, Reggie Roby, Jay Hilgenberg, Ronnie Harmon, Mike Haight, and Chuck Long.

Iowa's basketball team fared well during this period. Ralph Miller, who coached the team from 1965 to 1970, saw his last team go undefeated in the Big Ten and average over 100 points per game. Miller was followed by Dick Schultz (1971–74) and Lute Olson (1974–82). Olson's last four teams won at least twenty games per season, and each was invited to an NCAA tournament. George Raveling arrived in 1983 to stay three years and twice took the team to the NCAA tournament. In the spring of 1986 Tom Davis replaced Raveling. His players began the season by winning eighteen straight games and earning the top spot in national polls. The team, which won thirty games (a school record), advanced in the NCAA tournament to the West Regional Finals where in April 1987 it lost to the University of Nevada/Las Vegas, 84–81. Among the standout players from this

NCAA record crowd, Carver-Hawkeye Arena, February 3, 1985. On February 3, 1985, 22,157 fans squeezed into the Carver-Hawkeye Arena to watch the Iowa women's basketball team play Ohio State. The crowd, almost 7,000 larger than the arena's listed capacity, was by far the largest ever to watch a women's collegiate game. That year the Iowa women, coached by C. Vivian Stringer, had their first twenty-win season, and they followed that with twenty-two victories in 1985–86. The 1986–87 sea-son was better still. Iowa fin-ished tied for the Big Ten title (with Ohio State), won two NCAA tournament games be-fore losing by a point to even-tual national runner-up Loui-siana Tech in the NCAA Southeast Regional Final. The Iowa women finished the year at 26–5 and were ranked in the top ten nationally.

Wrestling coach Dan Gable puts a headlock on assistant J Robinson during a match against Oklahoma State, 1982. Dan Gable is a legend in the world of amateur wrestling. During his student days at Iowa State he won 100 straight matches, losing only his last collegiate match in the 1970 NCAA Finals. In 1972 he won a gold medal in the Olympics. Gable was Gary Kurdelmeier's assistant in 1975–76, when Iowa won its first NCAA wres-tling championship, and head coach the next year, when Iowa won its second title. In 1977 Iowa State won the NCAA championship, but starting in 1978 Iowa won an unprecedented nine straight NCAA wrestling champion-ships, a streak broken in 1987, when Iowa finished as runner-up to an Iowa State team whose assistant coach was Ed Banach, a three-time NCAA champion for Gable. Under Gable the Iowa wrestlers have had a remarkable 201-9-2 rec-ord in dual meets since the 1976–77 season.

era were Bruce "Sky" King, Candy LaPrince, Kevin Kunnert, John Johnson, Fred Brown, Ronnie Lester, Greg Stokes, Scott Thompson, and Bob Hansen.

Though none of them quite match up to the NCAA championship teams of the years from 1978 to 1986, Iowa had some very good wrestling teams before Dan Gable arrived. From 1947 until 1975 (the year Iowa won its first NCAA wrestling title), the wrestlers finished in the top ten at the NCAA tournament seventeen times. Since 1975 Iowa has had the best collegiate wrestling team in eleven of thirteen years, finishing third in 1977 and second in 1987. The program has produced well over a hundred all-Americans.

Iowa has produced some notable competitors in other sports as well. Its men's gymnastics team was ranked in the top ten nationally for four straight years beginning in 1984; an Iowa golfer, Dave Rummells, went on the PGA Tour; former Iowa baseball players such as pitcher Mike Boddicker and catcher Jim Sundberg joined the major leagues; and the men's swimming team was ranked in the top twenty nationally four times between 1981 and 1987.

The rise in women's sports at Iowa has been nothing short of extraordinary. Much of the success of women's field hockey, swimming, track, basketball, and other sports in the 1980s can be attributed to Christine Grant, who became Iowa's first women's athletic director in 1973. Grant started with a modest budget of $30,000 and began to build. By 1985–86 the budget had grown to $2.4 million, and a number of teams had earned high national rankings. The swimming team, coached by Pete Kennedy, went from ninth in the Big Ten in 1981 to second in 1986. The women's softball team under Ginny Parrish had its first better than .500 season in 1983 and the following year had a new facility, the four-diamond

Hawkeye Softball Complex. Judith Davidson's field-hockey team has been a national power for a decade, and after finishing as runner-up two years earlier, won the NCAA championship in 1986—the first in Iowa women's sports history, though Iowa women have been competing in the NCAA only since 1982—with a 2–1 double-overtime victory over the University of New Hampshire. In track, Nan Doak was the NCAA 10,000-meter run champion in 1985. The women's basketball program moved ahead with the hiring of C. Vivian Stringer as head coach in 1983. Beginning in 1984–85 the team won at least twenty games a year, advanced to the NCAA Southeast Regional Final in 1987, and earned a top-ten ranking for the first time in Iowa women's basketball history.

English Composition

The repeated complaint that "Johnny can't write" cannot be laid at the door of the University of Iowa, for Iowa has long been recognized as a center for the teaching of composition and the training of teachers of composition. Since the days of Clark Ansley and Percival Hunt early in the century, Iowa has had many fine instructors in composition, such as Carrie Stanley, Alma B. Hovey, and Richard Braddock.

In the early 1940s Stanley opened a writing laboratory for students with special difficulties. Her one-on-one type of instruction proved so successful that writing laboratories and clinics soon sprang up in other institutions. After Stanley retired, Lou Kelly took over the laboratory with a zeal that made it even more influential. In 1944 Iowa and Michigan State were the first schools to introduce a communication skills program that combined training in both writing and speech. This type of training continued at Iowa after the term *communication skills* gave way to *rhetoric.*

The outreach of Iowa's work in composition made it especially noteworthy. In 1950 the leaders in the Iowa program were the prime movers in establishing the Conference on College Composition and Communication, now a national organization with over five thousand members. In 1966 and 1967, with funds from the National Defense Education Act, the English Department and the Rhetoric Program jointly sponsored two institutes under the leadership of Professor Carl Klaus for directors of college composition programs. Then from 1977 to 1984, with a large grant from the National Endowment for the Humanities and again with Klaus as director, English and Rhetoric sponsored two other institutes for directors of freshman programs. This time the participants had to study for six months on the Iowa campus, plan and put into effect composition programs on their own campuses, and have the results reviewed and evaluated by Klaus and his aides. The best of the programs were described in *Courses for Change in Writing* (1984), a book that won the Mina Shaughnessy Award of the Modern Language Association as the best book of the year on the teaching of writing. Aiding Klaus during the seven-year project were Professors Richard Lloyd-Jones, Paul Diehl, David Hamilton, Lou Kelly, Cleo Martin, and, as an assistant on the book, Nancy Jones.

Grade school and high school teachers of composition were not neglected. Continued consultation on an informal basis was formalized in 1978 when Professor Cleo Martin from the Rhetoric Program and James F. Davis from the Grant Wood Area Education Agency organized the Southeast Iowa Writing Project, a three-week summer workshop at the University for teachers of writing in the public schools. This regional project became so popular that it soon expanded into the Iowa Writing Project, with over two dozen summer workshops scattered throughout the state and financed chiefly by local school districts.

The Arts

As one of the chief beneficiaries of the building program, the departments in the Center for the Arts prospered mightily during the 1970s and 1980s. For dramatic arts and music the addition to the University Theatre and the Music Building provided much-needed space for teaching, rehearsing, and performing, and the Halsey Gymnasium did the same for the dance program. Students and faculty of all the fine arts departments, and the general public as well, had their lives enriched by the new Museum of Art and Hancher Auditorium. To go with the new buildings, the center, under the direction of Philip Hubbard, developed a vigorous and imaginative faculty. Taking advantage of the work done by such earlier heads as Frank Seiberling in art and Himie Voxman in music, the new heads—Wallace Tomasini in art and art history, Robert Hedley and Cosmo Catalano in theater, Marilyn Somville in music, Judy Allen and Alicia Brown in dance—gave new force to Iowa's already-strong reputation in the arts.

Moreover, with magnificent gifts from the Owen Elliotts of Cedar Rapids, the Nathaniel Alcocks of Iowa City, the David Stanleys of Muscatine, and many others, Ulfert Wilke and his successors, Jan Muhlert and Robert C. Hobbs, continued to build the Museum of Art into one of the finest university museums in the country. When Hobbs resigned in 1986, Charles Davidson (law)

Museum of Art, 1969. In 1962 Owen and Leone Elliott of Cedar Rapids told Professor Frank Seiberling that they would give their extraordinary collection of modern art to the University of Iowa, but only on the condition that suitable housing be provided. The offer of the Elliotts' collection—seventy paintings, including works by Matisse, Kandinsky, Munch, and Goya; over one thousand prints; a large collection of French, English, and Irish silver; and several exquisite jade carvings—led to the University of Iowa Foundation's first fund drive and to the opening of the Museum of Art in 1969. The museum's first director was Ulfert Wilke, an art collector and artist known for his calligraphic drawings and lithographs.

University Symphony premiere, Hancher Auditorium, October 30, 1972. Though not opposed to the idea of an auditorium, President Hancher never proposed to the regents that funds, either public or private, be sought for such a project. President Bowen was the one who started the project, and President Boyd infused new life into the fund drive when it later began to falter. With the opening of Hancher Auditorium on October 30, 1972, the University gained the large-scale performance hall envisioned for the arts complex since the 1930s. Designed by the architectural firm of Harrison & Abramovitz (who also designed the University's Museum of Art), Hancher has 2,680 seats, none of which is more than 125 feet from the stage. The extraordinary acoustics and computerized lighting system have enhanced the pleasure of those who since 1972 have seen a rich assortment of internationally prominent artists perform on Hancher's stage. On opening night, conductor James Dixon and the University Symphony performed pieces by Brahms and Mahler and gave a world premiere to Charles Wuorinen's Grand Bamboula for String Orchestra.

became the acting head, and he was followed in 1987 by Fredrick Woodard, the associate dean of faculties.

The flagship of the center was Hancher Auditorium, which since its opening in 1972 has brought a steady stream of fine performers to the campus. Its first director, James Wockenfuss, began breathtakingly by scheduling such entertainment as Vladimir Horowitz and the Boston Symphony, but as the costs for such events skyrocketed he had to adjust his programs to the constraints of the budget. Nevertheless, the events brought to Iowa City by Wockenfuss and his successor, Wallace Chappell, have been brilliant and varied, often dazzling. For the 1987–88 season alone Chappell scheduled over three dozen events, including the Joffrey Ballet in their world premiere of *The Nutcracker*, the Chamber Music Society of Lincoln Center, the Royal Philharmonic, directed by André Previn, and *Big River*, the musical based on *Huckleberry Finn*. Chappell gave broad appeal to his programs by adding younger artists and foreign troupes. He also eased tensions within the center by working agreeably with the heads of the performing arts departments and with Mary Louise Plautz, whose outreach activities each year involved over 70,000 individuals, many of them grade school and high school students.

Programs in the literary arts experienced a boost in the mid-1960s when they were given control over their own curriculums and activities in the resuscitated School of Letters, directed by John C. Gerber. These included not only the Writers' Workshop, Comparative Literature, and Linguistics (later a department), but also such newer programs as the International Writing Program, directed by Paul and Hua Ling Nieh Engle; the Translation Workshop, by Daniel Weissbort; the Playwriting Workshop, by Oscar Brownstein and later by Robert Hedley; the program in Modern Letters, by William Murray; the Center for Textual Studies, by Paul Baender;

the Windhover Press, by K. K. Merker; and the *Iowa Review*, by Merle Brown and later by Thomas Whitaker and David Hamilton. In 1976 Richard Lloyd-Jones became director of the School of Letters.

One of the happy results of such a bursting of activities in the arts was that Iowa Citians could stun most New Yorkers by remarking—with studied casualness, of course—that they had had dinner with Horowitz, enjoyed a poolside buffet with Seiji Ozawa, and shared an outdoor picnic with the Joffrey dancers, not to mention entertaining such writers as John Cheever and Anthony Burgess on many occasions.

Teaching and Research

However crucial the role of the administration in the life of a university, it is the faculty that carries out the institution's dual functions of creating and transmitting knowledge. The faculty are the teachers and researchers, and they have the greatest effect on the students.

The University of Iowa has been fortunate in having a long tradition of fine teaching, which began in the nineteenth century with teachers such as Nathan R. Leonard and the feisty Gustavus Hinrichs, and continued into the twentieth century with C. C. Nutting, Thomas A. Macbride, and the flamboyant Benjamin Shambaugh. More recently there were such superior scholar-teachers as James N. Murray and Allan D. Vestal. These and the scores who were their equals were not only masters of their subjects but presenters who could stir the minds of the students and tantalize their imaginations. To the relative certainties of the known they added the mysteries and excitement of the unknown.

In research, especially since World War II, the faculty

has steadily enhanced the reputation of the University and kept the students aware of the newest revelations of scholarly and scientific investigation. Possibly the figures for outside funding offer the best measure of the institution's progress in research. In 1975, for example, the University received $16,645,000 in federal research and development support, and it was fortieth among universities receiving such support. In 1984 it received $48,378,000 and had moved up to thirty-first position. From 1966 to 1986, external funds from all sources (the federal government, foundations, corporations, and individuals) amounted to over $1 billion, and in 1986–87 for the first time such funds topped $100 million in a single fiscal year. Of these funds, at least 70 percent was earmarked for research.

Of funds intended for research, less than a fourth went for projects outside the physical and biological sciences. Researchers in the social sciences, education, and law did receive a sizable number of grants, but those in such fields as history, English, and art history acquired relatively few, partly because the sources for external funds for those departments were limited and partly because they needed less outside support for their kinds of studies. Their commitment to research was nevertheless firm.

Primarily, though, Iowa's reputation as a research university developed as a result of the investigations in the physical and biological sciences, including the medical sciences. Two programs outdistanced all others in generating external funds: the investigations into outer space of James Van Allen and his colleagues, and those dealing with the cardiovascular system by Dr. Francis N. Abboud and his colleagues. By 1987 outside support for Van Allen's work amounted to $6 million annually. External support for Dr. Abboud's Cardiovascular Center, created

in 1972, had by 1987 paid the salaries of close to two hundred faculty and professional and technical employees, had provided for the training of almost three hundred postdoctoral fellows from sixteen participating departments, and had paid for the building of a home for the center by the addition of fifth and sixth floors to the Medical Research Center. By 1987 the center's external support for research and training amounted to $13 million annually.

In the late 1960s and early 1970s, a total of $6.7 million from the National Science Foundation funded a Center of Excellence in the biological sciences. Fields that especially benefited were endocrinology, neurobiology, and genetics, and also helped were the anatomy, biochemistry, biology, botany, microbiology, pharmacology, physiology, and psychology departments. In the 1980s, projects attracting special attention included Drs. Antonio and Hanna Damasio's interdisciplinary center for the study of Alzheimer's disease; the studies of Kathleen Buckwalter (nursing) on aging (including Alzheimer's), that of Dr. Christopher A. Squier (dentistry) on a dental scientist training program, and that of John Lach (pharmacy) on dosage. In the applied sciences there were, to name only a few, R. Rajagopal's work on groundwater quality in Iowa, Eric H. Christiansen's on water channels on Mars, Edward Haug's on computer-assisted design, and John F. Kennedy's on dropshaft systems for storm runoff water. The list of projects in the basic and applied sciences undertaken in the 1980s is so long that it convincingly demonstrates that there had been a strong tilt in the University toward the natural sciences, both basic and applied. It is not surprising, therefore, that the next two major buildings on the campus were to be the Human Biology Research Facility and the Center for Laser Science and Engineering.

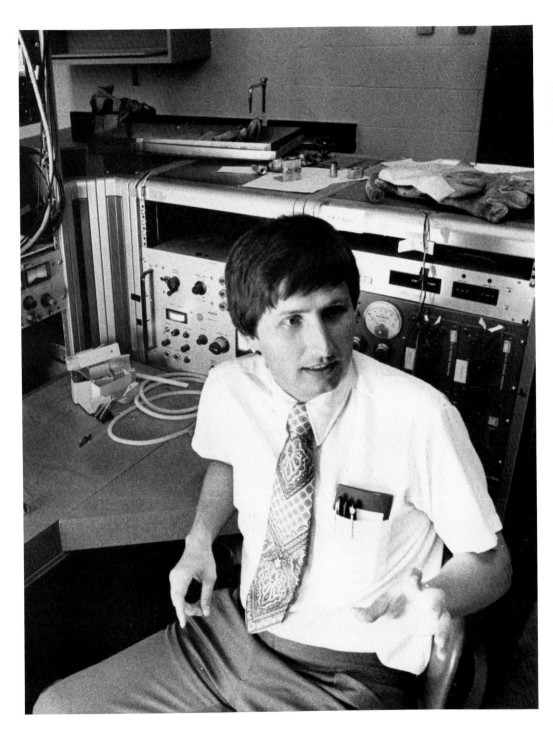

William Stwalley in the laser laboratory. The University's laser facility was established in 1979 to make laser-based technology readily available for such disciplines as medicine and engineering. The facility has assisted in bone research holography, in ophthalmology, and in the development of highly efficient sodium lamps. In 1987 a bill was passed by the Iowa legislature approving a bond issue of $25.1 million for the construction of a laser center on campus, which would bring together the Departments of Chemistry and Physics and the College of Engineering to conduct research and provide training in the application of laser technology.

The University of Iowa Foundation and Iowa Endowment 2000

Established in 1956 (when it was known as the Old Gold Development Fund), the University of Iowa Foundation has in recent years raised money for student scholarships, faculty development and research, laboratory equipment, and, of course, buildings. The Museum of Art (1969), the Health Sciences Library (1974), the restoration of Old Capitol (1976), the Cardiovascular Center (1982), Carver-Hawkeye Arena and the Field House renovation (1983), Iowa Hall in the Museum of Natural History (1985)—these are only some of the many capital projects made possible by the fund-raising efforts of Darrell D. Wyrick and the University of Iowa Foundation, which he directs. In 1986 the foundation received a record $43.8 million in gifts and future commitments from nearly 40,000 contributors living in all fifty states and in fifteen foreign countries.

The most ambitious effort undertaken by the foundation was the fund-raising campaign called "Iowa Endowment 2000, A Covenant with Quality." Assigned to the foundation by President Freedman, this was a campaign to raise $100 million for an endowment to create faculty chairs and graduate fellowships and an interdisciplinary center for advanced study. Marvin A. Pomerantz of Des Moines agreed to chair the drive. By May 8, 1987, when the campaign premiere was held in Hancher Auditorium, the foundation had already raised $51 million and the goal had been raised to $150 million.

Among the earliest gifts were those from the Elizabeth M. and C. Maxwell Stanley family in Muscatine for a Center for Asian and Pacific Studies, from the Iowa Alumni Association for a chair of liberal arts, from the Pomerantzes and Henry B. Tippie of Austin, Texas, for

Human Biology Research Facility, under construction, 1987. After ten years of planning, ground was finally broken for the Human Biology Research Facility in 1986. The $26 million, five-story building, paid for by private gifts and the nonprofit Iowa Facilities Corporation, should help keep the University competitive in the fight to attract research grants.

two chairs in business administration, from the Maytag Corporation of Newton for ten fellowships in the Writers' Workshop, and from the Grain Processing Corporation, Kent Feeds, and American Seeds of Muscatine for the James O. Freedman Chair in Letters. With the work of the foundation and the help of such friends as these, the University was indeed entering into a covenant with quality.

Gentle Thursday, May 1969. The "happenings" of the 1960s were not always angry. The first Gentle Thursday, on May 11, 1967, was declared a day of "gentleness, love, peace, and happiness." Sidewalks, Volkswagens, and bodies were painted with flowers and peace symbols, candy and hallucinogens were handed out, and thousands went to the Pentacrest to hear poet Allen Ginsberg read from his work and recite a ten-minute Buddhist chant.

Thieves' Market along the river near the Iowa Memorial Union, early 1970s.

Muhammad Ali speaking at the Iowa Memorial Union, 1969. A parade of nationally known speakers passed through the Union in the late 1960s, among them Dick Gregory, Ralph Nader, Jane Fonda, Julian Bond, Bernadette Devlin, William Kunstler, Alvin Toffler, John Kenneth Galbraith, and Gloria Steinem.

Commencement protest, June 7, 1968. Wanda Kaczynski (left) and Miss University of Iowa, Heidi Keir, were two of over four hundred graduating seniors who carried white crosses to protest the war in Vietnam during commencement ceremonies held at the Field House.

President Bowen concludes his address at services to honor Martin Luther King, April 9, 1968.

Head football coach Ray Nagel (left) and assistant coach Frank Gilliam at spring football practice, 1969. The 1969 football season began in controversy when sixteen of twenty black team members walked out of spring practice to protest what they considered to be discriminatory treatment in the program. After some candid discussion, most of the players rejoined the team for the fall season. The Hawkeyes posted a 5-5-1 record in 1969, a notable achievement in the lean years between 1962 and 1981, when no Iowa football team managed a winning season.

Fred Brown (32) shoots over Purdue's Rick Mount (10) as John Johnson (50) positions for a rebound during a game at the Field House, January 3, 1970. Iowa won 94–88 despite Mount's 53 points. After losing four of their first seven games, the 1969–70 Hawkeyes embarked on a sixteen-game winning streak, which ended at the NCAA Mideast Regional in a 104–103 loss to Jacksonville. The highest-scoring team in Iowa basketball history, the 1969–70 Hawkeyes had five players who averaged in double figures. John Johnson, who played eleven years in the NBA, led the way (27.9 points per game), followed by Chad Calabria (19.1), Fred Brown (17.9, later a star with the Seattle Supersonics), Glenn Vidnovic (17.3), and Ben McGilmer (10.3). Coached by Ralph Miller (in his last year at Iowa), the team went undefeated in Big Ten play, averaging 103 points per game, and was 20–5 on the season. In the consolation game of the NCAA Mideast Regional, Iowa scored more points than any other team in University history when it beat Notre Dame, 121–106.

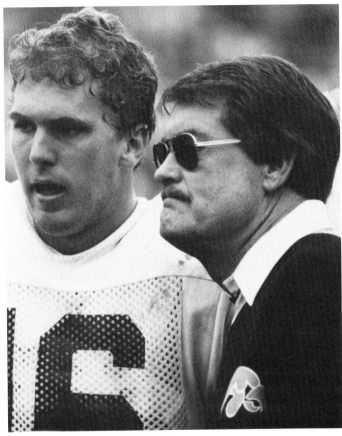

Celebration for the "Fabulous Few," Field House, March 1980. In the 1979–80 basketball season, Iowa finished at 19–10 but was still invited to the NCAA tournament. Coached by Lute Olson and led by Ronnie Lester, Kevin Boyle, Kenny Arnold, Steve Waite, Steve Krafcisin, and Vince Brookins, the team advanced to the East Regional Final in Philadelphia, where they stunned Georgetown, 81–80. Trailing by fourteen points at the half, Iowa made all fifteen of its free throws in the second half (and nineteen of twenty in the game), shot 70.8 from the field, and committed only one turnover. The victory put the Hawkeyes into the Final Four for the first time since 1956. Even though they lost to Louisville, the eventual national champion, in the semifinal by a score of 80–72, the road to that game was a memorable one for many Iowa fans.

Quarterback Chuck Long and Coach Hayden Fry confer on the sidelines, Iowa vs. Purdue, November 1985. When Hayden Fry took over in 1979 as head football coach, Iowa had not had a winning season in eighteen years. In 1981 Iowa went 8–3 and represented the Big Ten in the Rose Bowl. In the years that followed, Iowa once again became a national power, and one of the principal reasons was the play of Chuck Long. By the end of his colle- giate career in 1985, Long held the Big Ten career mark for passing yardage (10,142), and virtually every school record related to passing. In the 1984 Freedom Bowl, perhaps his finest performance in any game, Long completed twenty-nine of thirty-nine passes for 461 yards and six touchdowns as Iowa beat Texas, 55–17. A first-round draft choice in 1986, Long was selected by the Detroit Lions.

Iowa scores at the Peach Bowl in Atlanta, December 31, 1982. Iowa went on to defeat Tennessee, 28–22.

Michelle Murgatroyd (left) attacks the goal against Northwestern during a field hockey match at Kinnick Stadium, October 1985. In her nine years as head coach of women's field hockey, Judith Davidson's teams produced five Big Ten titles, thirty all-Americans, and an overall record of 168-47-14. Iowa has also made postseason tournament appearances every year since Davidson's arrival. In 1984 the team placed second in the NCAA tournament and won the National Indoor Field Hockey Championship. In 1986 the field hockey team won the first national title in Iowa women's sports history, beating New Hampshire 2–1 in double overtime.

The renovated Field House, 1985. After serving for over half a century as the home for many of the University's intercollegiate sports and endless intramural activity, the Field House was due for major renovation in the early 1980s. Work began in 1983 when the new Carver-Hawkeye Arena was completed. Funding for both projects came from the Hawkeye Arena/Recreation Campaign, conducted by the University of Iowa Foundation and 3,200 volunteers. Eighteen months and $7 million later, the Field House was almost entirely new from the walls in. Dedicated anew in 1985, the Field House has basketball, racquetball, handball, and squash courts, a weight room, a special activity area for the handicapped, a swimming pool, and a one-tenth-mile jogging track above the main floor.

Indoor Practice Facility, 1985. The facility is used by men's football and baseball, and by women's softball and field hockey.

Roy Carver (1909–81). Of all the men and women who have given to the University, few if any have given more than Roy Carver, who in 1957 founded Bandag, a Muscatine-based tire retreading company. Carver contributed substantially to a number of building projects at the University; those that bear his name include the three-story Carver Pavilion at the University Hospitals, the Carver Wing of the Museum of Art, and the Carver-Hawkeye Arena. Carver also funded the Green Room in Hancher Auditorium and the artificial turf in Kinnick Stadium, helped with the Bicentennial renovation of Old Capitol, and—a great wrestling fan—supported the Hawkeye Wrestling Club. All told, he gave nearly $10 million to the University, though he was an alumnus of the University of Illinois. In 1972 Carver was awarded the University of Iowa Distinguished Service Award.

Governor Robert Ray stands at left while Simon Estes sings at the rededication of Old Capitol, July 3, 1976. Estes graduated from Centerville (Iowa) High School in 1956, came to the University of Iowa on a partial athletic scholarship, and was a member of the freshman basketball team. While a member of the Old Gold Singers, however, he attracted the attention of voice coach Charles Kellis, with whom Estes began to refine his talent. In 1963 Estes spent a year at Juilliard, in 1964 he went to Europe, and in 1966 he won a silver medal in the Tchaikovsky International Vocal Contest. Known particularly for his roles in Wagner's Tannhaüser *and* The Flying Dutchman, *Estes eventually joined the Metropolitan Opera. There he has sung virtually all the bass-baritone opera roles, including a widely acclaimed performance as Porgy in the New York Metropolitan Opera's four-hour 1985 production of Gershwin's* Porgy and Bess. *Estes has returned to Iowa many times to perform, and in recognition of his contributions to the University, he was in 1986 awarded the Hancher-Finkbine Medallion.*

Center for New Music rehearsal, 1969. Established to support musical composition through performance, the Center for New Music opened in 1966 under the direction of Richard Hervig, with the support of a $100,000 grant from the Rockefeller Foundation. In the twenty-one years since its founding the center has been awarded the Commendation of Excellence, usually given to composers, from Broadcast Music Inc. and has performed modern works by such composers as Charles Wuorinen, Anton Webern, Milton Babbitt, Edgard Varèse, and George Crumb.

Opera theater director Beaumont Glass and student, 1981. As director of the Zurich Opera in Switzerland, Beaumont Glass worked frequently with Simon Estes, and it was on Estes's recommendation that Glass came to Iowa in 1980 as director of the Opera Production Unit. Among the major operas staged by Glass have been Boris Godunov, The Magic Flute, The Barber of Seville, *and* Agrippina. *All of Glass's work has involved great attention to detail, as is evident from this photograph, taken at rehearsals for his first production at Iowa,* The Cunning Little Vixen, *when he was showing a student precisely how to move like a squirrel.*

Joffrey II dancers perform in front of Hancher Auditorium, July 4, 1985. Dr. Lewis January was so pleased to see the Joffrey Ballet's first performance in Iowa City in 1974 that he immediately formed the Iowa Friends of the Joffrey. January, a cardiologist and devoted dance patron, had supported the Joffrey since the late 1960s, serving first as a member of the National Committee for the Joffrey and later as a member of the board of directors of the Foundation for the Joffrey. The enthusiasm of January and other Iowans led to the company's Joffrey II dancers coming to Iowa for residencies at the University in 1982, 1983, 1985, and 1987, when they also performed in *such communities as Tipton, Dubuque, and Cedar Rapids. In 1985 the Joffrey II company premiered* Tales from Hans Christian Andersen *at Hancher Auditorium, and in 1986 the Joffrey Ballet performed James Kudelka's* The Heart of the Matter, *commissioned especially by Hancher Auditorium for the fiftieth anniversary of the Iowa Center for the Arts. In December 1987 the main Joffrey company used Hancher Auditorium for its premier performance of* The Nutcracker.

Theatre Building, 1985. After almost fifty years of heavy, year-round use, the Theatre Building needed refurbishing, and additional space. The new facilities included an improved Mabie Theatre (new lighting and sound systems), and two new, smaller theater spaces. Theatre A has two hundred movable seats, while Theatre B is a fixed-seat, end-stage theater capable of seating 148. Among the building's many other features are the Gillette Design Studio, a new scene shop, sound-editing facilities, and infrared television cameras that allow technical personnel to "see in the dark" during productions.

Nijinsky, *1986. Nijinsky, a play by Glenn Blumstein, was performed April 1, 1987, at the American College Theatre Festival (ACTF) in Washington, D.C. After the performance, the Association for Theater in Higher Education awarded the University Theatre Department $1,000 for its continued support of student playwrights. The Iowa Playwrights' Workshop was founded in 1975 by Oscar Brownstein, but* Nijinsky—*the fourth play in nine years written by a member of the Playwrights' Workshop to be performed at ACTF—is one in a long line of original plays created and staged at Iowa since the days of E. C. Mabie.*

Film studio, Communication Studies Building, 1986. Dedicated in April 1985, the Communication Studies Building houses two television studios, a twenty-four-track recording studio, an animation studio, a film soundstage, and a broadcast-quality radio studio. These studios are linked through a master control center operated by the Communication Studies Department's chief broadcast engineer. Many classrooms have projection booths and videotape machines with converters that allow the translation of foreign broadcast signals onto tape.

Visitors to the International Writing Program (IWP) on a tour of John Deere headquarters in Moline, Ill., 1977. Formally established in 1967, the IWP was conceived by Paul Engle and his wife Hua Ling Engle as a means of bringing foreign writers to the United States. Typically, these writers are prominent in their own countries but work full-time and lack sufficient time to write. With the support of the State Department and such companies as John Deere, Maytag, Northern Natural Gas, Meredith Publishing, Quaker Oats, and the Ford Motor Company, the IWP has brought over five hundred writers to this country, given them the time to write, and helped them to travel in the United States as well. In con-junction with the Translation Workshop, the IWP has made it possible for some of these writers to publish their work in English for the first time in the Iowa Translation Series. Paul Engle retired as director of the IWP in 1977 and was succeeded in the position by his wife.

K. K. Merker, founder of Wind-hover Press, 1986. Kim Merker is the director of Windhover Press, which was established in 1968 to produce limited editions that are themselves works of art. But the University's rich heritage in fine book-making started earlier, in 1945, when Wilbur Schramm, head of the School of Journalism, established a typography laboratory. To run it he hired a printer from Muscatine named Carroll Coleman, who produced many award-winning books from 1945 until 1957 under his Prairie Press imprint. Harry Duncan, who in 1957 brought his Cummington Press to West Branch, took over from Coleman. When Duncan left in 1972, one of his students, Kay Amert, became director of the Typography Laboratory in the School of Journalism. In addition to the small presses operating within the University, there have also been many small presses in the Iowa City area run by students of Coleman, Duncan, and Merker. These presses have frequently published the work of students in the Writers' Workshop. Given this legacy, it seemed only appropriate that in 1978 Kim Merker would establish a fund in the name of the Center for the Book at the University of Iowa Foundation. In 1986 the center was formally established at Iowa. Its inter-disciplinary faculty included Merker, Amert, Timothy Barrett (papermaking), James Snitzer (art and art history), and William Anthony (master bookbinder and conservator at the University Library).

Raising the Picasso curtain, 1982. When the Centre Pompidou in Paris asked to borrow the University of Iowa's Jackson Pollock painting, Mural, *acting director Joann Moser arranged instead for an exchange. In return for the loan of its Pollock, a gift from Peggy Guggenheim in 1948, the Museum of Art received and displayed for three months Picasso's* Le 14 Juillet, *a 36-by-26-foot drop curtain executed in 1936 for a play of the same name.*

Drawing class, 1970s.

Hancher Auditorium and the Iowa River.

Afro-American Cultural Center, 1976. In 1967 there were approximately 150 black students on campus. That year, members of the Afro-American Student Association (AASA) established a center to provide a place in the University for black students to gather. A variety of events, including lectures, forums, poetry readings, and a jazz series, were held at the center, which, after several moves, located in the old Law Building in the summer of 1987.

Quadrangle dormitory, 1975. In the late 1960s, students saw dormitories as restrictive and archaic, as symbols of a system they wanted to separate themselves from. Because of this, in 1968–69 there were five hundred empty beds in the residence halls. Two years later there were over a thousand beds open. This low occupancy rate led to the "parietal rule," which required that every freshman, and later some sophomores, live in the dormitories. Because of the changing social climate, there were changes in the rules governing those who lived on campus. Closing hours were relaxed in the 1960s and by 1969 were dropped for everyone but first-semester women students. Bed checks disappeared, and men and women could visit one another's rooms freely. The first coed dorm, Rienow, was established in 1970, and soon almost every dormitory housed both men and women. By the end of the 1970s the parietal rule was suspended because of the tremendous demand for dormitory rooms. So great has the demand been since the late 1970s, in fact, that students camp out in dormitory lounges for weeks into the academic semester, hoping eventually to find a room of their own.*

Financial aid office in Old Dental, c. 1970.

Orientation, 1982. In June or July before their first year of college, most of Iowa's entering freshmen spend a day and a half on campus for orientation. They begin by attending small-group discussions about university life, then go on to get advice about course selection and finally register for the classes they will soon be taking. In conjunction with, but separate from, the student orientation is a parents' orientation designed to introduce parents to the campus, the faculty, and Iowa City and to address their concerns about "letting go" of their children.

Phillips Hall, 1965. Previously crowded into Jessup Hall, the College of Business Administration moved to new quarters at the corner of Clinton Street and Iowa Avenue in 1965. Phillips Hall, which was named to honor former dean of the college Chester A. Phillips, consolidated all the class-rooms, facilities, faculty, and staff offices for the college. But such has been the popularity of business classes in recent years—the college in 1987 had 1,800 undergraduate majors—that in two decades the College of Business Administration needed yet more space.

Checking the research schedule at Spence Laboratories, c. 1970. As part of their introduction to the psychology department, students participate in research projects during their general psychology course.

Lindquist Center courtyard. Completed in two phases—the south portion in 1972 and the north portion in 1980—the Lindquist Center houses the College of Education and the Weeg Computing Center. Lindquist, along with the Bowen Science Building and the Health Sciences Library, *was designed by Skidmore, Owings, and Merrill's Walter Netsch, who employed his complex "field theory" of interlocking architectural spaces. In 1981 Louise Nevelson's* Voyage, *a thirty-foot-tall sculpture made of Cor-Ten steel painted black, was installed in the Lindquist Center's courtyard.*

Religion professor George W. Forell and student. Forell came to the University in 1954 and that year developed a course called Religion in Human Culture. Although only forty-eight students enrolled then, the class became so popular that one year it enrolled 1,200 students. A fifth-generation *minister, Forell headed the School of Religion from 1966 until 1971 and became a Carver Professor in 1973.*

Bill Sackter in his coffee shop at the School of Social Work, North Hall. Bill Sackter was wrongly placed in a Minnesota mental institution at the age of seven and did not start to live on his own until forty-four years later, when he was released as part of a program to deinstitutionalize the mentally handicapped. Soon after his release, Sackter met filmmaker Barry Morrow, who befriended him, became his legal guardian, and brought him to Iowa City. With the help of Tom Walz, then director of the School of Social Work, Sackter found a job running Wild Bill's Coffee Shop in North Hall. Sackter's moving life story was made into the made-for-TV movie Bill, starring Mickey Rooney (who earned an Emmy for his performance), which premiered at Hancher Auditorium on December 3, 1981. A sequel, Bill: On His Own, was televised in 1983. Sackter died in his sleep in 1983, yet he remains for many a symbol of courage and determination.

*The giant sloth moves into Iowa Hall, 1984. The fifty-six displays in Iowa Hall (located in Macbride Hall) together constitute a walk through time, detailing the state's geologic, cultural, and natural history. Iowa Hall also tells the story of Iowa's native peoples and the ecology of the state to- day. One particularly dramatic exhibit reveals a nine-foot-tall Jefferson Ground Sloth (*Megalonyx jeffersoni*), a mammal which became extinct after the last ice age.*

Marquette-Joliet diorama, 1985. Many of the exhibits and dioramas in Iowa Hall are the work of nationally known museum exhibit designer Neal Deaton of Newton. Deaton assembled the Marquette-Joliet, Paleo-man, and Mesquakie Indian dioramas, and also the forest, prairie, and marsh exhibits depicting Iowa's ecology. Iowa Hall's attention to detail is exceptional and is the result of a great deal of fieldwork by museum director George Schrimper and his staff in conjunction with the designers. In the winter 1986 issue of the Iowan, *Deaton recalled photographing Pike's Peak (above the junction of the Mississippi and Wisconsin Rivers) for the Marquette-Joliet exhibit "at sunrise on the exact date of the event portrayed—June 17. We observed weather conditions and cloud formations and confirmed the exact position of the rising sun. We brought back hundreds of color photos in order to duplicate the landscape's colors and shadings in the early morning light at that time of year. University botanists and biologists helped select specimens so we could recreate replicas. Every plastic leaf, flower, and insect in the diorama looks true to real life."*

Robotics research, College of Engineering, 1983. Professor Dong H. Chyung (right) has conducted experiments in which three robots are programmed by computer to cooperate in a common task.

A. J. Odgaard (left) of the Iowa Institute for Hydraulic Research leads a group of visiting Japanese and American river experts on a tour of the first installation of the Iowa Vane Project on the Nishnabotna River near Red Oak, September 1986. Odgaard and John F. Kennedy of the Iowa Institute for Hydraulic Research devised the vane concept (now patented for worldwide application), which consists of a series of short, submerged panels that prevent rivers from eroding their banks, migrating over farmland, or undermining bridges. The institute is a truly international (and internationally known) program and has awarded advanced degrees to students from forty-three countries. Among the department's distinguished foreign graduates are Dr. Mikio Arie (president of Hokkaido University in Japan), Dr. Bingnan Lin (retired director of the Institute for Water Research in the People's Republic of China), and Dr. Chen-hsing Yen (chairman of the Atomic Energy Commission of the Republic of China).

The Plasma Diagnostics Package (PDP) extended from the spaceshuttle Columbia, March 1982. Designed by members of the University's Department of Physics and Astronomy, the PDP was launched aboard space flights in 1982 and 1985. The PDP's fourteen instruments gathered information on plasma—the electrically charged gas that makes up 99 percent of our universe—information that will be mined for years to come by students and faculty in Iowa's space physics program. A new, more complex PDP is scheduled for shuttle missions in the 1990s.

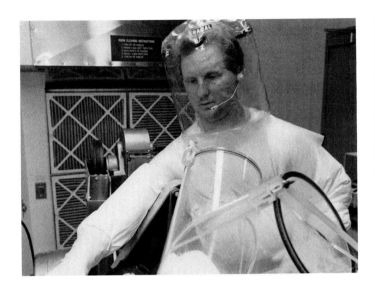

Cancer research at the College of Pharmacy, 1985. Since 1974 the University's Pharmaceutical Service has had as one of its major clients the National Cancer Institute of Bethesda, Maryland, for which it develops drugs to fight cancer. The Pharmaceutical Service, formally established in 1928, is the only FDA-approved university-based pharmaceutical manufacturing facility in the country. The "spacesuit" protects workers from the drug-testing environment and ensures that the laboratory remains sterile.

School of Dentistry, c. 1980. A legislative appropriation of $3.9 million, combined with a federal grant of more than $7 million, enabled the construction of a new building for the College of Dentistry in 1973. The two-part concrete structure, joined by a glass corridor, is located on the west side of the river near other buildings in the health sciences complex. Included in the building is the Dows Institute for Dental Research, established in 1976 to further study of the prevention and treatment of oral and systemic diseases.

Nursing Building. In 1949 the School of Nursing became the last of the University's professional schools to attain the status of a college, and Myrtle Kitchell (Aydelotte) was named as its first dean. The college became coeducational in 1950 when three men enrolled, and in 1953 it awarded its first bachelor's degrees (B.S.N.). Not only has the University trained thousands of nurses in Iowa City, but through its Continuing Education Outreach program it has for more than a decade helped practicing nurses in Iowa keep abreast of medical developments by offering one-day training programs at sites throughout Iowa. Nursing instruction in the 1950s and 1960s took place in Westlawn, but severe overcrowding there led to a call for a new building. The Nursing Building, overlooking the Iowa River, was occupied in 1971.

Family and Community Health Nursing, 1974. Nursing students at Iowa learn their profession not just by working at the University Hospitals and Clinics but also by caring for patients in their homes as part of their required course work.

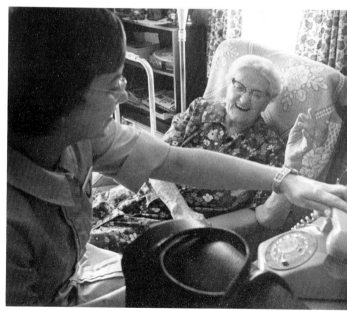

University Hospitals and Clinics and the health sciences complex, 1987. In the early 1970s University Hospitals began a three-phase renovation that would eventually make it the largest university-owned teaching hospital in the country. The first phase, Boyd Tower, completed in 1976, provided quarters for specialty clinics (dermatology, obstetrics, internal medicine, and others) devoted to ambulatory patient clinical services. The second major addition, the Carver Pavilion, was built in three stages between 1978 and 1984 and included a new Emergency Center, a Physical Therapy Department, and an expanded Orthopaedics Department. The third and last phase of the hospital's $184,000,000 expansion project, the Colloton Pavilion, finished in 1986, was designed to house the Iowa Children's Health Care Center of the Department of Pediatrics, with a staff of over a hundred pediatricians and 250 pediatric nurses. This addition was named for John W. Colloton, a native of Mason City who joined the hospital's staff in 1958 as business manager. Since 1971 he has been director of the University Hospitals, overseeing a staff of nearly seven thousand.

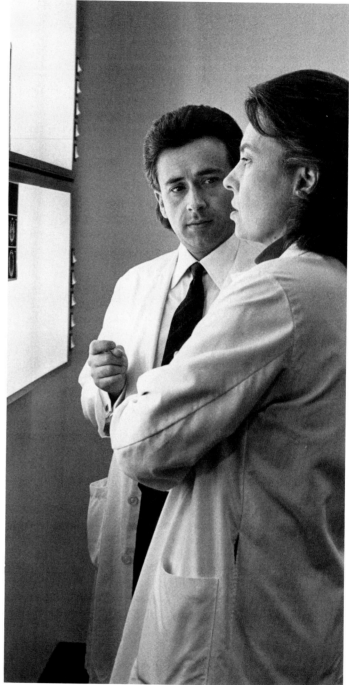

Match Day, 1981. Each spring, graduating medical students take part in the National Residency Matching Program, which matches more than 13,000 participating students across the country with private and university medical facilities. To qualify for practice in their specialties, most physicians take three to five years of residency training after medical school. Although the results could be delivered by mail, the gathering in the Bowen Science Building lobby to receive the sealed envelopes has become a rite of passage for Iowa's medical students.

Dr. Antonio Damasio and Dr. Hanna Damasio, neurology research, 1986. Dr. Antonio Damasio, chief of the division of behavioral neurology at the University Hospitals, has in recent years received grants totaling nearly two million dollars from the National Institutes of Health to study the neuro-anatomical foundations of human behavior. Among the recent research, which has application to the understanding of Alzheimer's disease and other dementias, is a "brain-mapping" project employing such sophisticated imaging devices as single photon emission computed tomography (SPECT) and nuclear magnetic resonance (NMR). Damasio has in recent years coauthored a number of articles with his wife, Dr. Hanna M. Damasio, professor of neurology.

Boyd Law Building, 1986. The University of Iowa's College of Law, consistently ranked among the top law schools in the country, moved into a new building in 1986. More than half of the space is given to the 420,000-volume law library, but the building also contains two full-scale trial courtrooms complete with a jury room and judge's chambers, and a 300-seat appellate courtroom which also serves as an auditorium for continuing education and special events.

Class of 1880 boulder, Penta-crest, 1980s.

Afterthought

In retrospect, the story of the University corroborates the old adage that the more things change, the more they remain the same. Most of the changes are obvious. They appear in university catalogs and in pictures such as those in this volume. A walk across campus reveals accretions of buildings, recreational spaces, and parking lots and such smaller additions as ramps and elevators for the handicapped. There are many more students and faculty members than in earlier decades, and they dress more informally and talk more casually. (Thirty years ago a faculty member almost always wore a suit and tie.) There are more women, proportionately, and more foreign students, especially students from the Far East. A closer look at faculty activities shows an increasing concentration on research and a continuing shift in the University's center of gravity away from the humanities and toward the sciences.

Such changes in size, scope, and complexity, however, cannot obscure the fact that most of the basic problems remain the same. There are the constraints of the budget, the concern over the quality of students, and the vexing problems of obtaining and retaining high-quality faculty. There are, moreover, the familiar oppositions that have persisted for decades: teaching vs. research, for example, the sciences vs. the humanities and fine arts, education for the life of the mind vs. education for the immediate betterment of society, the University as an instrument of theoretical research vs. the University as a means of improving the economy of the state, athletics vs. the academic, liberal education vs. vocational education, and the claims of undergraduate education vs. those of graduate work.

Presidents Amos Dean, George MacLean, and even Walter Jessup would be astonished by the campus of today, and yet if they could listen to the discussions over money, enrollment, the curriculum, student interests, and the needs of the state, they would feel right at home. Therein, we suspect, lies the heart of the appeal of a thriving university: it is forever new and forever the same.

Frederick W. Kent (1894–1984) with his camera and equipment. Many of the pictures in this book are the work of longtime Iowa City photographer Fred Kent. Kent came to the University from Dewitt in 1911 and as a freshman took pictures of Iowa football games with his postcard camera. He started his professional career by printing up pictures of the football crowds and game action and selling them at Whetstone's Drug Store downtown for five cents each. After graduating in 1915, Kent started a photo business at the University to serve faculty and staff. In 1947 he was appointed head of the University's Photographic Service. Kent took thousands of pictures documenting campus life—social occasions, faculty research, medical procedures, new buildings, and, of course, sporting events. A naturalist and birdwatcher, Kent devoted much of his later life to photographing the outdoors. Kent Park, west of Iowa City, is named in his honor.

Photo Credits

Negatives and prints made by Fred Kent during his years at the University are now on file at University Archives in the Special Collections department of the Main Library. Throughout the preparation of this volume, Robert McCown, Earl Rogers, and the staff at Special Collections provided access to these and other photographs and generously created workspace for the project. The encouragement, insight, and patience of Earl Rogers in particular were invaluable.

Also helpful were the assistance and expertise of Mary Bennett, photo archivist at the State Historical Society. Bennett and her staff went out of their way to insure that we obtained high-quality reproductions of the often-fragile materials in the collection.

In addition to these two major resources, photographs were gathered from many departmental and private collections. The following individuals provided photographs or were especially helpful in the preparation of the illustrations for this volume: Katherine Belgum, John Birkbeck, Richard Bovbjerg, Shirley Briggs, Barbara Buckley, Homer Calkin, Charles Calmer, William Casey, Joe Edens, Richard Eimas, Hua Ling Nieh Engle, Catherine Hahn, Palmer Howard, Carol Hunt, Tom Jorgensen, Margaret Keyes, L. W. Knapp, David Luck, Eleanor McClelland, Hermine McLeran, Jeff Myers, A. J. Odgaard, Warren Paris, Dorothy Pownall, Etta Rasmussen, Dotty Ray, Don Roberts, George Schrimper, Julie Scott, Joyce Summerwill, Kathleen Thomas, Will Thomson, James Van Allen, Jon Van Allen, Thomas Walz, and Everett Williams.

The copy negatives and prints necessary for this book were made by James Lindberg, University Photo Service, and the Office of Public Information (OPI) Photo Unit. All photographs are courtesy of the University Archives, with the following exceptions:

Winston Barclay: 242 right
College of Pharmacy: 207
Daily Iowan: 162 bottom, 198, 210, 249 right, 250 bottom

John Danicic, Jr.: 231
Department of Physics and Astronomy: 181
Department of Residence Services: 191 left, 192 top right, 192 bottom right, 193 top left
Joe Edens: 225 left
Drake Hokanson (OPI): 221 bottom, 237 left, 241, 246 top
Institute of Agricultural Medicine: 196 right
International Writing Program: 245
Iowa Lakeside Laboratory: 61, 81 right
Tom Jorgensen (OPI): 239 top, 243 left, 243 right, 244 right, 253 top left
James Lindberg: 232, 255 right
David Luck: 215 top left, 215 bottom, 218, 228 left, 233, 234 bottom left, 234 bottom right, 235 top, 235 bottom, 242 left
D. R. Miller (OPI): 253 bottom right
Jeff Myers (OPI): 244 left
National Aeronautics and Space Administration: 254 right
Office of Public Information Photo Unit: 173, 213 left, 221 top, 222, 247, 248 left, 248 right, 249 left, 253 top right, 255 left, 256 top, 256 bottom, 258 left, 258 right, 260
Omaha World Herald: 254 left
Warren Paris (OPI): 220, 257
Piney Woods School: 135
Dorothy Pownall: 133 right
School of Social Work: 252
State Historical Society of Iowa: 7, 11, 12, 14 far left, 17, 27, 29 bottom, 31 left, 37 top, 38 left, 38 right, 40 left, 46, 53 left, 53 right, 64, 70 left, 73, 84 left, 93 top, 98 bottom, 131 right, 150 bottom, 215 top right
University of Iowa Foundation: 213 right, 245 right, 251 left
University of Iowa Museum of Natural History: 80 left, 80 right
University Photo Service: 225 right, 237 right, 238 left, 238 right, 239 bottom
Jon Van Allen (UI Foundation): 259

Index